MW00648357

The Unchosen Me

the unchosen me

RACE, GENDER, AND IDENTITY
AMONG BLACK WOMEN IN COLLEGE

RACHELLE WINKLE-WAGNER

The Johns Hopkins University Press
Baltimore

© 2009 The Johns Hopkins University Press
All rights reserved. Published 2009
Printed in the United States of America on acid-free paper
2 4 6 8 9 7 5 3 1

The Johns Hopkins University Press
2715 North Charles Street
Baltimore, Maryland 21218-4363
www.press.jhu.edu

Library of Congress Cataloging-in-Publication Data

Winkle-Wagner, Rachelle.
The unchosen me : race, gender, and identity among black women
in college / Rachelle Winkle-Wagner.
        p.   cm.
Includes bibliographical references and index.
ISBN-13: 978-0-8018-9354-4 (hardcover : alk. paper)
ISBN-10: 0-8018-9354-2 (hardcover : alk. paper)
    1. Blacks—Education (Higher)—United States.   2. Sex
discrimination in higher education—United States.   3. Women,
Black—Education (Higher)—United States.   4. College students,
Black—United States—Social conditions.   5. Group identity—United
States.   6. Universities and colleges—United States—Sociological
aspects.   I. Title.
LC2781.W57 2009
378.1'982900973—dc22   2009012319

A catalog record for this book is available from the British Library.

Special discounts are available for bulk purchases of this book.
For more information, please contact Special Sales at 410-516-6936
or specialsales@press.jhu.edu.

The Johns Hopkins University Press uses environmentally friendly
book materials, including recycled text paper that is composed of at
least 30 percent post-consumer waste, whenever possible. All of our
book papers are acid-free, and our jackets and covers are printed on
paper with recycled content.

Lovingly dedicated to Eleanor and Mya—
That we may, in your generation, move toward a world where
race and gender can be re-created in a new way

To Mike—
with whom I have found more choice of self
than I thought possible

Contents

Acknowledgments

The writing of this book initiated, in many ways, an ongoing, transformative process. To the 30 women whose stories are represented in this book, I hope that the sisterhood fostered during the course of this research provided a safe haven, or at the very least a place to speak—a place to harness your own power—because you all have strength and a power that will transform society. I know this because you transformed me.

As a theoretical concept, the Unchosen Me was born on a hot summer morning in a small, stuffy classroom on a college campus where I met with other like-minded folks to discuss the philosophy of Jürgen Habermas and his critique of George Herbert Mead. What then became my doctoral dissertation, luckily for the readers of this book, has changed significantly. Yet I must thank those people with whom I discussed this project in those early days and who nurtured my idea, reading drafts as the research developed. A special thank-you goes to my dissertation committee—Deborah Faye Carter, Phil Carspecken, Edward St. John, and Quincy Stewart—who asked the difficult questions, supported my work, patiently read far less well-crafted drafts of this manuscript, and challenged me to be a better scholar and thinker. Your scholarship inspires me, as does your commitment to social justice.

This research project was graciously funded by an ASHE-Lumina Dissertation Fellowship. I am grateful both for the financial assistance this fellowship offered and for the networking and mentoring the program provided. I do better work for having been in this program. Additionally, this project was funded by the Office of Institutional Development and Student Affairs at Indiana University under the leadership of Charlie Nelms, whom I thank for his faith in my work.

Thank you to my editor at the Johns Hopkins University Press, Ashleigh Elliott McKown, for believing in my work and for helping me to structure and edit the book, making it more appealing to multiple audiences. Two anonymous reviewers provided thoughtful suggestions for which this is a better piece of work—thank you for your time and consideration. Thanks to the people who graciously read various chapters: Nana Osei-Kofi, Chris Linder, Debora Hinder-liter Ortloff, Cheryl Hunter, Barbara Dennis, and Dawn Michele Whitehead. A few people merit special thanks for reading multiple drafts of multiple chapters and for providing comments on the full manuscript: Marybeth Gasman, Pauline Reynolds, Carla Morelon-Quainoo, Susan Johnson, and Mike Wagner. Carla and Susan also served as peer debriefers, checking my analysis and interpretations for which these women's stories are better represented. All of these honest comments greatly aided in my revisions to the text. Any errors that remain are my own.

I am blessed to have many comrades in the area of writing and researching for social justice. Many people listened to my thoughts on this project and on the complexities of doing work across racial lines. This book is the better for it. In addition to those I have already mentioned, I am grateful to Mary Howard-Hamilton, Clif Conrad, Laura Perna, Barry Bull, Aki Yonehara, Lilia Santiague, Matt Hartley, Diana Slaughter-Defoe, Benetta Fairley, Adrea Lawrence, Joshua Hunter, Rob Aaron, Shaila Mulholland, Rashawn Ray, Dwyane Smith, Ghangis Carter, Ted Ingram, and John Kuykendall.

I am thankful to my colleagues at the University of Nebraska and specifically to my department chair, Larry Dlugosh, and to my dean, Marjorie Kostelnik, for offering me the gift of time that was necessary time to finish this manuscript. Accordingly, I am grateful for the Scholarly Enhancement Program and the teaching releases that were awarded as part of it.

My family provided ongoing support for the five years that this project took to complete. Thank you to my parents, Bill and Carola Winkle. Mom, your feminism inspired me to question the world around me, ultimately starting the fire within me that later became this project. Thank you also to my sister, Brenda, and my niece, Mya, for their support. Brenda, your incredible strength reminds me of the importance of this line of work. Thank you to my in-laws, Marilyn and Bill Wagner—I feel so lucky to have such wonderful support and family in you.

To Mike—my partner, husband, friend, and fellow scholar—I am eternally grateful to you for believing in me and in my work so wholly. Thank you for reading every version of every chapter of this manuscript, logging countless hours discussing this work, and for providing me the necessarily honest and yet somehow tactful feedback that one needs in the course of writing. I am in awe of your compassion, commitment, strength, patience, and intelligence, Mike. Thank you for choosing to spend your life with me each day.

I wrote the majority of this final version of the book while pregnant with my first child, Eleanor June. The anticipation of her birth made the importance of this work even more salient because I wanted even more to work toward the creation of a better world where race and gender would not continue to be created in such unequal ways. I received the contract for this book exactly one week before Eleanor graced our lives with her arrival. For the inspiration that Eleanor's wise soul brought and continues to bring into my being, writing, and life, I am unbelievably blessed.

The Unchosen Me

THE "PROBLEM" OF RACE AND GENDER

It is a peculiar sensation, this double-consciousness, this
sense of always looking at one's self through the eyes of
others, of measuring one's soul by the tape of a world that
looks on in amused contempt and pity. One ever feels his
two-ness.   —W.E.B. Du Bois, 1903/2003

College was both a dream and a promise for Michelle. At the age of seven, her
friend was shot in a senseless drug-related incident in their own urban Chicago
neighborhood. She remembers lying in the hospital bed with her friend and
making a pact—a promise that they would get out of their neighborhood, and
someday they would go to college. Michelle was heart-broken when her friend
died a few days later.

But Michelle kept her promise. She worked part-time jobs throughout her
adolescence, raising $4,000 for college. Her mother, who raised her as a single
mom, did not have a college degree. Michelle felt like her mom tried but
ultimately didn't know how to support Michelle's goal. Despite the odds,
Michelle studied hard and fearlessly told the cynics in her predominantly Black
neighborhood and school that she was going to college. And she did.

As a college senior, she reflected back on the shock she felt entering a
campus where so many students, primarily White students, had always
assumed they would attend college. Michelle's hard-earned $4,000 was gone
in her first semester, forcing her to struggle to stay enrolled—working

numerous part-time jobs, earning academic scholarships, somehow making ends meet. It was frustrating to see so many of her classmates who could simply call home and ask their parents to send them checks or cash when they needed money. This, however, was the least of the differences that Michelle experienced between herself and her classmates.

The truth was that Michelle just could not share her background at all. People would be too shocked, their eyes filled with pity and a complete lack of understanding. Or they would ignore her completely, as if it were impossible that someone could come from a place where she had to carry a hammer for protection when she walked to elementary school. She knew that 'fitting in' on campus was an impossibility. Worse yet, she realized in her first days on campus that being in college meant that she no longer fit or was accepted back home. She felt forced—as if it were the only way to succeed—to change her language, the way she dressed, her thinking, and the way she imagined herself, embracing everything that represented the "right" way to act on campus.

Michelle earned good grades, she joined clubs on campus (both those with mostly Black students like her sorority and those with mostly White students), she worked on becoming more outgoing—but always with the question of why she had to change so much about herself while many of her peers (particularly her White peers) did not. She was proud to be Black and talked about this openly, although she didn't feel this was accepted on campus. Her "previous self" still existed somewhere—perhaps in the shadows on campus and during the moments that she was alone—but she could pull it out and dust it off among certain groups in certain places. While she graduated with pride, Michelle still felt pain when it came to her college experience—this imposed, unshakable sense of two-ness, of being both things at once yet only feeling able to show one aspect of her self. Would there ever be a time when she could display both selves?

———

Leila was always the smart kid. There was never a time when she wasn't going to attend college. She remembers the question being "where" not "if" she would attend. Her parents had both struggled to get degrees—her mother an associate's degree, and her father a bachelor's degree—very late in life. But, these precious degrees changed Leila's life. After her parents earned their degrees, she was able to enroll in a special high school program for students who were gifted in math and science. In this gifted program, all of her classmates were White. Leila eventually got used to that and even made a couple of friends.

Upon graduation, she decided to attend a state institution in order to stay close to home. She was currently in the second year of her business degree. Her classes in business administration were in some ways just like high school, composed almost entirely of White students and mostly men.

By the end of her first year, Leila wasn't sure if words could possibly describe what was bothering her, but somehow she felt alienated, alone, isolated. She felt so much pressure—pressure to succeed in classes, pressure to act a particular way, to think certain things, and to appear a certain way. She tried so hard to do these things, straightening her hair and buying clothes that she saw her White peers wearing. She was careful never to arrive late to class so as to not be "the late Black girl." She kept her mouth shut most of the time, but when she did speak, she was careful never to use slang. This non-stop façade was all so exhausting.

Surprisingly, she found it difficult to make friends with other Black students. She attended Black Student Union meetings, but she just didn't feel like she fit there. At the same time, she also felt like her White peers wouldn't accept her. She was always the last picked for group work in her classes. Outside of class, the White women on her residence hall floor kept saying offensive things to her about her hair, about her complexion, or about stereotypes they had of African American students in general. She was trying to push through it, but sometimes it just felt so hard and so lonely that she had thoughts about leaving college. She didn't leave (her parents would never forgive her), but she had thoughts about it constantly. Why couldn't she fit with either Black or White students? Why did she always feel that she was being forced to be an outsider?

According to the majority of research about higher education, a woman like Michelle should be successful on campus, given her high level of involvement (Kuh & Vesper, 2000). Michelle is also highly interested and engaged in her academic work, striking a nice balance between involvement in the social and academic worlds of campus (Tinto, 1993, 2000; Astin, 1993, 1996). Yet, according to other evidence, her mother's lack of a college degree and her low-income socioeconomic background could impede Michelle's college success (Shapiro, 2004). Leila describes similar pressures despite having college-educated parents and self-identifying as upper-middle class. Leila is a very good student too, but her attempts to become involved on campus have not been successful. Both noted that they experienced alternating feelings of isolation and being "placed in the spotlight" during college. Both expressed feeling a sense of "two-ness."

That is, as Black women, they have to behave or "be" one way on campus and a different way in other settings.

In the early 1900s, W.E.B. Du Bois (1903/2003) first described "double consciousness," the notion that African Americans in the United States had to navigate two selves: one in reference to the White[1] American norms and one in reference to being Black.[2] More recently, Charisse Jones and Kumea Shorter-Gooden (2003) suggest in *Shifting*, their study of Black women's lives in America, that Black women in particular feel caught in a constant state of moving back and forth between Black and White norms or ways of being. Both Michelle and Leila, participants in this study and students at the same predominantly White university, referred to this sense of two-ness when reflecting on their college experiences. Why, despite their many differences, did Michelle and Leila describe the same pressures to be a particular way on this predominantly White campus?

The primary literature about college student success ignores the effect of the pressure—the two-ness—that Michelle, Leila, and the other women in this study described. Through their depictions of two-ness (or more-than-oneness), the 30 women in this study described an interactive process that creates race and gender in unequal and primarily negative ways. Ultimately, the effect of this isolation and the pressures that the women felt regarding a sense of who they *had to be* on campus in order to succeed remains an open question—more than a hundred years after the issue of two-ness was first considered by Du Bois.

Do African Americans in the United States still negotiate this double-consciousness? If so, how is it manifested within social institutions such as higher education, especially when current understandings of college success ignore it? How is double-consciousness experienced as an imposition on identity by college students? How does this imposition facilitate the process of creating race and gender? The central concern of this book is to understand the *process* whereby race and gender are created. Using a predominantly White institution of higher education as my laboratory, I examine race and gender theoretically and empirically through an ethnographic study with African American college women.

The African American women's voices represented here do indicate a sense of double consciousness. They did claim dichotomous impositions on their sense of self that influenced their experiences in college. The women felt pressure to navigate between their past and present, their hometowns and the college campus; between their minority groups and the majority group; and between the norms of being a "good woman" and those representing a "bad woman." Their experiences suggest that they "ever felt [their] two-ness." The two-ness they felt affected

their perceptions of their educational and social experiences, their sense of belonging on and off campus, their success in college, and their desire to persist
through college in ways that call into question the degree to which the widely
accepted predictors of college success are applicable to African American women.

PERSISTENT RACIAL INEQUALITIES

Race is one of the most studied issues in the United States. Sociologists, psychologists, economists, education scholars, and political scientists have attempted to
understand the persistent inequalities and implications associated with race.
Despite decades of exhaustive research, America is today, as it was upon its
founding, a racially divided country. Often descriptions of these inequalities
are centered on Black-White disparities as they relate to opportunities and outcomes. This comparison is understandable, given the depth and breadth of historical relationships between these two racial groups. But why does Black-White
inequality persist? Within the fields of education and sociology, race has primarily been studied in two ways: as an input, considering the impact of race on
subsequent life experiences and chances; and as an outcome, examining results
such as racism, discrimination, or cultural pathologies related to race. Both the
input and output perspectives of race provide useful insights about the ways that
race can influence life chances and the perpetual pathologies of race in society
(e.g., racism, discrimination, or victimization). However, they too often ignore
the *interactive processes,* individual and societal, subtle and overt, that work to
create race in everyday life.

Scholars emphasizing race as an input have considered the influence of race
or racialized contexts (i.e., neighborhoods, peer groups, culture) on subsequent
life chances such as educational or occupational attainment (Lee & Burkam,
2002; Massey, Charles, Lundy, & Fischer, 2003). Some scholars have linked race
and class as inputs, indicating that the lack of intergenerational wealth and cultural assets helps to account for persistent Black-White inequalities (Keister &
Moller, 2000; Oliver & Shapiro, 1997). These studies attempt to elucidate issues
such as the intergenerational disparities in wealth and assets between African
Americans and Whites as explored in *The Hidden Cost of Being African American*
(Shapiro, 2004).

A politically and scholarly contentious line of research spearheaded by Rich-
ard Hernstein and Charles Murray's *The Bell Curve: Intelligence and Class
Structure in American Life* (1994), controversially emphasizes alleged genetic
differences in intelligence or IQ, assuming that race is an input that results in

differential educational achievement. This is not a new way of conceptualizing racial difference. The biological[3] and pseudo-scientific (i.e., typically not empirically grounded or having data to support the arguments) notions of racial difference, propounded largely with the goal of demonstrating the physical or intellectual inferiority of non-White people, date back at least to the sixteenth and seventeenth centuries (Banton, 1998; Graves, 2002).

On the other hand, some scholars question the decision to treat race solely as an output, resulting in predictable inequalities. These scholars focus on race as an outcome, highlighting the influences of racial categorization, racism, and discrimination (Bonilla-Silva, 2003; Feagin, 1991; Omi & Winant, 1994). This work highlights what Feagin and McKinney (2002) call the costs of racism, such as racial inequalities in education, income, the workplace, and public spaces more generally. The consideration of race as an output, resulting in predictable inequalities of status or power is longstanding, dating back to at least the 1930s, to studies about interracial relations and the inequalities resulting from these relations (Banton, 1998).

A contrarian to this perspective, John McWhorter (2001), argues that one of the outcomes of race is a culture of victimization, leading to Black self-sabotage. This argument has resonated with some mainstream writers like Juan Williams, a senior correspondent for National Public Radio (Williams, 2006), and high-profile members of the Black community such as Bill Cosby, leading to further debate on the outcomes of race as related to victimhood among young Blacks. In their recent book, *Come on People* (2007), Cosby and his coauthor, Alvin Poussaint, maintain that Black youth particularly must begin to move from "victims to victors" and begin to "take back" their communities and neighborhoods. Victimization, these leaders suggest, offers Black people a way to deflect the blame of their misfortunes onto others.

But these discussions, whether considering race as an input or an outcome, fail to consider the ongoing processes that create and reinforce race and racial inequality in everyday life. If the *creation* of race is continuously misunderstood or ignored, it is likely that efforts toward equality will only delay rather than eradicate the effects of racism, an insidious social disease. Race is not something that simply "happens to" someone (race as an input) or "results in" a particular outcome (race as an outcome), but it is in many ways an action and interaction that occurs on the everyday level and is reified or created through institutions and social structures. That is, if race is created in everyday interactions, one must begin to identify what it is about these interactive processes that continues to perpetuate existing and unequal notions of race.

One example that mixes the input and outcome of race is the study of Black-White disparities in standardized testing, indicating that Black students continually receive lower standardized test scores and thus differential educational or occupational attainment (Jencks & Phillips, 1998). In this case, the "input" of being Black results in the "output" of lower test scores and subsequent life chances. Racial bias in test construction is often cited as one reason for this discrepancy, focusing on the outcome of being Black, meaning that African Americans often earn lower test scores than do their White counterparts (Jencks & Phillips, 1998). While this is one example of an attempt to understand race in two ways simultaneously, the process that creates and reinforces race is still left untapped. Thus, one may begin to understand how one's race can predict life chances (as an input), or how one's race can result in negative experiences (as an outcome), leaving unconsidered the way race is continually created and perpetuated.

It is not that race has been studied in ways that are wrong, although I do argue strongly against the biological determinism model as presented in Hernstein and Murray's (1994) work. These studies are generally important and necessary to help reveal a complete understanding of how racialized categories perpetuate inequalities. However, there are limits to studying race as either inputs affecting life chances and opportunities or outputs/outcomes affecting experiences because of racism and discrimination or victimhood. In particular, these perspectives miss the chance to cast a revealing light on the *process* whereby race and gender are created. By "create," I do not mean to imply that race is being created for the first time. Rather, the study of the way race is continually created in everyday life sheds light on the perpetual, longitudinal, cumulative nature of racial inequality. At times it may seem as if race is being created for the first time, but as this book demonstrates, most often race is being created over and over again through interaction in old and perpetually unequal ways.

This project takes as its charge the consideration of the everyday process of race and gender—the ways in which they are continually *interacted* to maintain and reinforce existing inequalities. If the process of the continual creation and reinforcement of race and gender can be understood, it may be easier to ameliorate the persistent inequalities and to alter the way race and gender manifest themselves at both the individual and societal levels. The setting for this study is a large, predominantly White university in the Midwest, but the experiences that the women in the study express transcend the Ivory Tower, transferring to other social institutions and even to interpersonal relationships.

EDUCATIONAL INEQUALITIES

Persistent racial inequalities are consistently illustrated in education. The struggle for educational equality in the United States has been volatile at best. Racial
and gender inequality remains at all levels of education but particularly in higher
education (Allen & Jewel, 1996; Blau, 2004; Pascarella & Terenzini, 2005). The
input and outcome notions of race transfer to the way education is studied and
the way it is practiced in terms of pedagogy, curriculum, and experiences. Those
who have historically been disadvantaged in the larger social structure still often experience inequality in educational attainment, opportunity, and outcomes
(Blau, 2004; Carey, 2004; Carnoy, 1995; Oliver & Shapiro, 1997). There is growing evidence of social, economic, and psychological barriers to higher education
based on race, class, and gender (Carnoy, 1995; R. D. Myers, 2003).

As an illustration of the continuing disparities between historically advan-
taged and disadvantaged groups, the number of 18- to 24-year-old African American students who were enrolled nationally in institutions of higher education
increased by less than 7% between 1976 and 1997 (R. D. Myers, 2003). While
some strides have been made in providing access to college for African American students since then, the number of African Americans aged 18-24 enrolled
in college still only increased by 5% (from 27% to 32.3%) between 1996 and
2006 (Census Bureau, 2008a).[4] The enrollment of White students was consistently at least 5% higher during this time (Census Bureau, 2008b). The African
American students that do enroll in institutions of higher education are less
likely to complete their degrees than are their White peers, indicating that there
is a problem with retention (DesJardins, Ahlberg, & McCall, 2002; R. D. Myers,
2003; Pathways to College Network, 2003). Less than half of the African American students who begin college actually complete their degrees in six years.
Among the freshman class of 2000-2001, only 41.2% of Black students com-
pleted their degrees within a six-year period as compared to 59.4% of White
students (U.S. Department of Education, 2008).[5] What is happening during
college to lead to such poor retention rates among African American students?

This discrepancy in persistence is chronicled in *The Agony of Education* (Feagin, Vera, & Imani, 1996), which describes the educational choices of African
American college students and their parents. There is growing evidence that underrepresented students, particularly African American students, continue to
report feelings of isolation, experiences with racism, and a lack of support or
negative experiences in predominantly White institutions (PWIs) (Allen, 1992;
Branch Douglas, 1998; Davis et al., 2004; Feagin et al., 1996; Fries-Britt & Turner,

2002; Loo & Rollison, 1986; Nilsson, Paul, Lupini & Tatem, 1999). This book uses these studies as a springboard for uncovering *why* underrepresented students still report such negative experiences in college more than 50 years after the *Brown v. Board of Education* decision abolishing desegregation in public schools. In particular, this study is an effort to understand the ways in which these experiences, these interactive processes (between students, their peers and professors on campus, and the larger social structure), influenced and shaped student identity and subsequent educational opportunities, successes, and failures.

Generally, programs geared toward increasing the persistence and success of students of color in higher education stress the importance of academic and social integration: if a student successfully integrates into an institution, she is more likely to persist through her degree program (Astin, 1996; Beil et al., 1999; Guifridda, 2003; Kuh, Hu, & Vesper, 2000; Tinto, 1975, 1993, 2000). This academic-social integration model was developed by Vincent Tinto (1975, 1993), using an interpretation of Durkheim's (1897/2006) notion of Catholic and Protestant suicide.[6] Durkheim concluded that people were less likely to commit suicide if they were integrated into society, finding that Catholics were less likely to commit suicide than Protestants because they were more integrated into the moral code of their religious tradition.

Vincent Tinto (1993) used this theoretical discussion to suggest that college students, like the Catholics and Protestants in Durkheim's study, would be more likely to persist in college degree programs if they integrated into the academic and social traditions of campus. Tinto's model has been critiqued for lacking diversity in his population sample and the perspectives of minorities (Howard-Hamilton, 1997; Rendòn, Jalomo, & Nora 2000; Taylor & Miller, 2002; Torres, 2003); of needing revision (Braxton, 2000; Braxton & McClendon, 2001; Braxton & Mundy, 2001; Padilla, Trevino, Gonzalez, & Trevino, 1997); and for assuming the assimilation[7] of minority students as a prerequisite for success in a majority environment (Tierney, 1992, 1999, 2000).

Building on these critiques, this book explores how integration affects students of color, specifically African American women, in potentially negative, though often unintentional, ways. Feagin, Vera, and Imani (1996) argue that "'integration' has, in practice, been a major failure. Indeed, 'integration' has been designed for the most part as a one-way assimilation process in which Black students are forced to adapt to White views, norms, and practices" (p. xi). With this in mind, I propose an alternative to the integrationist model.

The academic and social integration model suggests an underlying assumption that a *student* must integrate into the institution rather than challenging *institutions* to adapt to the needs of new populations of students. To bring new populations of students to the proverbial table of higher education in meaningful ways and to continue to retain students from underrepresented groups, institutions and the people that serve in them must be willing to re-imagine what it means to provide an "inclusive" environment. This argument is crucial to a deeper understanding of issues of access, retention, and student success in higher education.

The integrationist model, encouraging underrepresented students to integrate into institutions, results in requiring those who have been underrepresented and historically disadvantaged to change and sometimes to lose themselves by assimilating into existing institutions—the same institutions that create race and gender in persistently unequal ways. This book uncovers the ways in which race and gender are created within social institutions—in this case, institutions of higher education. My hope in taking on this challenge is that this knowledge will facilitate the process of beginning to revolutionize persistent inequalities not only in education but also in the larger social context.

Research about inequalities in higher education focuses on the campus climate (Hurtado & Carter, 1997; Hurtado, Carter, & Kardia, 1998; Locks, Hurtado, Bowman, & Oseguera, 2008); race (Allen, 1992; Davis et al., 2004; Nilsson et al., 1999; Stewart, 2008; Zhang, 2008); and gender (Jacobs, 1996; Whitt et al., 1999; Zhang, 2008). Campus climate research (Hurtado, Carter, & Spuler, 1996; Hurtado, Milem, Clayton-Pederson, & Allen, 1998; Museus, Nichols, & Lambert, 2008) and research regarding financial aid (Hu & St. John, 2001; Ness & Tucker, 2008; St. John, Cabrera, Nora, & Asker, 2000; Tilghman, 2007)[8] are alternatives to the academic / social integration framework. However, research regarding the possibility of institutions' imposing identity on students—particularly, research that examines the interactive process that may greatly affect students' experiences in college—is essentially nonexistent. Moreover, there is little research examining the subjective experiences that students have with the campus climate (i.e., the way students interact with this climate) (Hurtado & Carter, 1997). By focusing on students' experiences, this study provides a glimpse into an often overlooked aspect of the campus climate: the way institutional norms, policies, and practices impose identity on students and the influence of these impositions on the student experience.

Although inequalities in educational attainment and outcomes have been demonstrated in empirical research, there is still relatively little research focusing particularly on the experiences of African American students in college.[9] There is even less work related to the unique experiences of African American *women* in college.[10] Many of the recent books regarding African American students' educational experiences focus on primary and/or secondary schooling. For example, in *Learning While Black: Creating Educational Excellence for African American Children* (2001) Janice Hale argues that the solution to the Black-White achievement gap lies in the interaction between students and teachers, advocating for institutional change. Also at the K–12 level, Signithia Fordham's *Blacked Out: Dilemmas of Race, Identity and Success at Capital High* (1995) probes her concept of "acting White" among African American adolescents, claiming that positive images of successful African Americans are "blacked out" in American society and in education.[11] Also examining the "acting White" phenomenon among African American and Latino students in K–12 schooling, Prudence Carter's *Keepin' It Real: School Success beyond Black and White* (2005), found that African American and Latino youth do in fact value education as a key component of economic mobility, maintaining that the "acting White" issue is really a rejection of the "White" American norms of interaction, speech, dress, and musical tastes.

In higher education, much of the work that considers the experiences of African American students centers on comparisons of predominantly White and historically Black institutions (Allen, 1992; Allen, Epps & Haniff, 1991; Fleming, 1984; Fries-Britt & Turner, 2002). These studies, such as *Blacks in College* by Jacqueline Fleming (1984) and *College in Black and White* by Walter Allen and his colleagues (1991) indicate that African American students may perform better and have greater success in historically Black colleges and universities. Or more recently, Sarah Susanna Willie's *Acting Black* (2003) considers the reflections of African American alumni who attended either a predominantly White institution or a historically Black institution, exploring their experience related to race and the performance of race in college. Focusing on experiences within a predominantly White institution, *The Agony of Education* (Feagin et al., 1996) considers the educational choices made by African American students and their parents. Sharon Fries-Britt examines the experiences of high-achieving African American students (Fries-Britt, 1998; Fries-Britt & Griffin, 2007; Fries-Britt & Turner, 2002). Other research emphasizes the experiences of African American males in particular (Harper, 2006, 2008; Harper & Quaye, 2007).

Yet there remain relatively few studies that highlight the experiences of African American women. One that merits mention is an edited volume by Mary Howard-Hamilton (2004) in which she compiled chapters focusing on the needs of African American female students, administrators, and faculty in higher education. One suggestion of this volume is that more empirical work needs to focus on African American women. Considering at least in part the experiences of African Americans, Dorothy Holland and Margaret Eisenhart (1990) investigated the ways that peer culture influenced both White and African American women's experiences at two universities. As the book's title suggests, the women are *Educated in Romance,* experiencing in college society's gender hierarchy that places heavy emphasis on appearance and male interest in them and less importance on academics and intellect. But even this work does not focus solely on the distinctive experiences of African American women, and in some ways the act of comparing Black and White women may unwittingly devalue the unique experiences of Black women, reasserting White women as the "norm" or standard against which all others should be measured.

One reason for the importance of studying the experience of African American women on their own (without comparisons to White women, for instance) is that African American women are consistently outpacing their male counterparts by 2:1 in terms of higher education enrollment and graduate rates (De-Sousa, 2001; NCES, 2005; Wilds, 2000). Still, there remain many questions about the experiences that African American women are having in higher education, largely because there is little research that focuses specifically on this population. Understanding African American women's struggles and successes in college, particularly at predominantly White institutions where the majority of African American students are enrolled (DeSousa, 2001), could help to identify ways to better support African American students and perhaps other underrepresented students more generally.

While there has not been much research focusing specifically on African American women's college experiences, there has been extensive research regarding the general impact of college experiences on identity (Evans, Forney, & Guido-DiBrito, 1998; Torres, Howard-Hamilton, & Cooper, 2003). Left unexamined is the important possibility that institutions of higher education may in fact *impose* identity on students, forcing them to choose between their historical selves and their new imposed identity. I address this issue head on, asking: Do institutions of higher education impose identity on students differentially by race or gender? If so, how does this shape the students' experiences and success in college?

In addition, the field of higher education has predominantly centered on psychologically based theories of identity development (Evans, Forney, & Guido-DiBrito, 1998; Torres, Howard-Hamilton, & Cooper, 2003). These theories generally assert that identity development occurs in a series of stages or phases through which a student will progress. I pause here to introduce the predominant frameworks for identity in higher education and my argument for an alternative way to consider identity.

IDENTITY MODELS AND THE UNCHOSEN ME:
TOWARD A SOCIOLOGICAL PERSPECTIVE

There are two branches of scholarship and thinking about identity in the field of social psychology (Hogg, Terry, & White, 1995). One, called *social identity theory*, developed from the psychological tradition (see Tajfel, 1982; Tajfel & Turner, 1985) and is the origin of the majority of the student development theory in higher education.[12] The preponderance of the literature regarding college student identity maintains a linear process through which students progress, often in a series of stages/phases (Evans et al., 1998).[13] Relative to race, the psychological tradition most closely implies an input perspective—the input of one's race influences the development of one's identity.[14] Another perspective, *identity theory*, is rooted in the field of sociology (see Stryker, 1980). This perspective implies neither an input nor an outcome perspective of race or identity, but rather shifts identity work toward an interaction-based approach whereby race and identity are manifested through interactions between self, others, and society.

Many of the psychologically based theories of college student development have been critiqued for focusing too much on students in majority groups such as white, male, and heterosexual students, to the exclusion of students not in these groups. As the demographics of institutions of higher education continue to change, it is necessary to understand the needs of new populations of students, and these earlier theories may not adapt well to these groups (Torres, Howard-Hamilton, & Cooper, 2003). While the foundational theories of college student development theory are rooted in psychology, the underlying assumptions of the psychological tradition and the limits of this perspective have largely been unexamined in higher education, resulting in the assumptions and limitations of this perspective being largely ignored.

The foundational student development theories in higher education have been criticized for lacking racial/ethnic and gender diversity in their methods and implications (Gilligan, 1993; Torres et al., 2003).[15] More recent work in college student development theory strives for the inclusion of racially underrepresented students and women (Gilligan, 1993; Josselson, 1973, 1987; Torres, 1999). The predominantly White campus environment may actually be counterproductive to student development for African American students, constraining the development of identity (McEwen, Roper, Bryant & Langa, 1990; Taub & McEwen, 1992). To address some of these critiques, there have been more recent advances in college student development theory that focus on some of the populations that were largely excluded from the foundational theories.[16]

During the past two decades of research, some scholars have suggested that college students, particularly students of color, may experience multiple components or categories of identity.[17] Yet in the main, even these advances and alternative theories continue to use a linear, stage-based model of development whereby an individual progresses through a series of stages, phases, or statuses toward an idealized endpoint of development.[18] Given that my work shifts toward a new perspective, in the following sections I provide a comparison of the psychological perspective on identity with the sociological perspective.

The Psychological Perspective on Identity

The psychological perspective on identity maintains the following (Hogg, Terry & White, 1995; Stryker, 1997):

1. It begins by assuming the theoretical priority of the individual and not society.
2. Work on identity, called social identity theory (see Tajfel, 1978; Tajfel & Turner, 1985), emphasizes cognitions or mental processes.
3. The self is rooted in cognitions that arise out of a person's experiences.
4. There is an assumption of a single self, a singular identity.
5. Psychological theory discusses traits, characteristics, and personality.
6. Studies often examine perceptions of membership within groups.

The psychological perspective begins with the individual, single self. While some theories may consider the environment, the individual self would exist *before* the self is influenced by environmental factors—emphasizing the individual rather than society's influence on the individual. The studies rooted in the psychological perspective, as many college student development theories are, often explore membership in groups. This membership in a group may facilitate or create barriers to the development of self, but the underlying assumption is that the self exists before the group, and thus one's core identity would be there to discover or develop with or without the group. The group would then be a catalyst or a barrier to this self-discovery.[19]

There are several substantive and methodological limitations to the dominance of psychologically based theories, particularly stage/process-based theories. Many psychologically based theories, such as racial identity theories, assert a series of tasks one must achieve, setting up the theory instrumentally, as if one can have a *more achieved* identity if one can accomplish more tasks. This instrumentality is often value-laden, considering some as more advanced in their identity than others. As an illustration of this type of instrumentality, Cross's (1995) theory of Nigrescence (the process of becoming Black) maintains that a person may "regress," or be "fixated" in a particular stage, or may "drop out" of the stages altogether. These words connote that moving through the stages is better than not moving through them, going backward through them, or choosing not to go through them at all.

Similarly, because identity in racial identity theories is often constructed as a linear process, there is an assumption of an end point, as if one develops toward a goal. The inherent value judgment assumes that someone in an earlier stage is *less developed.* It is possible that one could progress through the stages in a non-linear fashion, moving in and out of stages/statuses in different contexts. Additionally, some stages could be considered to be very problematical, leaving someone to be considered *stuck* in a particular stage if he or she could not move out of it. This implies that one is more achieved if one moves linearly through the stages in a systematic way.

Perhaps most importantly, stage/process theories of identity run the risk of stereotyping or labeling. The generalized nature of these theories assumes that *all* people in a particular group will move through the same stages in a linear progression. Yet this does not allow for enough complexity for people to determine their own identity processes. For instance, Taub and McEwen (1992) indicated that African American women may experience the predominantly White college campus as a barrier or roadblock to their identity development. If a psychologically based notion of identity were used, these women would often be labeled as being lower in the stages of their developmental processes.

For qualitative data analysis in particular, using psychologically rooted perspectives like those in many racial identity stage theories implies *fitting* the data to particular stages in the developmental process. However, one could miss other forms of evidence or other issues that emerge through analysis. That is, a researcher looking for students to be placed within particular stages or statuses may lose sight of other identity-related factors within the students' experiences.[20]

Theoretically, the psychological perspective has limitations such as: (1) the assumption of a single self; (2) a lack of central consideration to the social structure; and (3) the root in cognitions. The psychological perspective begins with the individual single self, potentially leaving little room for considerations about the impact of the social structure, inequality, or discrimination on identity development. This perspective may ignore the influence of one's location in the social structure on the self because emphasis is placed on the individual first and the social structure second. One would *develop* her identity through cognitions or mental processes, as a task. This perspective does not seem to be consistent with the way in which many students, especially underrepresented students, describe a sense of multiple selves in college as compared to the way they are at home (Pascarella & Terenzini, 2005; Renn, 2000). The single self, in its extreme, would not allow for acclimation to multiple situations and contexts.

The centrality of cognitions or mental processes in the psychological perspective disallows, or at least makes less likely, considerations of the nuances of self: emotion, the impact of interaction on the self, roles, or the affect of the social structure on the self. In other words, the social structure is often secondary if it is central at all to these theories because the self arises out of cognitions—the self is primary to the society or social structure. Yet one's cognitions may not simply be within one's own mind but may be importantly influenced by the social structure (Stryker, 1997). The psychological perspective, and the primacy of the individual self and cognition over the larger society, does not readily allow for a theoretical consideration that the environment may alter cognitions in the ways that may actually happen in day-to-day life. The lack of focus on the social structure (because the individual is considered primary) may ignore, even inadvertently, the way that social inequality may affect identity processes. That is, all may not have equal access to their own identity development in a particular setting. For example, an African American woman may feel that her identity development is constrained in a predominantly White setting due to current and past racial injustices (Taub & McEwen, 1992).

All this said, there is no need to throw the baby out with the bathwater. These limitations become problematic only when the psychological perspective is used in *absence* of another perspective, such as the sociological perspective, or when the psychological perspective is used as the *only* way of viewing college student development. I suggest that the research, thought, and dialogue within the field of higher education should be expanded to include a sociological perspective as employed in the remainder of this text. The theoretical development of the Unchosen Me is rooted in the sociological perspective.

The Sociological Perspective on Identity

The sociological perspective on identity has the following characteristics (Hogg, Terry & White, 1995; Stryker, 1997):

1. The self develops out of interaction.
2. Society develops first, and a person's identity stems from socialized roles.

3. The self is located in social structures.
4. The self works to organize social life.
5. There are multiple selves.[21]
6. Reflexivity is a central aspect of the self; one is able to reflect on oneself.
7. Sociological work in identity is called identity theory (see Stryker, 1980).
8. The sociological perspective underwrites identity theory's emphasis on roles, commitment to roles, and identity salience.

In the sociological perspective, the self develops out of interactions between one's self, others, and the larger social structure rather than initiating in one's cognitions or mental processes.[22] In the sociological perspective, society develops first and then one's self initiates within that society. Sheldon Stryker (1997), considered the father of the sociological perspective on identity, wrote: "In the beginning, there is society," meaning that the self is entirely linked to and initially located within the existing social structure. Once the self has developed out of the social structure, this self or set of identities works to organize social life. The primacy of the larger social structure allows a deeper consideration of the influence and connection of the social structure with identity. One's racial category, for example, and identities more generally, would initiate in the social structure—developing out of and in response to it. The central consideration of the social structure is vital to examinations of the experiences of underrepresented students. This perspective allows for explorations of the way social inequality outside of higher education may influence students while they are in college, placing the primary responsibility for inequality squarely on the social structure rather than on the individual student.

Perhaps one of the most marked differences that the sociological perspective provides is the assumption of multiple identities. Because the self initiates in the social structure or develops out of society, there are numerous identities associated with different aspects of the society.[23] These multiple identities relate to the roles one plays within social groups. In the case of higher education, one could have an identity associated with being a college student, with being a family member, or with being a friend. These identities may overlap a bit or may be more or less salient in particular settings, but there could be as many identities as the roles one takes within a society.[24] Contrarily, the psychological perspective ultimately would limit the discussion of multiple identities because of the assumption of singular identity.

The sociological perspective is often empirically tested through the study of one's roles, commitment to roles, and identity salience.[25] Comparatively, the psychological perspective often studies the effects of group membership on an individual. The sociological perspective, on the other hand, could provide insight into this group membership through understanding the roles one plays within that group versus those played outside of the group, what this says about one's commitment to particular groups, and the salience of particular identities within each group.

As an individual's self develops, he or she can accept or reject the socially constructed identity through self-reflection/reflexivity. Group membership, the topic of many psychologically based studies, is an organizational tool in social life—a way for the self to be recognized or for the self to continue in its development. In the sociological perspective, identities are *socialized* or *learned* through one's connection to groups and to society. Alternatively, with the psychological perspective, there is an implicit assumption that others, perhaps expert-others, can locate and describe one's identity as being in a particular stage/phase/ trait-cognition level.

Given the socialized or learned nature of the sociological perspective on identity, education, broadly conceived as more than just schools or classrooms, plays a central role in identity. That is, education within society, both formal and informal, both inside and outside of classrooms, is a driving force of identity construction. One's identity is integrally linked to the social structure because one's identity initiates in that social structure. Identity is fluid and malleable, leaving room for education's central role in *constructing* that identity, rather than facilitating or impeding identity development (as in the psychological perspective). Yet there is still room for agency of the individual to accept or reject these socially constructed identities because of the centrality of self-reflection within this sociologically based identity development.

The sociological perspective of identity theory provides the field of higher education an opportunity to more centrally locate issues of social justice and equality within discussions about college student development because identity initiates in the social structure (Stryker, 2000). Thus, one's identity, in essence, would mirror existing social stratification, and the study of identity could shed light on the reasons for this stratification. That is, if one's identities initiate in the *already stratified* social structures (e.g., stratified by race, class, gender), the study of identity development could provide insight into the social structure itself in a way that the focus on the individual's cognitions / thought processes within the self as primary (as in the psychological perspective) could not. The influence of and inequalities inherent in the social structure as it relates to postsecondary student access, transitions, and retention in higher education would become more explicit with this perspective because identity comes second to the existing social structure.

Currently, there is little if any work in college student development theory that uses a sociological perspective. I am not necessarily advocating for the replacement of the psychological perspective with the sociological perspective in higher education.[26] However, I am asserting that the *dominance* of one theoretical perspective over the other may limit the possibilities for understanding the identity and development of college students, particularly students of color in predominantly White institutions. If the psychological perspective provides the foundation to nearly all student development theories, there is ostensibly only room for considerations of a singular identity, giving primacy to the individual self, an outcome or endpoint orientation, and cognition. What about college students who describe their identities in multiple ways, as the women in this book do? What about the role of the social structure in identity development? The sociological perspective is needed for a full theoretical development of these issues.

I part ways with psychologically based models of identity with an original theoretical concept I call the Unchosen Me, which is rooted in sociological perspectives of identity.[27] Through this perspective, I argue that identity is rooted in interaction between self, others, and society, allowing for a focus on the process of interaction that creates race and gender and the manifestations of these concepts within identity processes. This allows for a multiple-identities perspective that is similar to the way many of the Black women in this study ended up describing themselves—as if they experienced a two-ness or multiple selves at once and some of these selves felt unwelcome in some settings on campus. The central inclusion of the social structure within this perspective is integral to my discussion of the affect of social inequality on identity.

This book provides a new theoretical notion of identity, race, and gender through the theoretical discussion and empirical application of the concept of the Unchosen Me. It also offers an alternative theoretical foundation for student development and the success of underrepresented students in higher education. I argue that race- and gender-related identity processes in many ways mirror existing social stratification related to race and gender. That is, if society is stratified or racially unequal, for example, one's identities may also be stratified or feel as if they are treated unequally within different social settings. This may create a feeling that one's identities, or aspects of one's identities, may not be chosen as much as they are ascribed or imposed by a social institution—in the case of this book, predominantly White institutions of higher education.

A NEW PERSPECTIVE ON RACE AND GENDER

I begin with the notion that race and gender are intimately and inextricably linked. As many Black and Latina feminist scholars have maintained, the concept of gender is often considered only from a White-centered perspective (Hill Collins, 2000; hooks, 2000; Hurtado, 1996; Zinn & Dill, 1999). On the other hand, those studying the concept of race often ignore the notion of gender, although perhaps tacitly or even unwittingly. Here, I am immediately bonding these two concepts together, maintaining that in everyday life one is continually racialized and gendered simultaneously. While one category may feel more salient in a particular context, these categories may never be separated in meaningful ways. Class, I argue, presents itself differently as a category because it is not necessarily physically embodied in the way that race and gender are. For instance, while one may be born into a particular class category, this may not be a distinction that one physically embodies in the way that one does with race and gender. Thus, I consider class distinctions as related to race and gender, but I do not link class with race and gender in the inextricable way that I intersect the concepts of race and gender.

To fully understand inequality related to race and gender, one must examine the *process* in which race and gender are created in everyday life. One way to shed light on this is by studying interaction. I examined the interactive process of the creation of race and gender through a study of the identity of African American college women. Identity, in this case, is initiated through interaction and can be defined as one's interactions between one's self, other people, and society. The study of identity (as interaction between self, others, and society), which focuses on issues of race and gender as they relate to identity processes, becomes a way to uncover the interactive process that creates race and gender.

I examined this interactive identity process as related to race and gender both theoretically and empirically. Theoretically, I developed the concept of Unchosen Me, which is fully explained in chapter 2. The empirical portion of the book (chapters 4–7), outlines my critical ethnographic study, which examined the college experiences of African American women and the affect of these experiences on identity. By "critical," I mean that this study had an explicit orientation toward social justice and the empowerment of the women involved in the study. Chapter 3 provides a reflection on my role as a White woman conducting research with African American women. Additionally, Appendix B provides a detailed discussion of the data analysis and validation techniques.

The setting for this study was a postsecondary institution that I call Midwest University (MU). It is representative of many large, predominantly White institutions in the United States. I chose MU because of its similarity to many predominantly White institutions nationwide that struggle to recruit and graduate students from underrepresented groups. Located in a small midwestern city, MU enrolls approximately 35,000 undergraduate students. It was an ideal research site because of the relatively low minority population (approximately 9% of the total student population: 4% African American, 2% Latino, 3% Asian American).[28] However, there is a strong institutional commitment to admit and integrate students of color into the campus through policy and practice such as financial aid decisions, a mission of diversity and inclusion, centers on diversity, and diversity-related student organizations. A variety of support programs at the institutional and departmental levels provide a cross section of efforts to encourage student success. MU also provided an interesting site because, although it is a public institution, it is not a land-grant university and has more selective admissions criteria than many public state institutions. Thus, MU provides an interesting case of the delicate balance between elite admissions criteria and a desire to serve the state's citizenry.

I met with the 30 women of color (27 African American, 2 Black Latina, 1 Multiracial) for a period of nine months in a series of focus groups called "sister circles." At first I found it extremely difficult as a White woman to gain the trust of the women, but as we spent time together, trust solidified (chapter 3 fully explains this process). Once women on campus started to hear about the groups, other women started approaching me to become involved. The women were primarily first-generation college students (24 of the 30), that is, their parents did not have college degrees. They were from all over the United States and from many different departments on campus. I include a more thorough description of the women in Appendix A.

As the project progressed, it became clear that the sister circles filled a need that was not being met by the institution. The women found support in these groups, and they often noted that they did not find this support elsewhere on campus. We met bi-weekly over pizza, and eventually, after three or four months, the women took ownership of their groups, determining the topics of discussion. Generally, the discussion centered on their challenges and successes on campus and on helping each other to navigate the campus, often described as an unsafe, unwelcoming, and hostile place for students of color. Sometimes the groups met without me (though of course those meetings did not become part of the research). I also conducted individual interviews with the women and observed them in a variety of settings such as lunches, dinners, conferences, classes, and social settings. As time went on, I became more of an observer and a mentor to the women—meeting with many of them outside of our group meetings to talk about their classes, applying for jobs, or applying for graduate programs. This approach complements a critical advocacy perspective on research. I was changed through this process, and so were they.

I analyzed the data in a variety of ways, primarily using Phil Carspecken's (1996) critical ethnographic data analysis techniques in an effort to delve deeper into the meaning, both explicit and implicit, within the statements (see Appendix B for further details on analysis and validation). The results of the analysis suggest that African American women experience multiple impositions, or pressures, on their identity related to race and gender. These descriptions of impositions on identity uncover ways that race and gender are created on campus and in the larger society. The study provides an alternative way of thinking about the support and success of students of color at predominantly White institutions. But beyond higher education, this study reveals a new way of thinking about race and gender—as an interactive process—and this may allow scholars and practitioners to consider new ways to work toward racial and gender equality.

"EVER FEELING [HER] TWO-NESS . . ."

Inquiring about race and gender as an interactive process necessitates new theoretical concepts. Building on the identity work in social psychology to provide a theory for the interactions of race and gender, I developed the Unchosen Me, intersecting opportunity, privilege, and choice (i.e., choices related to identity, educational, and occupational attainment). I maintain that social institutions, like educational institutions, may impose a form of identity that works to create racialized and gendered categories in unequal ways. In particular, I argue that identities mirror the larger social stratification that exists in America. If the social structure and institutions within that social structure are stratified by race and gender, identities too will be stratified, not because one chooses a superior or dominant identity per se, but rather because the interaction between oneself and the social structure, institutions, and those within institutions (i.e., peers, those in superior or dominant positions, cultural artifacts, etc.) work to create these stratified identities. This is a fluid, continual process.

The stratification of identity itself is something that, I argue, is outside the realm of choice—thus the term "unchosen." As such, the Unchosen Me is an imposition on one's identity whereby one perceives a need to accept and portray particular ways of thinking, acting, speaking, or being in order to belong within the social realm. Perhaps everyone is influenced by various forms of unchosen identities. However, I contend that one's interaction with this phenomenon will be different depending on whether a person is in a majority or minority group within a particular context. If one is in a minority group, such as the African American women enrolled at the predominantly White college campus in this ethnographic study, she is likely to experience *more* impositions on her identity or a greater influence of the Unchosen Me. This would lead to a perception that she would need to change more aspects of herself, of her identity, than would her majority (White, in this case) peers.

The interaction of race and gender was demonstrated in the data from the ethnographic study upon which chapters 4–7 focus. While the setting for this particular study was a large, Research Extensive, predominantly White institution of higher education, the experiences and findings could be transferred to other social institutions. I compare the Unchosen Me concept to the data to deem whether or not the data relate to the concept and whether they help to evolve the concept.

African American women experienced dual or dichotomous pressures on campus—a two-ness or multiple-ness that had serious implications for their college experiences. These dichotomies were not of their choosing. Rather, they resulted from the interaction the Black women had with their sense of self (identity); their peers, administrators, and faculty on campus; the larger postsecondary institution (i.e., policies, practices and culture); and the larger social structure (i.e., media portrayals, social norms).

African American women experienced unique feelings of culture shock and isolation, presented in chapter 4. They also described experiencing a dichotomous pressure either to speak on behalf of their racial group or to remain silent in the classroom as discussed in chapter 5. This duality between being in the "spotlight" or being "invisible" was created by the interaction between the African American women and their peers and professors on campus. Simultaneously, the women perceived a need to "perform" (e.g., represent, defend, support) their racialized category while also feeling ignored or avoided because of it. Race was dichotomous, as evidenced in chapter 6, whereby the women felt that they needed to balance between being perceived as either "too White" or "too ghetto" (i.e., "too Black") among their peers. As a result of this "too White" / "too ghetto" duality, the Black women altered various aspects of their behavior, speech patterns, thinking, or tastes in an effort to indicate their racial classification or membership to their peers from both majority and minority groups. Ultimately, race and gender were inextricably linked, race was gendered, and gender was racialized, as demonstrated in chapter 7. The women's stories illustrate how these tensions affected their educational success, overall experiences in college, and, eventually, their ability and/or willingness to persist in their degree programs.

While grappling with the implicit interaction of race on campus—an interaction between the Black women's sense of self, their peers, their professors and administrators, and the institution and larger social structure, I also present more explicit evidence of racialized interactions, namely, the women's conversations about race. These conversations about race also created the meaning and ordering of race on campus. Indeed, the conversations highlighted both subtle and overt racism and sexism on campus, underscoring the feelings of isolation that the African American women commonly experienced.

What about gender? I weave evidence about gender throughout the book, offering multiple illustrations of the ways in which gender connects to race. Gender was largely constructed within the boundaries of what it meant to be a "good woman"—yet another imposed identity. The requirements of being a "good woman" were often described in ways that are antithetical to the notions of achievement and success on campus, relegating the women to grapple with either being a "good woman" or a successful student. Ultimately, gender was constructed in racialized terms; that is, the notion of being a "good woman" was constructed with Whiteness (i.e., being like a White woman) as the norm. That is, being a "good woman" was really associated with being a good *White* woman. As the African American women reflected on their own gender, they struggled with the racialized nature of gender constructions on campus and its imposition on their own identity as shown by their conversations in chapter 7.

The Unchosen Me explores privilege and power as these concepts relate to identity, race, and gender. I focus on the ways that race and gender are created every day on a college campus, not for the first time, but in a cumulative, perpetual way. This book thus provides both theoretical and empirical evidence of the *interactive process* that continually creates and reinforces these categories. While the setting for this discussion is a college campus, some of the findings could relate to many of the social institutions within the United States.

The women felt continually split, pulled in multiple directions at one time in the interaction between their own sense of self, those on campus, their peers, and the larger social structure. Ultimately, as W.E.B. Du Bois predicted, the women "ever felt [their] two-ness . . ."

CHAPTER TWO

THE UNCHOSEN ME

The Intersection of Opportunity,
Privilege, and Choice

We would pull ourselves up by our bootstraps if only we
had boots.   —*Martin Luther King Jr. (1968)*

Are all identities created equal? Beverly Tatum (2000) argues that in American society some identities, namely, those associated with Whiteness, are privileged over others. If this is the case, who has the power to determine which identities are privileged? In a nation built on notions of meritocracy, such as the United States, there is an inherent assumption of equality of opportunity—if one works hard, one will earn opportunities—particularly related to issues of educational opportunity (Lemann, 1999; Turner, 1960). Those scholars employing the input and outcome perspectives on race have examined issues of opportunity and equality (Blau, 2004; Bonilla-Silva, 2003; Feagin, 1991; Lee & Burkam, 2002; Massey, Charles, Lundy, & Fischer, 2003; Omi & Winant, 1994). Yet, can equal opportunity coexist among unequally privileged identities?

Tackling the issues of identity, perceptions of choice related to identity, and perceptions of opportunity within the context of higher education, this theoretical chapter raises the question: Does one have choice regarding identity? If choice of identity does exist on some level, does everyone have equal choices, or are there barriers to choice for some? I argue that all do not have equal access to alternatives, particularly alternative identities—calling into question the notion of choice related to identity. Choice is an integral part of equality. If there are fewer alternatives for some, there are fewer choices. If one can better understand the inequality of choice, one can gain further insight into ways to ameliorate inequality. Since identities are integral to the process of widening behavioral choices with regard to opportunities, then if one can better understand the inequality of choice related to the development of identities, one can better understand inequality of opportunity. That is, if some perceive there to be fewer choices regarding *who* they can become, they may have fewer opportunities or a perception of fewer opportunities. I argue below that identity choice—and subsequently, choice of opportunity—is constrained, or limited, due to racialized and gendered categories. I employ a sociological notion of identity that places interaction at the center—interaction between one's self, other people, and the larger social structure. This interaction-based notion of identity allows for a deeper consideration of the concepts of race and gender as phenomena that are created through interaction. A deeper understanding of the creation of race and gender could provide insight into ways to transform the inequalities associated with these categories.

This chapter provides an alternative, complementary framework for understanding college student development.[1] This addition more centrally considers the social structure and the way existing social inequalities *outside* of higher education may influence the experiences of students, particularly underrepresented students, *within* higher education—namely, through a concept that reveals those identities or aspects of identities that are imposed, or experienced as not chosen. This has important consequences for policies and practices aimed at supporting underrepresented students since it could allow for a more thorough understanding of the unique issues that underrepresented students face in higher education and ways that those in postsecondary education can work to alleviate these challenges. This could inform work related to college student retention, recruitment, campus culture and climate, and pedagogy. At the very least, it might provide new theoretical insight into identity work about students in higher education while simultaneously offering a new perspective on the creation of race and gender more generally. The remainder of this book focuses on a predominantly White institution (PWI) of higher education, and thus often provides examples related to higher education. However, the concepts described here could ultimately transcend higher education and could be present in numerous settings within society writ large.

THE "ME" AND THE SOCIOLOGICAL
PERSPECTIVE OF IDENTITY

The sociological perspective of identity is rooted in the philosophical work of pragmatist thinkers William James (1890/1968), Charles Cooley (1902), and George Herbert Mead (1934/1967). These thinkers focused on interaction, and the tradition is aptly called "symbolic interactionism." Mead (1934/1967), for example, examined the interaction between one's self and society. Stryker (1980) developed these initial symbolic interactionist theories of identity to make them empirically testable. Mead (1934/1967) argued that the source of the mind and self were *ongoing processes* entirely linked to others. Thus, the study of interaction became the study of the interaction between self, others, and society.

This interactionist perspective differs from the dominant psychologically based theoretical perspectives in higher education in that it maintains a multiple-identities perspective where both individuals and society are continually created in and through social processes. Rather than passing through a series of stages, one's identity is being created constantly through interaction. As opposed to a particular stage-based endpoint, the sociological perspective emphasizes the *process* and *interaction* between the individual (self), other people, the larger society, and in this case, the college campus.[2] To build a foundation for my own theoretical concept, the Unchosen Me, I begin by reviewing these foundational theories of identity.

The Self in the Sociological Perspective: Foundational Theories

The sociological perspective on identity, rooted in the work of James, Cooley, and Mead, created a shift from the behaviorist psychological perspective, which studied only the observable self, to the self as a product of one's reflection. Mead (1934/1967) still considered himself a behaviorist, but his work greatly altered notions of identity: from being solely that which can be observed, to including one's own reflection of her or his sense of self. Cooley (1902) and Mead (1934/1967) used an evolutionary framework, noting the processes of change in society. They also maintained that communication is fundamental to society. However, Cooley differed from Mead in his conception of self, asserting that the self is a process occurring within the confines of the individual human mind. For Cooley, the self and society are two sides of the same coin.

Mead, on the other hand, asserted that the self is derived from *interaction*. This conception of self developed through interaction led to the elaboration of

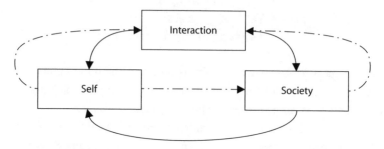

Figure 2.1 Mead's interaction, self, and society

the symbolic interactionist perspective in social psychology. For Mead, interaction creates both the self and society. The self, ultimately initiated within social interaction, is dependent on society; that is, the social structure is central to the development of identities. Figure 2.1 provides a visual representation to explain the interaction between self and society as put forth by Mead (1934/1967). While the self does affect society in some ways, for Mead, society has a greater influence on the self than the self has on society, as represented by the dotted line between the self and society (fig. 2.1).

Mead's I/Me Differentiation

William James (1890/1968) was the first to consider two parts of self: the directly observable, empirical parts of self, developing the concept of the socialized "Me" aspect of self and the unpredictable, innovative "I" aspect of self. George Herbert Mead's development of self elaborated on James's two aspects of self, the "I" and the "Me" (hereafter referred to as simply I and Me without quotation marks).[3] For Mead, the self is dialogic, in that the language process of dialogue and interaction is integral to the development of the self. He proposed that the I and the Me are separated, but they belong together in the sense that they are parts of a whole self (Mead, 1934/1967). As such, the I and the Me could be considered to be two parts of a circle. At one end of the circle is the "pure I," which has no qualities because it is not objectified in any way; while on the other end is the socialized part of self that is dependent on culture, language, and others. Yet they are both part of the same circle. While there is really only one I aspect of self, there are multiple Me parts of self—perhaps as many social selves as there are groups of others to respond to a person (see James, 1890/1968).[4] While my theoretical work primarily centers on the Me aspect of identity, I explain both here to provide a background of Mead's dialectical[5] notion of identity.

The "pure I" is associated with pure subjectivity. In that sense, it is the part of the self that can never be objectified, the source of always unexpected activity, or the sense that we "surprise ourselves by our own action" (Mead, 1934/1967, p. 174). The I is where free will and desires reside. It is the principle of action and of impulse, and in its action it changes the social structure (Morris in Mead, 1934/1967).

The I is a free factor, meaning that it can be related to awareness and creativity. While the I can become aware of the entire feature of the Me and the "roles" one plays, it is more than any particular role or Me, unpredictable in some ways and not fully known by others, even to oneself (Mead, 1934/1967). In some ways, the I is the *not*. In other words, the I is the state of knowing that one is *not* this; *not* that, even if one does not know what one *is*. The I is said to have no qualities in that it is possible to *feel* the I, but the moment that one begins to consider it, the I seems to vanish,[6] or it becomes a Me, because it would be bound by a cultural reality. Mead maintains that the I comes into being as a historical figure. By this he means, "It is what you were a second ago that is the 'I' of the 'me.' It is another me that has to take that role" (1934/1967, p. 174).

The I is the deepest, innermost part of self, and no one, not even oneself, can ever completely and infinitely know the I, though most long for this type of infinite recognition.[7] Considering the I in terms of a desire to be recognized,[8] the self is subject to a motivation to have its I recognized, ultimately by its own self, though it is always more than any objectification that can be formed or used for it.

As is the case with dialectics, the I aspect of self is needed to fully understand the Me. Mead's depiction of the Me part of self is derived from interaction (1934/1967). It is dependent on cultural forms, language, and the ability to interact with others. One relies on culture, group norms, and roles to obtain the Me. Mead uses two stages of self-development to describe this interaction: play and game. In play, a child assumes one role after another of persons or animals that have entered his or her life (Morris in Mead, 1934/1967, p. xxiv). In game, all of the attitudes and roles of all others who are playing the game are taken into oneself (p. xxiv).[9] These generalized attitudes that one takes into oneself become what Mead calls the "generalized other." It is through this generalized other that one knows how to define her own conduct. The Me is what others recognize about a person; it is constituted of the "attitudes of others" (1934/1967, p. 175), making it highly dependent on the generalized other for its existence. In that way, one's Me is highly dependent not only on interaction with others and the larger society, but on an internalization of the roles and attitudes, and in many ways the socialized expectations,[10] of others. Linking the Me to recognition desires (Hegel, 1977/1952), the Me is the part of the self that longs for recognition by others as a part of a community/group.

Consistent with James's (1890/1968) notion of multiple selves, it is possible to have multiple "Me's," or Me components within oneself. Using college students as an example, one Me may be associated with being a student, and another Me may be associated with being a partner or a friend. In each different Me, a person may act and feel differently as he or she makes different claims to identity. A person may often have a particular Me component present within multiple Me's. As an illustration, a female may have a female Me component in many of her Me's. However, being entirely defined by cultural forms or by any particular Me does not fulfill the needs for the recognition of individuality or uniqueness; thus, there is a deeper, more elusive part of self—the I. This underscores the interplay and the dialectical, intimate connection between the I and the Me; they are two aspects of the same whole self.[11]

In this I/Me circle, the self has two tendencies that could be considered to be in tension with one another, using the notion of a Hegelian dialectic:[12] a tendency toward conforming so that others do recognize one and so that one may belong to a group, community, or culture; and the tendency to differentiate from others, to be unique, and to be an individual. A person develops identity through a process of differentiation from others as well as through conformity with others. In other words, to apply Hegel's concept of recognition desires and dialectical tensions (1977/1952): the self longs for recognition from others, producing a tendency to conform, and at the same time longs for the recognition that acknowledges its individuality and uniqueness, creating a tendency to differentiate. Moreover, recognition is a fundamental need. When a self emerges within this dual structure, the motivation complex of gaining recognition (either through conformity or individuality) also emerges.[13] Table 2.1 illustrates the I/Me differentiation to articulate the differences between these two aspects of self.

Structural Symbolic Interactionism

Sheldon Stryker (1980, 2000),[14] the father of structural symbolic interactionism, adapted Mead's symbolic interactionist framework to empirically specify and test ideas relating to social structures, selves in the form of multiple identities, and social behavior. The sociological perspective on identity theory largely grew out of Stryker's work (1980, 2000). Stryker began by conceptualizing society as a congeries of social relationships and the self as a hierarchical structure of multiple identities. His work in part attempted to uncover the motives and ratio-

TABLE 2.1
Mead's I/Me Components of Self

	The "I"	The "Me"
Location of	Free will and desires, pure subjectivity, principle of action and of impulse	Socialized sense of self, the roles one plays
Level of Objectification	Cannot be objectified	Objectified sense of self
Dependent on	Pure subjectivity	A generalized other for recognition, cultural norms and values, language
Source of	Always unexpected activity (surprise oneself by own activity)	What others recognize about a person, the roles one plays
Number of	One "I" that is never fully known by others or oneself	Multiple Me's or Me components within oneself
Recognition Desires	Desire to be unique and individual	Desire to be accepted as part of a group/community

Source: I/Me Components adapted from Mead (1934/1967). Recognition desires adapted from Hegel (1952/1977).

nales behind one's choice of a particular identity. In structural symbolic interactionism, the strength of one's commitments to one's social networks is affected by the relative salience of one's identities linked to the roles[15] one plays in the networks in which one is imbedded.[16] In turn, the relative salience[17] of one's identities affects the probability of opting, in choice situations, for behaviors consistent with those identities (Stryker, 1980).

Stryker's formulation of identity provides excellent insight into the external conditions of identity development (e.g., the situations, environments, and groups affecting identity). The terms of Mead's formulation as shown in figure 2.1 (self, interaction, society), are specified by Stryker's work (as shown in figure 2.2) through the notions of commitment, identity salience, and role choice. This specification allows for what Mead's formulation does not: the empirical test of theoretical arguments implied by Mead. To give an example, if an African American woman was highly committed to being perceived as Black, she would likely display behaviors that she perceived as "Black" when she was among other Black students. Or, if a student was very committed to being perceived as a "good student," she would likely display this identity in the classroom by taking copious notes, sitting at the front, and answering questions when asked by the professor.

Building on Mead's notion of the Me aspect of self and Stryker's empirical formulation of Mead's concepts, I turn my attention toward those aspects of

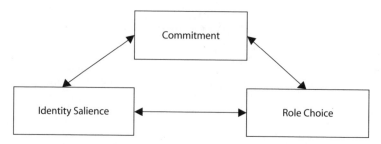

Figure 2.2 Commitment, identity salience, and role choice

identities that are *not* freely chosen. This shifts from Stryker's focus on the instrumental aspects of identities (i.e., motives, goals), calling into question the notion of role choice. Additionally, with the Unchosen Me I begin to consider both the internal and external aspects of identities.

THE UNCHOSEN ME

I developed the Unchosen Me (fig. 2.3), rooted in Mead's socialized aspect of self, the Me, as a concept to understand the intersection of perceptions of opportunity and privilege structures with perceptions of choice, specifically one's choice of identity. I examine the differential freedom and constraints resulting from the social structure and the way these concepts affect identity processes. The Unchosen Me is a theoretical concept with which to consider the possibility of interactional characteristics of identity (interaction between self, other people, and society) that work to either empower or disempower people. While the theoretical concept could be applied to a larger social setting, I limit my discussion of the concept here primarily to institutions of higher education. But first I provide brief explanations for the concepts of opportunity, privilege, and choice.

Opportunity, Privilege, and Choice

As the self develops both as a unique entity and as a socialized being, it is bounded by institutional and cultural structures. The self, particularly the Me aspects of self, is influenced by one's perception of and access to opportunity structures. Also, the self is affected by socially ascribed privileges or lack of privileges. The intersection of these opportunity and privilege structures influences the choices of identity that one experiences as available. Specifically, this influences the development of one's identities.

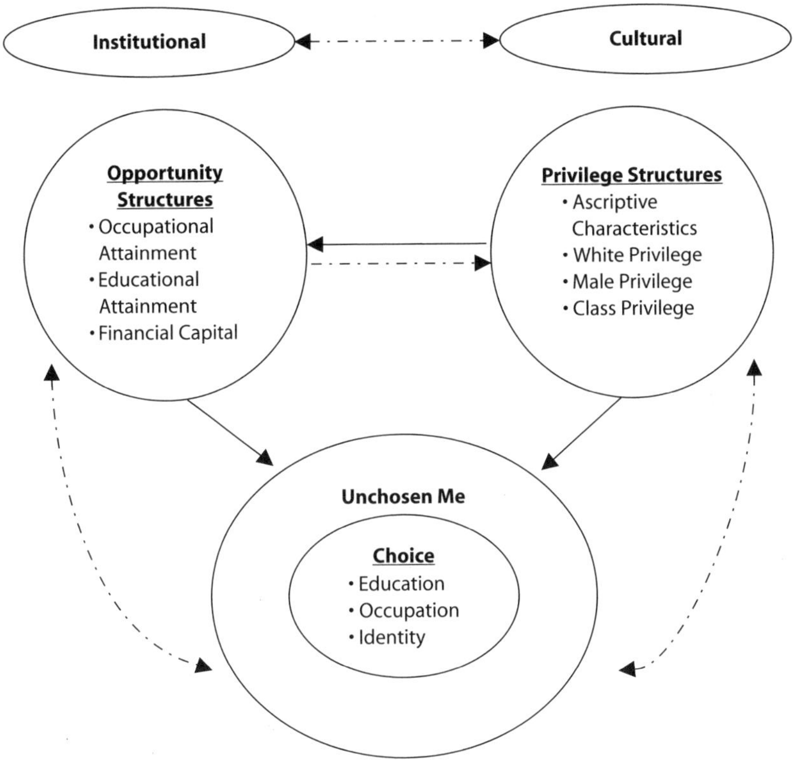

Figure 2.3 The Unchosen Me: the intersection of opportunity, privilege, and choice

Institutional Influence—Opportunity Structures

While it is sometimes stated that people have equal access to opportunities in the United States, people's perceptions of these opportunities may differ, as will the opportunities themselves. For the purposes of this discussion, I am considering opportunity structures with regard to occupational attainment, educational attainment, and financial background (Kerckhoff, 1995; Knotterus, 1987; Sewell, Haller, & Portes, 1969; Sewell & Hauser, 1972). These structures are often institutionalized as policies and legislation. For example, financial aid as an institutionalized structure attempts to provide financial access to postsecondary education. Affirmative action, another example, is an institutionalized policy encouraging diversity and equal opportunity within occupational structures and institutions of higher education (Guinier, 2000).

There are both subjective and objective aspects of opportunity structures. Objectively, opportunity is constrained for some due to economic, racial, or gender stratification in society. Subjectively, as one interacts within the social structure, one develops a perception of the availability of opportunities. This perception of opportunity availability is often bounded by racialized or gendered categories. For instance, until the 2008 presidential elections, when Hillary Clinton and Barack Obama both ran for president, many women and African Americans did not see the run for the presidency as an opportunity that was available to them. The Obama presidency may make the presidency a reasonable aspiration for African American youth in a way that it was not before. Or in the area of education, if a student does not have parents, friends, or family members who attended college, postsecondary education may not seem like a viable opportunity. Ultimately, this perception of opportunity can influence one's action and choices. Here, I am primarily concerned with how one perceives opportunities—the way one does or does not experience opportunity related to education as accessible. But opportunities are also constrained or facilitated by privilege structures.

Cultural Influences—Privilege

Privilege can be defined in multiple ways. For the purposes of this discussion, privilege refers to the unearned status and/or characteristics that provide advantages or disadvantages to people. Thus, privilege refers to a favored state conferred by birth, luck, or unequal social structures (Blum, 2008; Garvey & Ignatiev, 1997; McIntosh, 1992). Here, I am particularly interested in privileges related to race, class, and gender.

White privilege, a form of racialized privilege, refers to the privileges of White people in the United States associated with superiority and dominance (Mahoney, 1997). With many types of privilege, including White privilege, there are characteristics of near invisibility, making it difficult to see because, as in the case of White privilege, Whiteness becomes the standard or the norm with which all other people or ideas are compared (Giroux, 1997; Keating, 1995). For example, the phrase "a Black doctor" implicitly indicates that it is abnormal for a person with a medical degree to be Black. Or research that constantly compares White and Black students can implicitly imply that White students are the norm against which Black students should be measured. White privilege manifests itself in many ways within educational institutions. One example is early tracking in schooling, often linked to ascribed racial characteristics, which potentially results in less access to higher education (Blau, 2004). This may be experienced by people of color as if White people are the standard against which all others must be measured.

Male privilege refers to the advantages conferred upon males within a patriarchal society (Case, 2007; McIntosh, 1992). In higher education male privilege manifests itself by creating a climate that is less inclusive to females (Case, 2007; Jacobs, 1996; Whitt et al., 1999). There has been debate in popular news media regarding the possibility of female advantages in education (Zarembo, 2002). While there is evidence that females are beginning to outnumber males in many postsecondary institutions, this may not be an indication that male privilege is lessening. Male privilege connotes privileges afforded to males in both subtle and overt ways. For instance, although many females obtain similar or more education than males, the pay gap between males and females continues to exist, indicating that the rewards of education still privilege males (Reskin & Padavic, 1994; Zhang, 2008). This may be experienced by females as if males are the norm or standard against which they are measured.

Class privilege, for the purposes of this analysis, connotes the subtle and overt advantages awarded to a person for demonstrating particular class-related tastes, preferences, norms, or values. This learned taste distinction, called cultural capital, works as an asset through attitudes and behaviors associated with high-class status that are rewarded in social settings (Bourdieu, 1979/1984).[18] Cultural capital is coupled with peer influences or subgroup structure whereby all members of a particular subgroup have similar tastes, attitudes, expectations, and aspirations, creating privilege for some based on class (Bourdieu, 1979/1984). These tastes, attitudes, values, expectations, and aspirations work as a form of capital in educational settings where students are rewarded for demonstrating that they have high-status tastes, preferences, and norms or values (Lareau, 1987, 1993, 2003). One way that class privilege is manifested in education is through the differential preparation for higher education along class lines in K–12 schooling (McDonough, 1997; Perna, 2000; Roscigno & Ainsworth-Darnell, 1999). Privilege, whether it is White privilege, class privilege, or male privilege, could influence one's perceptions of opportunities and, ultimately, the choices one sees as available.

Choice—Freedom and Constraint

Choice, as I am using it for the purposes of this discussion, refers to one's volition or one's *perception* of volition. I am primarily interested here in the limits or boundaries around choice. This relates to Stryker's (1989) assertion that choice is a function of the degree to which one has multiple selves and the extent to which one feels one can display those selves. Even if one has a particular identity, one may feel that this identity is not recognized or that it is *mis*-recognized in certain settings. For example, if an African American student uses slang or an informal dialect in a college classroom, some professors may misrecognize this as a sign that the student is not as smart as those students who are speaking more formally. Such a student may not feel she can act the same way in all settings. But more importantly, she may not feel as if her identity is properly recognized in some settings.

Stryker (1994) investigated the dialectical process of freedom and constraint to better understand the alternatives one has available in making choices about identity. He argues, "If alternatives are not symbolically present, attached to salient identities, or supported by networks of relationships to which persons have high levels of commitment, alternatives are minimal or will have low likelihood of enactment" (1997, p. 323). In this way, choice is bounded by the social structure of which one is a part. While this is the case for all people, I am interested here in the unequal ways that the social structure influences identity relative to race and gender.

Depending on one's location in the social structure, perceptions of opportunities, and level of privilege, one will experience as available a differential set of choices. Regarding identity, one is only able to *choose* an identity if there is a level of freedom of options available or if there are fewer constraints on that identity. Furthermore, one is only able to choose identities that are socially recognizable in a given context. For those who are underrepresented in a particular context, such as students of color on predominantly White college campuses, it may be difficult to have recognized those identity choices that are outside of the mainstream.

Using the concepts of opportunity, privilege, and choice, I now turn to an explanation of the Unchosen Me concept as an attempt to elucidate the ways one experiences identity relative to the existing social inequalities and stratification within the social structure.

The Unchosen Me Defined

The Unchosen Me depicts a Me or Me components that are institutionally bounded, culturally and institutionally imposed, and thus not necessarily freely *chosen* by people. The Unchosen Me reveals the *process* of accepting these aspects of identities into one's notion of self. At times this process occurs before one has the opportunity to choose, while at other times one may consciously accept these unchosen identities or identity characteristics as a strategy for success in a particular setting. Or one may unknowingly accept Unchosen Me characteristics over a period of time even though the change is nearly imperceptible until much later. This is a fluid and dynamic process—changing through the course of one's interactions between one's self, others, and society.

While I call this concept the Unchosen Me, I still maintain a multiple-identities perspective. One could have multiple Me's at one time and could have multiple Unchosen Me's within one's identities simultaneously. The Unchosen Me could in theory be an entire identity in and of itself. However, in general, I am conceiving of the Unchosen Me as related to particular *aspects* or *characteristics* that influence identities.

The Unchosen Me refers to the aspects of identities or entire identities that one questions or senses are unfit. The Unchosen Me also includes those aspects of identity or identities that one does not consciously recognize as unchosen, yet one did not readily make a decision to accept. One example of such identities is those that are ascribed (e.g., race, gender).[19] At its limit, the Unchosen Me could imply that in some ways, at least implicitly, all Me aspects of self or Me identities are unchosen. In order for a Me to exist, it must be socially recognizable—one must interact with others and the larger society to have this identity recognized. Given that the Me part of an identity is initiated in the already existing social structure, the Me is limited by that social structure. That is, one is bounded by the available Me's in that social structure. Or, perhaps more accurately, one is really bounded by the availability of recognition of one's identity by others and through the larger society. Thus, only particular socially recognized roles seem available, and for some, the available roles do not seem to fit.

Of course, one could challenge the existing social structure eventually, pushing at the boundaries to make it possible for new Me's to exist. But in some ways, one would always be bounded by the social structure—one could only go so far in the *choice* of a Me before running into the boundary of what is recognizable by others through the already-existing social structure. While I appreciate this feature of the Unchosen Me, that is, that in some ways all Me's have an unchosen component, I am focusing here particularly on the limits of volition with regard to the Me aspect of identities as they relate to inequality and stratification within the social structure.

Through the Unchosen Me concept, I am arguing that some identities are privileged over others for individuals and society as a whole. Given that the social structure is already stratified by race, class, and gender long before one interacts within that structure, and because the Me parts of one's identities originate in that stratified social structure, identities are also stratified. That is, one is born into existing social stratification by race, class, and gender; and then one's identities (Me aspects of self) develop within this stratification—mirroring social inequality. In some ways, the roles that one is offered as a socialized being are already determined before one has the opportunity to consider choosing them. To provide an example of how early this can begin, one is born and named either a "boy" or a "girl" and then placed, without one's own volition, into the social stratification. A person does not have the opportunity to choose what others will impose based on his or her sex. Almost immediately one is assumed to have certain temperaments, preferences, and behaviors based on one's sex. When my daughter Eleanor was born, for instance, some of my friends already started talking about her playing traditional female roles (e.g., cooking, cleaning, being married to a man, rearing children), or being "sweet," "pretty," "so quiet," and "caring." The gifts that many people offered were gendered too—dolls and pink outfits rather than cars and trucks or blue outfits. Since she was only a few days old, these were largely impositions on her, preparing her for her role as a female in a society that historically has favored males. While she can push back on these assumptions and on the role of "female" (and I hope she does!), she will constantly have to grapple with the already existing role and notions of "female" identity.

This existing social stratification intimately links to the way one's identities develop—as an interaction between one's self, others, and society. As one interacts in this way, one is interacting with the existing social stratification at many levels. This interaction then influences one's identity. Identity may be an illustration of one's interactions within a socially stratified society. Hence, identity itself may be socially stratified, or experienced as unequal. Eventually, some identities may be considered "normal" or "mainstream," while other identities may be deemed alternative or even socially unacceptable. In the process, the boundaries around Me's are created so that only some Me aspects of self are socially acceptable or available.

This is the place where privilege becomes central—some identities may be privileged over others even if one doesn't exactly choose those identities. At least initially, one does not choose into which sex, race, or class category one is placed. Yet some categories may be privileged in society over others (i.e., male over female, White over non-White, higher socioeconomic status over lower socioeconomic status). As one's identity develops within this privilege structure, one's identity is unknowingly placed into this stratification. While a woman may not desire to have an identity as a female that receives fewer privileges than would a male identity, she is not given this choice—the stratification existed long before she was labeled "female." Hypothetically, she could decide not to identify as female in order to avoid this stratification, but this has consequences too, such as not being socially accepted or recognized by those around her.

The Unchosen Me illuminates both the freedom and the constraints (Stryker, 1994) that people experience in their choice of identity. These constraints could be one's perceptions of opportunities or objectively constrained opportunities (e.g., economic social stratification). To belong within an institution, at some level, most people accept a Me or Me characteristics that are heavily encouraged, rewarded, or recognized by the institution. In the case of higher education, students accept certain ways of thinking, writing, speaking, and acting as a way to navigate the institution successfully.

The Unchosen Me relates to the boundaries or perceptions of boundaries that are placed around opportunity structures and privilege within the social structure. Through this, I ask: Are some people more free or more socially constrained than others? To the extent to which the Me aspects of self are embedded within a cultural milieu, they are racialized, gendered, and influenced by class statuses. Consequently, some identities may be experienced as easier to express or more privileged than others, while other identities are constrained. One may not experience a sense of choice with these freedoms and constraints. It is as if the freedoms/constraints existed long before one had the opportunity to interact with them. Thus, freedoms and constraints could represent the existing social stratification within the social structure—some people have certain, sometimes subtle, freedoms that others may not enjoy. Others may have more constraints. Admittedly, those who do enjoy more freedoms or privileges may not have initially chosen these benefits. Yet this differential freedom and constraint may limit access to identity projects, or "Me's" that are not in the mainstream. One may experience this as feeling like alternatives to the mainstream identities are either not present, not viable (meaning that they would not be socially accepted), or not rewarded (there may be a sanction for not having a mainstream identity).

The lack of access to viable (i.e., socially accepted) non-mainstream identities may encourage people to accept Unchosen Me's or imposed aspects of self linked to racialized or gendered categories. For example, in a dichotomous (oppressor/oppressed) racialized society like that in the United States, someone does not necessarily *choose* to be Black in America; they are born into this ascribed category with all of the inequality or stratification that comes with it. The category imposed on a person based on skin pigmentation brings with it a cultural milieu of historical oppression. From the time that race is recorded on one's birth certificate, one is ascribed particular characteristics based on the category listed. At least initially, one does not choose one's racial classification; thus, it is an Unchosen Me aspect of self. Then there are boundaries around what it means to be Black, to exist in this racialized group, and what it means to *not* be White in this social structure that often privileges White people. But, how does this notion of boundaries and the issue of the Unchosen Me relate to institutions such as post-secondary institutions?

The boundaries around one's choice of identities or choice of Me's is enacted through rewards, sanctions, and recognition. As one interacts in a particular setting or situation, one acts within an already existing set of boundaries. Thus, there are particular ways of acting, thinking, speaking, or being that are recognized in that setting, and these ways will be rewarded with recognition from those in that setting or situation. Alternatively, there are ways of thinking, speaking, acting, or being that will either not be recognized or will be misrecognized and therefore sanctioned in that situation or setting. In this way, there might be different aspects of self that are not chosen or Unchosen Mes in various situations or settings.[20]

Predominantly White institutions (PWIs) of higher education provide a good example. I am arguing that the Me components privileged by many social institutions, including higher education, are inherently racist, classist, or sexist because institutions are within a cultural milieu that can be racist, classist, and sexist. Consequently, while there may be a variety of Me formations within an institution, along with some semblance of choice, the Me characteristics that get respect and result in having one's voice heard will likely have essential characteristics representing dominant Me components. In the case of PWIs, many of the dominant Me characteristics would be associated with Whiteness—with being White, or "acting White" (Horvat & Lewis, 2003; Spencer, Noll, Stoltzfus, & Harpalani, 2001).

While college students, for example, are not necessarily forced to accept these ways of being, they will be more rewarded or recognized if they do—and potentially sanctioned if they do not (e.g., receiving a lower grade, being reprimanded by a professor, not feeling socially accepted in peer groups). In this way the institution and those within it could privilege some Me characteristics over others, making the alternatives less appealing or even less available. In other words, while there are many ways to be a "college student," there are certain ways of speaking, thinking, and acting that are rewarded or recognized by the institution more than others. Thus, there is a cultural milieu that privileges certain Me components or characteristics over others.

While institutions do not exactly force identities on people, they and those within them may place significant pressure on people, through institutional processes, people, and policies, to adopt Me components linked to the dominant characteristics valued within the institution. Thus, people from underrepresented groups may be forced to make a choice to either accept the Me characteristics to help them navigate the institution,[21] to avoid the Me characteristics imposed by the institution and subsequently be punished or unrecognized, or to leave the institution. In higher education, this has serious ramifications for student retention, especially for underrepresented students as they attempt to be recognized within the mainstream culture of an institution (Arroyo & Zigler, 1995; Rendòn, 1994; Tierney, 1992). Often success in higher education is predicated on one's *disassociation* from one's previous culture or past, suggesting that a student must acclimatize, assimilate, or adjust to campus by severing ties with past, families, or communities (Arroyo & Zigler, 1995; Tierney, 1999; Winkle-Wagner, 2009a). This may be more difficult for some students (i.e., students of color) than for others.

The issue of recognition of identity, along with the system of rewards and sanctions, creates a necessity of self-monitoring. As one acts, there is a level of self-monitoring that occurs almost simultaneously with the act. One monitors the act so that it fits within existing socialized norms, values, or ways of being. I argue that in certain contexts particular people will be encouraged, if not coerced, into self-monitoring in ways that are unequal to ways required of others. For instance, an African American student at a predominantly White university may feel the need to self-monitor in ways that are inconsistent with previous Me parts of self or with previous social ties. Consequently, a student may not talk about her past or about her family. Or a student may use different language on campus than he would use off campus or with others from his racial group. These changes may be painful and even detrimental to the success of students of color in college (see Winkle-Wagner, 2009a).

So, how does the Unchosen Me relate to the concept of choice more generally? If some aspects of identity are imposed or unchosen, are there other aspects that are in fact experienced as chosen?

Locating the Unchosen Me with Choice

I locate the Unchosen Me in a circle around choice—before, during, and after choice (fig. 2.3). The Unchosen Me explicates the limits of choice or volition within the development of identity, revealing those aspects of self that one experiences as both internal and external to volition. The Unchosen Me provides insight into those aspects of identity that are external to volition through a focus on those identities or aspects of identity that are imposed, coerced, or forced upon a person through external conditions (e.g., situations, people, policies, environments). Yet the Unchosen Me simultaneously refers to those aspects of identity or identities that are internal to volition in that there are instances where a person may consciously accept aspects of identities or identities in general that do not readily fit with her larger notion of her sense of self.

The Unchosen Me occurs external to or before choice in that as one makes claims to identity through action or interaction, there are imposed or ascribed characteristics of race, class, and gender that occur *before* one makes a choice about identity (fig. 2.3). In other words, if an African American woman, for example, were to make a claim to identity, there would often be an ascribed (not chosen) racial category associated with the claim to identity (e.g., you are Black because you have dark-colored skin). In fact, the ascribed racial identity might not be the identity that one would claim for oneself. But the ascription occurs *before* the choice of the claim to identity. For instance, a person from Jamaica might be considered African American in the United States, even though her national identity is not linked to an African country.

The Unchosen Me is also located in a simultaneous position with choice (fig. 2.3), as internal to volition. Here, a person would knowingly accept particular Me characteristics to navigate one's way through an institution. In the case of higher education, students may learn to think, speak, or act in particular ways in order to navigate the system. The student would *knowingly* make these changes and would potentially act differently when not on campus (e.g., she would speak or act differently among a peer group off campus). Using the example of Black students at a PWI, a student would accept Unchosen Me aspects of self because of a lack of alternatives, because other Me components might not be readily available, because alternative Me characteristics would not be rewarded or recognized, or because alternative Me characteristics would be sanctioned. Ultimately, the Unchosen Me may affect everyone, but some students, likely students of color in the case of predominantly White institutions, would experience more identity impositions than others.

Finally, the Unchosen Me is located after choice, as either internal or external to volition. As such, a person could accept an entire Me part of self that is not chosen, perhaps without even realizing that he or she has done so (external to volition). Or at times, one may actively choose this entire aspect of self due to coercion or the lack of viable alternatives (internal to volition, below the conscious level). Discussions about internalized racism are relevant to the location of the Unchosen Me after choice. For example, Helms (1995) developed a racial identity model for people of color (African Americans, Latinos, and Asian Americans) with the ego statuses ranging from conformity to integrative awareness.[22] Conformity represents a dependence on White society for definition and approval, with negative attitudes toward one's own racial or cultural group. As a person internalizes messages about him- or herself, trying to integrate into the White mainstream, potentially denying one's own racialized group, the person could ultimately become a socialized being that was imposed or that possesses an entire Me part of self that was imposed. The same could hold true for gender/class categorizations.

Self-reflection provides a hopeful layer to the Unchosen Me concept. Ultimately, when one notices the sense of Unchosen Me characteristics, this self-awareness or reflection is linked to one's memory of former Me's or Me parts of self that are still rooted in social reality.[23] If one found recognition within a particular cultural group and then was removed from that group, the memory of this earlier recognition would guide one's reflection on later identities, or Me's. Additionally, through self-reflection one may begin to push at the boundaries around identity choices—ultimately leading toward the creation of new viable Me alternatives.

Figure 2.3 illustrates the Unchosen Me concept and the interaction between opportunity structures and privilege. Institutional structures and cultural norms or mores are located at the top of the figure to connote the way institutional and cultural concepts interact with each other and also affect both opportunity and privilege structures. The dotted line represents an indirect effect, meaning that institutional and cultural concepts may influence one another, but at times indirectly or without one's consciousness of it. Privilege directly influences people's perceptions of opportunity structures and then, eventually, opportunity structures may affect people's perceptions of privilege (indirectly, as represented by the dotted line). Privilege and opportunity structures, and people's perceptions of these concepts, directly influence imposed identity or Unchosen Me characteristics of identity and one's choices or perceptions of choice related to identity. Ultimately, one's choice (or lack of choice) related to identity also affects one's choice and perception of education and opportunity—eventually having an indirect influence on the creation of opportunity and privilege structures within the larger social structure.

The Unchosen Me, Responsibility, Victimization, and Resistance Identities

Two challenges in the development of the Unchosen Me concept are the issues of responsibility and ownership. To develop an identity, at some point one must say "yes" to the identity and claim it as one's own. With the Unchosen Me, the name itself connotes the inability to freely choose. However, if a person is unaware of alternatives due to oppression, either subtle or overt, he or she may find it harder to really *choose* the identity, so there is a façade of choice. The Unchosen Me is particularly relevant when something about a person (i.e., gender, race, and class of origin) already limits the possible identities or Me's available to him or her. The unique longings, desires, orientations, or creativities do not then have a way to be expressed, and the result can be a feeling of oppression. If one's Me qualities are always already valued less in the culture because of something unchosen (e.g., race, gender, class, sexual orientation), then the desire for being fully validated comes into conflict with the Me components and structures available. While there are multiple Me's, there are constraints and boundaries, and certain Me components do not receive recognition: one's freedom to choose is limited.

What about victimization? In the discussion of issues of racial privilege, or even gender or class privilege, especially if done by members of the dominant group, the less-privileged groups are often characterized as the victims. I need to stress that the Unchosen Me is not an effort to undermine the idea of agency and free will. Also, it is not my intent to create victims in the disadvantaged. The Unchosen Me could be accepted as a form of identity for both privileged and underprivileged groups. White people in the United States, for instance, may accept an identity that is related to racism, or a racist identity (Helms, 1994). Likewise, a person of color in the United States may develop an identity that is initially based on the dominant racial identities because of a lack of access to alternatives (Cross, 1995; Helms, 1994). Through the Unchosen Me, I am attempting to clarify the way that existing inequalities have a meaningful effect on the identities one views as available or recognizable. Ultimately, some may find it easier, given existing opportunity and privilege structures, to receive social recognition for their identities. It is this inequality that I desire to explain here.

There is room for agency even with the potentially gloomy picture portrayed by the Unchosen Me. The creation of support networks or socialized groups where people can resist impositions on identity or Unchosen Me characteristics may be helpful in facilitating agency. If one can find a group with whom to feel recognized in one's alternative identity, this group may actually become a form of agency or resistance in itself—a way of resisting unchosen pressures.

Some people would say that those experiencing oppression have developed identities of resistance to counter the oppression or to be unlike the norm or those in power. This counter-identity is often a way of inverting the values and norms of the dominant culture. This dependency on the dominant culture may or may not result in another form of oppression. If the values chosen only have meaning because they are trying to resist dominant culture, they probably will not result in self-realization and could continue to be oppressive (see MacLeod, 1987; Willis, 1977, for examples). However, if these resistance values are in some way sustainable on their own, regardless of the dominant culture, the resistance identity could lead to a form of liberation of identities for those who choose it. Additionally, in those cases when the Unchosen Me aspects of self are knowingly accepted as a navigational tool, one may actually be accepting these identity characteristics as a form of agency. A student at a PWI who knowingly accepts Unchosen Me characteristics as a strategy to navigate an institution may feel empowered in knowing this and then be able to have agency in her identity.

Another possibility for resistance to Unchosen Me characteristics in higher education is holding identities in social units outside of or within the institution. For example, an African American student at a predominantly White college who belongs to the Black Student Union may find agency within this group because she finds a place to belong and, potentially, a group with which to subvert the White-centered campus norms. This is also consistent with the multiple Me's stance in the sociological perspective. One's memory of former Me's or identities held outside of the institution or within other groups within the institution may aid one in navigating, if not denying, Unchosen Me characteristics.

Applying the Unchosen Me to Higher Education

On predominantly White college campuses, it is important to consider this imposition of ascribed characteristics. Is there a mainstream that is considered "normal" on campus? If so, does it relate to a particular racialized, class-specific, or gendered group? In what ways are in-groups and out-groups defined or bounded? The characteristics one feels he or she must adopt as a way to fit within an in-group, or to self-monitor in a given context, are related to the Unchosen Me.

I developed the idea of the Unchosen Me in an effort to better understand the biased identity that an institution may impose on students. One way to apply this concept to predominantly White institutions of higher education is through the retention and persistence debate (Bean & Eaton, 2001; Christie & Dinham, 1991; Rendòn, 1994; Tierney, 1992; Tinto, 1993, 1997). Of course this is just one of many possible applications for this concept.

Many college student retention theories argue that student persistence in degree programs is linked to the academic and social integration of students (Bean & Eaton, 2001; Christie & Dinham, 1991; Tinto, 1975, 1993, 1997). I challenge this model within predominantly White institutions because there is an underlying assumption that a *student* must integrate into the institution rather than challenging *institutions* to change to meet the needs of new populations of students. To bring new populations to the proverbial table of higher education in meaningful ways, institutions must be willing to change, particularly when it comes to the inclusion of those from underrepresented groups. This argument recommends a fundamental shift in the way research is conducted, asserting that research may in fact be unwittingly part of the oppression.

In the student retention literature, for example, scholars have criticized retention theories regarding their lack of consideration for minority students (Howard-Hamilton, 1997; Rendòn, 1994; Tierney, 1992). The academic-social integration model, which maintains that students should be socialized into institutions, could facilitate imposed identities or Unchosen Me characteristics. This issue needs further consideration, given that ethnic minorities have a higher probability of leaving college prematurely than ethnic majority students (DesJardins et al., 2002; Hatch & Mommsen, 1984; Mehan et al., 1994; R. D. Myers, 2003; Pathways to College Network, 2003). Could this perhaps be in part because students of color are asked to give up more of their pasts or identities in order to integrate than are White students?

The idea that institutions of higher education impose standards and/or provide categories by which identities or Me components are judged and evaluated could lead to a feeling of either entitlement and privilege or disempowerment, depending on whether or not these standards provide a feeling of recognition for the students (recognition of conformity versus recognition of individuality). For instance, if the dominant Me components imposed by a predominantly White campus are "White Me" components, this could leave non-White students feeling marginalized or disempowered as they try to gain recognition through conformity. Alternatively, this could subtly empower White students since they may find it easier to gain recognition on campus.

If students feel empowered or privileged because the mainstream Me characteristics are in line with their previous culture, they will likely persist in pursuing a degree. If students feel disempowered or underprivileged because their Me characteristics do not connect to their previous culture or former Me's, they may accept the dominant Me characteristics as a strategy to navigate the institution, resist the dominant Me characteristics and be unrewarded/unrecognized by the institution, or eventually leave the institution. Alternatively, if those who feel disempowered, or allies of those who are underprivileged, can come together, there is a possibility of change to the institution.

Retention policies, programs, and theories need to take the cultural background of students seriously and include discussions about cultural differences within the efforts to integrate students academically and socially. Retention programs cannot be solely based on the molding of students to fit the institution. The institution likewise must change to fit the new populations of students. As institutions of postsecondary education become increasingly diverse, the need for this shift in thinking becomes even greater. The retention example is but one instance of the potential manifestation of the Unchosen Me in higher education. In this project I was also interested in better understanding other ways that the Unchosen Me presents itself, such as through the general student experiences on campus.

Autonomy and Self-Reflection as Hope

Does the existence of the Unchosen Me represent a downward spiral of oppression with no hope of remedy? Recall that Mead's (1934/1967) development of the Me was linked to one's ability to reflect on oneself. Reflection and autonomy have the potential to mitigate this gloomy picture. One can use reflection as a way to differentiate oneself from others and as a way to say "no" to the Unchosen Me. Durkheim explains: "To be a person is to be an autonomous source of action. Man acquires this quality only insofar as there is something which is his alone and which individualizes him, as he is something more than a simple incarnation of the generic type of his race and his group" (quoted in Habermas, 1987, p. 84).

This self-realization is linked to the heightened awareness of the memory of former Me's, or even of possible selves that have yet to exist. So could the heightened awareness or recognition of former Me's or possible future selves liberate one from the imposed institutional identity of the Unchosen Me? I maintain hope that one may be able to accept Me's that feel right, or through which a person can recognize him- or herself through fostering self-reflection. Habermas elaborates: "Once reflection is awakened, it is not easy to restrain it. When it has taken hold, it develops spontaneously beyond the limits assigned to it" (1984, p. 84). Reflection is akin to the self-realization described by Mead (1934/1967), who describes the power of spontaneous self-realization as freeing. I concur that the self-realization that one is more than Unchosen Me characteristics could be the key to freedom.

Consciousness-raising groups are a good example of ways in which one could try to facilitate the self-discovery of the Me's that feel true to oneself. There is something to be said for groups or relationships in which one can commune, or share a part of oneself in a way that is deeper than anything that a person has previously known. There are many examples that seem in some way to facilitate the discovery of oneself: the intimacy of a lifetime partnership, the sharing of a creative expression such as playing a musical instrument, or even the intense community formed by those who are oppressed as a way to overcome the oppression. All of these relationships have a commonality in that they in some way validate or recognize the self in such a way that one is able to move to higher levels of thought and/or of being. One may then be able to accept Me's that feel right or through which one can recognize oneself.

However, there is a fine line between a community or a relationship that is liberating and one that shackles the self to accept a pre-constructed Me. An example is a highly dogmatic religious community. Those who join the community may find that questioning the tenets or the dogma of the community results in marginalization or even, as it is internalized, in self-loathing. In time, the person loses the ability to question and in turn is no longer able to take a critical position on the tenets of the community. People within the community often profess a belief in the dogma without doubt or questioning. But while doubt has been removed, is there, in fact, choice?

CONCLUSION: HOPE AMIDST THE UNCHOSEN ME?

So how can one keep the process of self-discovery and self-reflection awake? Can one ensure that the communal relationships that are entered into are not determining a pre-constructed, Unchosen Me that will deny the self? Perhaps one answer is to awaken one's own autonomy and self-reflection, or the ability to *choose* the Me, or to at least remember former Me's or consider future selves that are more congruent to one's true identities. Yet there must be places where these Me's will be socially recognized. The larger social structures must also be called into question or else the affects of autonomy and reflection will be limited.

Martin Luther King Jr. once said, "We would pull ourselves up by our bootstraps if only we had boots" (King, 1968). He was referring to the widely accepted "bootstraps mentality" in the United States, the belief that if people just try hard enough, they will succeed. It is possible that the "boots" are a metaphor for the techniques necessary to navigate society. If so, does everyone receive standard-issue boots? Perhaps the metaphorical boots are really the necessary identity structures or ways of being that are rewarded or recognized by mainstream society. So can autonomy and self-reflection become the boots by which people can pull themselves up? The point is to critically examine social structures to allow for alternative boots instead of only recognizing the standard-issue boots, or identities, allowing for people to choose boots that fit, and recognizing those boots as valid.

CHAPTER THREE

RESEARCH ACROSS
THE COLOR LINE

*Empowerment, Mutual Learning,
and Difficult Decisions*

Contemporary society [is] unfair, unequal, and both subtly
and overtly oppressive for many people. We do not like it,
and we want to change it.   *—Carspecken, 1996*

I remember feeling a knot in the pit of my stomach as this research project began. Weeks had passed, and I had been waiting in dorm lounges, coffee shops,
pizza places, conference rooms, and the campus union alone with stacks of pizzas, over and over again—waiting for the women to come. I had worried about
how, as a White woman, I would gain trust with African American women, and
these solitary meetings enlightened me that perhaps the customary way of re-
cruiting participants into my research project would not work in this case. I sent
more than 400 e-mails to African American women across campus, using contact information I received from a merit-based financial aid program, a statewide
need-based financial aid program, an African American learning community,
and a mentoring program on campus. I posted fliers all over campus. I attended
meetings of various student organizations like the Black Student Union where I
knew there would be African American students present. Many students agreed
to participate, but when it came time to actually meet me, I remained alone with
my stacks of pizzas. So, how did I go from these empty rooms to nine months of
biweekly focus group / sister circle meetings with 30 women?

I got real. That is, I let myself become an integral part of the research process
while I simultaneously focused on building meaningful relationships in which

I spent time with the women in various aspects of their lives rather than simply in a researcher-participant relationship. I had long ago chosen to conduct my project using critical qualitative methods, because I found the advocacy approach[1] of critical inquiry so fitting for my project about the imposed identity of African American college women. I also enjoyed the active role that the participants would play in the research process within critical methods. But perhaps most importantly, I found the specific attention to identifying and fighting oppression in this method not only to fit my own ideas about research but also to suit my project that so centrally concerned itself with race and gender oppression on college campuses and in the larger society.

By getting real, I mean that I realized that as a White woman attempting to gain the trust and participation of African American women, I couldn't simply attend a meeting here and there and beg for participants. I couldn't only be interested in doing research *about* African American women. I had to do research *with* them, in *their* way if I were to gain insight into their experiences or if I wanted to begin to encourage them to remain involved in the project. I had to make myself vulnerable if I ever wanted them to share their stories with me.

This chapter provides a description of the process that I underwent in this research. It is not a chapter about methodology per se, although I do provide a brief summary of the methodology here. Rather, this is a place for me to reflect on the process of conducting research across color lines. My hope is that this chapter personalizes the research process, tackling the reality of gaining access to a group of people different from oneself and summarizing my role and the decisions I made in a personal as well as a scholarly way. This reflective process is also an integral aspect of the critical style of research that I used in this study. In addition, I provide a more thorough description of the methodology, particularly the data analysis and validation techniques, in Appendix B.

THE CRITICAL ASPECT OF CRITICAL METHODS

Since critical research became one of the primary ways that I "got real" in this research process, I will provide a brief overview of the primary characteristics of this style of research. Critical inquiry or research is concerned with social inequality and social justice. It directs itself toward social change. Critical researchers "find contemporary society to be unfair, unequal, and both subtly and overtly oppressive for many people. We do not like it, and we want to change it" (Carspecken, 1996, p. 7). I used critical inquiry for this research because I was attempting to uncover and begin to remedy social inequalities, related particularly to race and gender, within higher education and in society.

Perhaps one of the most unique facets of critical inquiry is the placement of facts and values within the research process. In critical research, the ideologies of the researcher, including values, "enter intrinsically and inseparably into methods, interpretations, and epistemology"[2] (Carspecken, 1996, p. 5; Kincheloe & McLaren, 2003). This does not mean that the research is necessarily more biased than those forms of research that are considered to be value-free or neutral. Rather, the critical research method suggests that the researcher outwardly describes his or her values in the research process. This still allows for surprises: participants may or may not have the same values as the researcher.

The issue of facts and values in the research process is the topic of much debate in the field of research methodology (Hammersley, 2005; Korth, 2005). Many scholars who employ critical research argue that it is not possible to separate values from the research process. For example, in a discussion about critical inquiry Kincheloe and McLaren assert that "facts can never be isolated from the domain of values or removed from some form of ideological inscription" (2003, p. 452). This fusion of facts and values could be dangerous, if not irresponsible, in research. If facts and values are inextricably linked, as Kincheloe and McLaren suggest, how can one know that research findings are not just reflections of the values of the researcher? Moreover, this fusion could be oppressive. For instance, if one were to recall a racist act that was perpetrated against her, would not the fusion of facts and values suggest that this racism was just a tension between values? In short, the fusion of facts and values could undermine real, observable oppression as simply a matter of perception.

Carspecken takes issue with this fusion of facts and values, arguing that the values that participants and researchers hold are not exactly "chosen" (1996, p. 6). Highly value-driven researchers often feel compelled to conduct research as a way to ameliorate oppression, and it is often a deep and powerful personal need rather than a real choice for the researcher. Furthermore, Carspecken notes that the values involved in research findings "need not be the same as the values defining our orientation" (1996, p. 6). Importantly, well-done critical research should not be biased and does not guarantee finding the "facts" or "values" that match what one had hoped to find. I concur with Carspecken's discussion about the nuances and complexity of facts and values, and I approached this research with a meaningful understanding of my own values, realizing that my findings were not always as expected,[3] nor were my values always the same as those of my participants.[4]

Critical researchers, because of the advocacy involved in the research process, assert the importance of clearly stating their own value orientation. The general value orientation of critical inquiry is as follows:

- Research is a form of cultural and social criticism.
- Certain groups in society are privileged over others.
- The oppression that characterizes contemporary societies is most forcefully reproduced when subordinates accept their social status as natural or inevitable.
- Oppression has many faces.
- Mainstream research practices are generally, although most often unwittingly, part of the oppression. (Carspecken, 1996, p. 7; Kincheloe & McLaren, 2003, p. 452)

The numerous data analysis techniques used in critical research, particularly the analysis techniques developed by Carspecken (1996), add both rigor and validation to the research process (see explanation in Appendix B, examples in Appendix C). Research conducted from a critical perspective attempts to neutralize power relations within the research process. I attempted to neutralize power through the inclusion of participants in the research design and data collection process, the type of analysis used, and member checks where participants reviewed transcripts, analysis, and interpretation. Stemming from this critical approach, I provide a brief description of the research design below (see Appendix B for a longer description of the data analysis, limitations, and validation).

A BRIEF RESEARCH DESIGN SUMMARY

The overarching research question for this study was: How are race and gender created through interactions between self, others, and society? I chose to study the interaction that creates race and gender through an examination of an interaction-based notion of identity (defining identity as the interaction between self, others, and society) that explicitly allows for considerations of identity impositions (the Unchosen Me). The study of experiences with identity impositions sheds light on one's interactions with others and society. Therefore, the investigation into how race and gender are created on a college campus led to other specific questions explored in the pages that follow, including: Do policies and practices within higher education facilitate institutionally imposed identity / Unchosen Me characteristics that are racially, gender, or socioeconomically biased? If identity is imposed, how does imposed identity affect students' transitions into and through college, their college experiences, and their retention in degree programs?

This critical ethnographic study included 30 Black women (27 African American, 2 Black Latina, 1 Multiracial), most of whom were first-generation college students (24 women), that is, their parents were not college-educated. I collected data for a period of nine months. Appendix A includes the demographics and information about all of the participants.

Using purposeful sampling (Creswell, 1998), I selected three groups (an early-intervention need-based aid program, a merit-based aid program, a peer mentoring program, and a living-learning community in the residence halls) from which to select African American women[5] (ages 18–22) for voluntary participation in the project. To recruit the women, I sent e-mails to all of the women in the four groups. In addition, I worked with my African American colleagues (faculty and administrators) on campus, who then put potential participants in contact with me. The participants also began to recruit subsequent participants.

I separated the women into eight groups, called "sister circles," that met regularly (biweekly or monthly) for a period of nine months. Each group determined its own size, meeting place, and number of meetings. These sister circles were a good technique for gathering data related to racial issues because the group process fostered a feeling of support. This technique also allowed for observation of social processes and collective discourses (Morgan, 1997). In addition, I interviewed women one-on-one if it became apparent that they were less comfortable talking in groups or to follow up on conversations (Denzin & Lincoln, 2003). I also observed the women in a variety of settings such as classes, social outings, and moments with their friends.

The research site was a large, predominantly White, public, midwestern, Carnegie Research Extensive institution of higher education that I will call Midwest University (MU). There were 35,000 students enrolled at the institution, approximately 25,000 of whom were undergraduates. The university had a relatively low minority population (approximately 9% of the total student population: 4% African American, 2% Latino, 3% Asian American). The demographics of MU are representative of other PWIs nationally. MU is located in Brady, a small city of 85,000 people that prides itself on having numerous musical and arts events, lovely homegrown restaurants, and a charming town square. Brady is approximately a one-hour drive from a larger metropolitan area that boasts a vibrant and relatively established middle-class African American community.

Sister circles and individual interviews were audiotaped and transcribed verbatim, using pseudonyms chosen by the participants to protect confidentiality.

Before the coding process, I employed a variety of analysis techniques to delve deeper into the meaning within the women's statements. That is, rather than only coding data, I used five related data analysis techniques, mostly developed by Carspecken (1996), that built on one another to both delve deeper into the meaning within the data and to validate that the findings were representative of the participants' intentions (data analysis is explained fully in Appendix B, and examples are provided in Appendix C). The analysis techniques employed were: (1) meaning field analysis that considers the range of possible meanings within a statement; (2) hermeneutic-reconstructive horizon analysis that deconstructs the data to explicate objective, subjective, normative-evaluative, and identity references in each statement;[6] (3) coding that separated the data into themes and sub-themes; (4) the duality of identity, that is, an imposed identity analysis combining subjective, normative, and identity references within a statement (an analysis technique developed through this study); and (5) systems analysis that considers broad general patterns that relate to macro-level concepts (e.g., the social structure, larger inequalities). These numerous techniques served to deepen the meaning of the codes. They also served as a validation technique to ensure rigor in the analysis process. (I provide a detailed explanation of the data analysis, with examples, in Appendixes B and C.)

I employed a variety of validation techniques[7] to ensure that the data analysis was trustworthy (Carspecken, 1996): (1) peer debriefing (African American colleagues reviewed the analysis); (2) member checks (participants reviewed the analyses and the transcripts); (3) long-term engagement in the field (biweekly meetings for 9 months); (4) assessing my own biases and value orientations; (5) strip analysis (analyzing strips of data to ascertain if the findings were consistent with larger findings); and (6) negative case analysis (examining those aspects of the data that did not fit in the larger analysis.

Yet how did I gain and keep trust? What was my role as a researcher, given the critical approach? In what follows, I provide a narrative on some of the decisions, dilemmas, and surprising outcomes of the research process.

GAINING AND KEEPING TRUST

After my seemingly endless weeks of sitting with stacks of pizzas waiting for participants who didn't come, I decided that I needed help gaining trust. Fortunately, I had a relatively large network of African American friends and colleagues with whom I could be really honest about my struggles with doing cross-racial research. These women were invaluable in helping me to gain trust with my participants. One woman in particular sent e-mails across campus to African American faculty, staff, and students to tell them about my project. She called those who responded and talked with them about me and about her own sense of my authenticity in doing this work. She opened the gate for me. It was after her e-mails and phone calls that some of the women I had originally contacted began to contact me. In three weeks time, I had more than 30 women involved in the project, almost all of whom had *asked* to be involved. Ironically, they were from the groups I had initially targeted: the need-based financial aid program, the merit-based financial aid program, an African American learning community, and a mentoring program on campus. Many of the women were involved in more than one of these groups. In later conversations, I found out that the women had received my initial invitations but were waiting for someone to validate that the project was worthy of their time and that they would not be exploited or mistreated.

Once the women contacted me, I set up informal one-on-one meetings with each of them so that they could ask me questions. The purpose of these meetings was to gain mutual trust. I met in places the women suggested and bought them lunch or coffee as we talked. I answered any questions that they had of me, about the project, personal issues, or professional issues. Then I told them about the project, my vision of it, and asked them about their own vision for a project such as this. I did not specifically tell the women that I was interested in imposed identity because I didn't want them to bias their stories or to feel pressure to help the study or me. Thus, when the women described imposed identity in their description of self, it was unsolicited, not from any direct reference that I made to it (protocols are included in Appendix D). Rather, I told them I was interested in their experiences and the way they described themselves / their sense of self. At that time, they could ask questions as to what this meant, but generally, the women were interested in simply having a place to share their experience.

After the informal meetings, I began to group the women into focus groups called sister circles. Depending on the women's comfort levels, I grouped them with their friends and acquaintances or with strangers. For example, if the women said they would be comfortable meeting new people, I put them with women they did not know. Otherwise, I grouped them with at least one woman with whom they were friends or acquaintances.

As the sister circles began to meet, I checked in with the women individually (not as part of the data collection, but to build and maintain trust) and often within the groups and one-on-one conversations over the phone, by e-mail, or in person. I began meeting with many of the women outside of the groups to talk with them about their classes, applying to graduate school, their personal lives, or their professional aspirations. This creation of a meaningful relationship with each of the women was integral in the building and keeping of trust—as many of the women indicated to me when I asked them about the project later. Ultimately, I tried to demonstrate to the women that I cared about them as people, not just as research subjects. This went a long way in gaining and maintaining trust.

The last part of building and keeping trust is a bit difficult to write softly. So I will just say it right out loud. To do really good critical research, one must in many ways *live* the research process. That is, if someone like me, a White woman, is doing work with African American women, it is important that her friendship network not be made up only of other White people. This is perhaps more difficult to prescribe to others because it could result in an insincere adaptation: White researchers trying to make friends with Black people just to appear more authentic. But I need to mention it here because I was told by the women in my study that it was important to them that I was interested in building relationships. In many ways, this was an easier part of the research process for me because I am blessed with some deep and meaningful African American female friendships. I was also involved in the larger African American community off campus. Thus, when participants saw me outside of our meetings, they often saw me with African American friends and colleagues. This was not planned but happened organically and authentically because of naturally forming friendships in my personal life. It turned out to be one of the most important factors in building and maintaining trust.

THE SISTER CIRCLES: FROM RESEARCH GROUPS TO SUPPORT NETWORKS

Initially, I had an idea for a long-term focus group methodology that would bring women together in a safe place so that they could talk about their college experiences. The term "sister circle" seemed fitting because I wanted to connote to the women that this was a place where they would be supported, where they were equals, and where they were valued—almost like a family. I first heard the term a year earlier from a colleague who was involved in a group of African American women that called their group a sister circle. The groups soon took ownership over this term, and when I used the term "focus group," they would correct me and remind me that this was a *sister circle*. The term also came up during our meetings. For example, Isis, a first-generation student and a senior nonprofit-management major said, "This is Sister Circle. We are your sisters. You can tell us anything." The name for the groups eventually was a trust-invoking term.

Each of the eight sister circles took on its own personality and style. The groups were formed relatively organically. As mentioned above, I met one-on-one with each woman as she desired to join the study and placed her in a group where she had friends or acquaintances (if she requested this), or in a group which needed participants. Since many of the women recruited other women to the project, bringing the new people to a sister circle meeting, some of the groups were larger than others. I did not turn away anyone who wanted to join. Thus, some sister circles were naturally forming friendship groups that had known each other for a long period of time (e.g., circles 1 and 2). Other groups were initially acquaintances but not necessarily friends (e.g., circles 4, 5, and 7), and the others were made up of women who were initially strangers (e.g., circles 3, 6, and 8).

It is possible that the women self-selecting into these groups were choosing to become members of the sister circles because they needed and desired support that they were not getting elsewhere on campus. Many of the women mentioned that this was one of the first places on campus where they felt wholly supported or where they were able to really discuss their college experience in honest and meaningful ways. If this was the case, I consider this an important aspect of the study. It demonstrates the need for such support.

The groups each had a unique communication style, and the women bonded differently in each group. Because each group took on its own form, the types of conversations that the women had in their groups differed, as did the level of self-disclosure among the women. Interestingly, there was a higher level of self-disclosure among women who were initially strangers or acquaintances before being in the group together. In groups where women were long-time friends, it seemed that they assumed an understanding or that they had already shared aspects of their experiences outside of the group.

Once the groups were formed, the women determined where we would meet, how often we would meet, and the type of food that they wanted during the meetings. Generally, I purchased pizzas and sodas for the women, and I found that giving them something to eat helped them relax as they talked. Usually the groups met during lunches and dinners, and I would order enough food for them to take leftovers with them after the meeting.

I came to the first five sessions with well-planned ideas for facilitating the discussions. (Appendix D provides examples of the protocols used in these meetings.) However, I found that after the first five sessions, the women were so bonded that each group took its own direction. In some groups (e.g., circles 4 and 7), the women started to take turns facilitating the group. The woman in charge would come with questions or ideas, and she would lead the group in that meeting. During these sessions, I began to serve more as an observer than as a facilitator. Other groups shared the role of facilitation with me, sometimes taking charge of asking questions themselves and sometimes asking me to facilitate. In these instances, I was flexible and came prepared either to facilitate or to observe. Then, depending on the mood of the group, I would either serve in a moderator role or just watch while the women led their own session. When I did serve in a moderator role, I took cues from the group and often let the conversation go in the direction that the women initiated.

The topics that the women chose to discuss varied, often relating to previous discussions, allowing the women to further discuss the previous issues in more detail. In some groups, they began to self-disclose some of the painful issues from their pasts (e.g. child abuse, sexual abuse, being shot). When this occurred, the women helped each other to heal, and they surprised me in their ability to find meaning in the situation and in their compassion for one another. In one session, a participant, showing her scars and talking about horrific events, confided that she had been shot twice before the age of 15. The women in her sister circle used that session to find meaning in the situation, delving deeply into their religious beliefs and values. They described this as a transformative event—something that provided strength and even motivation to push beyond adversity. Generally, as in this example, once a session like this occurred, the group became very close.

In another example, one woman shared a painful past that involved sexual abuse, not an uncommon story among the women in the study. The sister circle used that session to discuss this experience, and ultimately the women in the group encouraged her to seek out professional counseling, which she did. After this session, other women in the group began to disclose similar experiences and to help each other seek out professional help (counseling and therapy) for these issues.

The women were the ones who kept the groups meeting for the nine-month period of time. I initially set out to meet with each group only five times. But the women did not want to stop meeting, so we continued. In all eight of the sister circles, if we didn't meet for more than two weeks, I started receiving phone calls and e-mails asking when we would meet again. Some women did change groups, but in general, the membership stayed the same.

I was amazed at the way that these sister circles became meaningful support networks for the women involved. Circles 4 and 7 met for the longest period of time. When some of the members in Sister Circle 4 graduated, the women invited new members into the group, forming Sister Circle 7. I chose to number these groups separately because the group dynamics changed as new members were added. This group had an intense bond. Through the bonds they made with one another, they literally helped to guide each other through the college experience. Some of the women studied together, helped each other fill out job or graduate school applications, or simply provided one another the much-needed support that they were not getting elsewhere on campus. This group kept meeting on their own time, unrelated to this research, for nearly a year after the end of the project.

I became a personal mentor to many of the women in all of the sister circles, meeting them individually for coffees and lunches unrelated to the research project. I helped three of the women apply for graduate school and two of them apply and prepare for internships. I also tutored some of the women or found them tutors in academic subjects. But perhaps the most long-lasting and meaningful outcome of these groups was the eventual incorporation of the sister circles into a mentoring organization on campus so that the sister circle meetings would continue as support networks for African American women beyond this research project.

THE MANY ROLES OF A RESEARCHER:
THE MANY ROLES OF ME

I played numerous roles as a researcher: facilitator, observer, mentor, listener, learner, and friend. The women described me and my role in many different ways throughout the study, using all of these words. My role within the sister circles changed during the course of the study. At the beginning, I was actively the facilitator, asking questions that the women in turn answered. As time went on, I tried to foster more leadership in the women within each group, encouraging them to ask questions of one another and to pose topics for the group. Some women began to bring their own questions and to lead their own groups. The women described this as an empowering process and also as a place to gain leadership skills. I eventually became an observer, hardly uttering a word as the conversation and the group took on a life of its own. I found this to be particularly helpful in facilitating trust with the women. I was attempting to foster a space where they could honestly and openly discuss what it felt like to be a minority on the predominantly White campus. I often found that when I played a less-active role within the group, it fostered more honest discussions about race.

I was aware that my own presence as a White woman among African American women may have changed the level of self-disclosure, so I attempted to take steps to create a safe space for the women. I tried to ensure that the demographics of each sister circle were the opposite of campus, meaning that I was the only White woman in the room most of the time (unless one of the participants invited a friend who was White, although this rarely happened). Additionally, at the beginning of each session I told the women not to worry about offending me or each other, and if someone did take offense to a comment, we talked about it immediately. Initially, the women often apologized when making negative comments about White women, but in time, when I told them this was unnecessary, they stopped apologizing and began to openly discuss their opinions. When racial discussions did occur among the women, I attempted to lessen my leadership role in the group, talking less and just listening to their comments. Often, I would ask the women if they thought that they would have disclosed differently had I not been a White woman, and we would talk about that. In general, the women said that they would not have self-disclosed differently; however, it would be an interesting future inquiry to test this.

Admittedly, in the groups where personal disclosure was high and women shared painful experiences, I had to seek the counsel of friends and family to debrief and to get emotional support. I also spent many hours observing the women, following them through their days and activities. Sometimes I witnessed racist experiences that the women had with peers and professors, and this also heavily affected me personally.

In a way, the project moved toward action research, or critical research with an action component, in the final months of the study. That is, I actively attempted to change the experience that some of the women were having in school, trying to help them navigate their way through campus. I met with top administrators on campus (vice presidents, deans, directors of various units) to discuss with them ways that the campus could better serve African American female students. I also wrote reports to various administrative units in this regard. Given that this study was rooted in critical ethnographic methods (Carspecken, 1996), my role as an active supporter of the participants was not contrary to my research methods because the empowerment of the participants was a significant goal of my work.

Continued Self Analysis: The Study of Race Begins Early

The importance of self-analysis as a researcher in critical qualitative inquiry cannot be emphasized enough. Kincheloe and McLaren (2003) assert, "Critical qualitative researchers who understand the relationship between identity formation and interpretive lenses are better equipped to understand the etymology of their own assertions—especially the way power operates to shape them" (2003, p. 447). Thus, it was necessary for me to continually consider my own biases, ideologies, and background.

I am a White woman who grew up in a middle-class, Protestant, two-parent home in a small midwestern town that was approximately forty-five minutes from one of the poorest American Indian reservations in the United States. My first experiences with race in this setting were largely framed by stereotypes and by the continued discrimination and oppression of indigenous people in this country. People in my town were outwardly discriminatory to the native people in our area, calling them derogatory names, mocking them openly, and often not serving them in restaurants. I saw teachers in my classes in elementary school and middle school make fun of students who were from the reservation. Not surprisingly, there were very few American Indian students in my high school; the majority of the students left school as soon as it was legally possible for them to do so. Yet my grandparents on my father's side were actively involved in trying to bring justice to the reservation—spending much of their adult lives on a Lakota Sioux reservation working with the tribe on issues of education, religion, and the local economy. They were ceremoniously given tribal names by the tribe—a way of "naming" them as tribal members. Although I did not know it at as a child, these conflicting notions began my study of race. It was likely that these experiences shaped my sense of racial injustice, and it is often these experiences upon which I reflect in considering the insidiousness of racial inequality in this country.

As I have studied race and race theory over the past several years, I am increasingly convinced that racial categories as we commonly use them in Westernized society are socialized, if not ascribed. What I mean by this is that I do not adhere to a biological foundation of racial difference in my work or my thinking. In fact, I am challenged by the notion of *choosing* racial identity, and I wonder if race is ascribed to us before we have a chance to make a choice. For example, because the United States has a color-coded classification system, someone is assumed to be White or Caucasian or Black or African American because of skin tone and pigmentation, not necessarily because of culture or background. However, I am a product of the environment in which I was raised, so there are times when I may have unwittingly assumed racial categories rooted in biological theory, that is, based on physical markers of difference. Also, the idea of racial ascription is not without its problems, namely, that it could in fact work to disempower people, failing to account for chosen racialized identities. Nonetheless,

I do tend to believe that we do not *choose* the racial classifications used to categorize, at least in the very initial stages of racial classification.

Further questions regarding racial categories that I continually asked myself throughout my research include: (1) Do I sometimes inherently take racial categories for granted as if they are unproblematic? (2) Am I able to claim or not claim my own White racial identity while others do not have a similar choice? (3) Do I assume that race is central to the lives of my participants when this may not always be the case? (4) Does considering race a social construction deny the lived racialized experiences of participants?

To keep these potential biases and ideologies regarding racial categories at bay, I continued to examine the historical accounts of racial categories and the consequences of these categories during the research process. I consider my own racial category and claim it daily. I accept my own White racial identity even though Whiteness has a history of oppression of those who are non-White. This is often uncomfortable for me. While I sometimes wish that I could decide *not* to claim my White identity, I feel that I have a responsibility to claim it, with all of its positive and negative qualities, if I am going to study the racial experiences and identity of others. It is with this sense of reflexivity or reflection that I now consider some of the difficult decisions that I made during the course of this research process.

DIFFICULT DECISIONS
Reporting, Comparisons, and Inclusion

Despite the active involvement of the women in this project, the responsibility for reporting the data still remained with me. This is not a responsibility that I take lightly. It means that I got to choose how to present the study, including the language that is or is not used, and that ultimately, I will get the credit for the study. While I did include the women in the study to review transcripts, analysis, and drafts of the writing, in an effort to maintain the women's confidentiality, their real names are not given.

Related to the issue of the reporting of the study were the issues of who to include in the manuscript and whether or not to compare the Black women in this study to other demographic groups. The initial study did include 11 White women (constituting Sister Circle 9, although this group did not meet for the entire time). However, I chose not to include these women in this research for a variety of reasons. Most importantly, there has been a long-standing trend in research to compare groups across color lines. The result is often a comparison between White participants and Black participants.

The White participants in these comparisons often become the center of the study—the norm against which all "others" are compared. The Black participants are often relegated, even if unwittingly by the researchers involved, to a position as other, as abnormal, or as somehow substandard. I worry that Black participants, particularly Black women, are not provided a forum to let their experiences stand *on their own*. That is, the Black/White comparison often leaves readers wondering why Black folks can't just become more like White folks instead of wondering why White folks should always be framed as the norm. The Black experience more generally becomes subordinated to the White experience, almost as if it is somehow less important. Here, I am attempting to shed light on Black women's experiences in their own right, emphasizing their relevance and importance to both the larger social fiber and to the institution of higher education. This was a conscious effort to reframe the way research about people of color is done and to keep from recreating Whiteness as the norm.

The 30 Black women in this discussion include women who self-identify African American or Black as their primary racial classification (27 women); women who are Multiracial, claiming Black as one of their racial groups (1 woman); or women who are Black Latina, claiming Black as one of their racial groups (2 women). I chose to involve the Multiracial and Black Latina women in this discussion because of their clear self-identification as being Black and because they typically related to the experiences of the African American / Black women. Many of the women did not fully disclose their full racial/ethnic identity until they were involved in the project for weeks (calling themselves African American or simply Black until trust was built), and I felt that it was not my role to determine that they were or were not "Black enough" to fit in this study.

Language and Grammar Issues

After careful thought, I made the decision not to edit the women's speech patterns or grammar. This was following numerous conversations with African American female scholars across the country and with many of my African American female friends—who in fact did not agree with one another on this issue. Some of my colleagues felt that *not* changing the women's slang or grammar might misrepresent the women, perpetuating stereotypes that the women were somehow unable to speak "properly." Others felt that my changes to the women's grammar or slang would in many ways represent a personal judgment of the women—as if I thought that I knew *better* than the women what they were trying to say. Ultimately, I attempted to strike a bit of a balance on this issue. The women did have the opportunity to change their own speech patterns or grammar, and some of them opted to do so (as is reflected here). But if the women did not request changes to their speech or grammar, then I have decided to represent exactly what they said, exactly the way they said it. This means that at times the women did use colloquial language or slang. The women often code switched, speaking differently in the sister circles that were primarily Black than they did when I observed them in groups that were primarily White (e.g., in classrooms, among White peers). Yet what is presented here comes mostly from the sister circles, so there is more slang and informal language than the women used in other settings.

Another language issue was the capitalization of the words White and Black. Some of my African American colleagues and friends felt that capitalizing them gave them inappropriate levels of power—reifying existing color divisions. Others felt that *not* capitalizing these words undermined the very real (even if not desired) power that the color line indeed has in this country's history and current times. Eventually, I decided to capitalize these words for this very reason. While I hope that someday we can move beyond the color line[8] in the United States, there is still a very real division when it comes to the nation's history, existing power structures, and interactions. The women often describe a "color line" on campus, explaining that students did not generally associate with peers outside of their own racial/ethnic group. The cross-racial interactions that did occur were primarily framed as negative in these stories.

Finally, I refer to the women as both Black and African American. The women in the study often debated these terms. Some women felt that Black was a more inclusive term because it allowed for the inclusion of Black Latinas, Multiracial women, and those women who did not have African ancestry. Others reasoned that African American is a better term because it highlights the majority of the group's ancestry from Africa and also the involuntary immigration of many people into the United States. Because these terms were debated without a consensus being reached among the participants, I chose to use both terms in this book.

CONCLUSION: RESEARCH AS TRANSFORMATION

I was once told and have read a few times that a qualitative researcher must prepare to be wounded in the field.[9] Yet this did not prepare me for my level of personal attachment to the women in this study. I felt pain when the women stumbled academically or decided not to return to campus the following year. I went to bed thinking about the women individually, and I woke up still thinking about them. Even as time has passed after the research process, I continue to think about them often.

I was deeply transformed by this research process. I gained a better understanding of African American women's experiences in college and in society. I also questioned, grappled with, and ultimately became more accepting of my own White identity. This research forever changed how I see my own place in the world and provided me a new impetus for my entire research agenda. It also gave me a call to action in my advocacy work outside of the research process. I may spend the rest of my life doing this work, and much of that can be attributed to this project and the effect that these women had on my life, both personally and professionally.

My hope is that the women in this study were also positively changed by this work. Many of the women did indicate that the sister circles were transformational experiences during their time in college. These groups, largely due to the women's commitment to the project and to one another, provided the women with support networks that they had not found in other places on this predominantly White campus. The women in the groups motivated each other to succeed in their classes and to become more involved on campus and in their communities.

It is my view that research should influence the participants in a positive way above and beyond (and more important than) what a researcher gains from the project in terms of publications or prestige. Yet only in my wildest dreams would I have imagined that the sister circle groups would become institutionalized and thus continued long after my research project ended. I attribute this to the women, to their tenacity, and to their own empowerment of one another. I hope that this project, continues to affect women (even those who do not self-identify as Black women) in this positive way through the ongoing sister circles at Midwest University as well as through this book.

CHAPTER FOUR

WALKING IN ENEMY TERRITORY

Being Black on Campus

What did I get myself into? You just keep holding on. It's
such a cultural shock.

—*Claudia, first-generation senior psychology major*

To be an African American woman at a predominantly White institution like Midwest University means "isolation," "alienation," and navigating "culture shock," according to the women in this study.[1] Once students made the decision to attend college and chose a particular institution, they faced the sometimes arduous process of transitioning into and through the campus environment. Generally, the women talked about their initial campus experiences as a "shock" or a "surprise." This shock fostered a sense of not fitting into the existing mainstream, White-centered campus culture or of needing to change oneself to fit in. The culture shock and isolation were experienced by the African American women as being imposed externally, in reference to the predominantly White majority of campus life (table 4.1). It was as if the isolation and culture shock formed an atmospheric haze over their experiences and all interactions were inseparable from the fog that surrounded them. The imposition was external, but the women felt the effects internally, almost as if *they* were somehow not normal.

Interestingly, the sense of shock and isolation was an issue for the women regardless of their high school demographics. Whether they had attended a predominantly White or a predominantly Black high school, they still described their campus experience in terms of culture shock and isolation. Even the

TABLE 4.1
The Culture Shock and Isolation Imposition

	Type of Imposition	Source of Imposition
Culture Shock and Isolation	External	Majority groups

women who thought they were prepared for the predominantly White environment described these feelings.

THE SHOCK OF BEING OUTNUMBERED

Brandi, a sophomore biochemistry major, remembered her transition to campus: "I knew that there wouldn't be that many . . . people of color. That we would be outnumbered. I already knew that. I mean I figured that. I mean it was kind of a shock when you come here, but you kind of know." Brandi had attended a predominantly White high school and both of her parents held advanced degrees. She had tried to prepare herself for what it would be like to be in the minority in the predominantly White college setting, yet she still felt that her transition onto campus was a "shock."

Tina, a senior psychology major who was a first-generation student, reflected on her initial impression of campus: "When I got here in the fall, it was such a culture shock. There were no minorities at all! Oh my God!" For Tina, who had also attended a predominantly White high school, the overwhelming White presence on campus made it seem like she was the *only* minority student in the environment.

Claudia, a first-generation college student and a senior psychology major in her final semester on campus, agreed: "No, you're like, 'Oh my God!' Like, for me that's how it was I was like, 'Oh my God.' And like I was in class and I would be the only minority and I'm like, Oh my God. You know, what did I get myself into? No, seriously it was like that. It doesn't prepare you to come back. You just keep holding on. It's such a cultural shock." Claudia, who had attended a relatively racially mixed high school according to her description, provided a compelling account of her intense discomfort during her college transition process, where she felt that she was barely "holding on." Claudia's experience influenced her decision about whether to return to campus, making it more difficult to want to come back and affecting her academic success.

Nearly all of the African American women described their transition to campus as "culture shock." It was as if they felt that they were going to a foreign country. For first-generation students, the campus was in many ways experienced as a foreign culture. While many students describe some discomfort in their adjustment to college, for these women their negative experiences were significantly compounded by factors such as their race and gender.[2] As was exemplified by Claudia, the intensity of the shock was not diminished even as the women progressed through their degree programs. She still felt the shock in her senior year.

The transition process was largely considered an uncomfortable, painful process. The pain of this process was often associated with a sense of loss for many of the African American women. The discomfort associated with the transition led many students to wonder, like Claudia, "What did I get myself into?" This indicates that the campus is not a welcoming place—it is a place where one must change oneself in order to fit in. The "culture shock" of the college transition process is evidence that students feel an imposition as they enter campus. To fit into campus norms and decrease this "shock," the women felt pressure to change aspects of themselves or their behavior, as will be evidenced in the later chapters of this book.

The feeling of difference, of "being the only one," of "being outnumbered" resulted in a sense that the women ultimately did not belong on campus—or worse, that they were among enemies. The overwhelming presence of White students on campus diminished the sense of belonging for many African American women. Isis, a first-generation senior, captured the kind of isolation that many women felt. For her, identity was constructed around fighting, being a survivor, and trying to find allies on campus:

> The first time I took a class, there were just like so many White people, every time. I felt alienated. After that happened, I just looked to see a Black face. You know? Like, I'm walking across campus and all I can see is White people. And then, like, I went to the bus stop and there are like 100 White people at the bus stop. I was like, "Where is there a Black face?" I hadn't been around so many White people until I got here. It was like I was walking in enemy territory.

Isis's sentiment that campus was an "enemy territory" was influenced by the sense that she was the only one, that everyone on campus was White. She experienced the campus as unwelcoming, as if everyone around her on campus was the "enemy."[3] Not surprisingly, she speaks in the past tense to describe this experience, except when she says, "I feel alienated," indicating that she continues to feel alienated even at the end of her college career.

The word "alienation" generally connotes a sense of estrangement or separation from something, in this case, the mainstream campus. It is as if the women are present but don't feel they are an integral part of the campus. The feelings of isolation that the African American women experienced were related to the racial separation at Midwest University. Students were often informally separated, choosing peer groups with others from their racial/ethnic groups. But there were also formal separations by race on campus. For instance, the campus offered an African American learning community in the residence halls, there were many racial/ethnic organizations (e.g., the Black Student Union), there were numerous cultural centers (e.g., a Latino house, a Black culture center, an Asian center, etc.) and the Greek-letter organizations were generally separated racially (e.g., historically White, Black, or Latina groups). The Black women generally discussed feeling as if White students did not want to be around them— not the other way around. While the sense of being so greatly outnumbered created feelings of isolation and culture shock for the women, so did the sense that they were separate or somehow outside of the mainstream on campus.

THE ISOLATION OF BEING SEPARATE

The MU campus was described as a separated, segregated place by many of the African American women. In the women's stories, White students and Black students were not together either socially or academically. This was sometimes by choice, but sometimes the women felt like it was institutionalized. Ultimately, the separation facilitated isolation for Black students. Krystal, a first-year student, described the African American learning community (a floor in the residence halls dedicated to a particular issue or topic) in which she lived as an "alienating" place. She felt the physical location of the residence hall (located on the fringes of campus), coupled with being grouped together with other students of color, to be alienating:

> Nothing against the [learning community] program here, but, the fact [is that it is] out of the school. Being out here . . . being away from so much. Like, if I lived in [Smith], I know I would be more interactive than what I am now. That's why I changed some of that stuff for my sophomore year. Because it was like I was alienated from everything else. And I didn't really care about [anything]. . . . I didn't try to go out and other things. I was like, forget it, I live too far. In order for us to work at the library, I am like, man, I live too far, I can't go all the way over there.

Krystal was not only physically separated from the mainstream of campus, but she also felt emotionally separated. Even the library felt inaccessible to her.

While the learning community was intended to provide a safe place for African American students to congregate together, some of the women in the program felt as if they had been "ghetto-ized"—removed from the heart of campus—sending a message that African American students were not welcome or that they needed to be sectioned off into their own space on campus. This is an example of the way many programs for underrepresented students are not incorporated into the mainstream campus. The structure and the actual implementation of the program undid the potential or intended good that might have come from it. While the program itself was initially attractive to Krystal as a "safe place" to commune with other African American students, the placement of the program on the fringes of campus sent a message to her that the program was unimportant or even unrecognized by the mainstream campus. The residence hall became a symbol of the way African American students and students of color more generally felt in this study: while African American students faced thousands of White students, they felt like *they* were on the fringes of campus, undervalued and unrecognized through the mainstream campus. In this case, even a program that was designed to create safe communities for Black students fostered a feeling of isolation in practice. This also worked to create race in a way that constantly placed Black students outside of the "norm," or mainstream.

While communities that were intended to be safe spaces for African American students may have unintentionally alienated students, informal cross-racial interactions also fostered isolation. Ultimately, there was a major racial divide among students on campus, a racial separation that was initiated long before students came to Midwest University, in high schools or neighborhoods. Yet this separation often led to racial stereotypes or biases due to a lack of exposure. For the African American women, the lack of exposure to diversity on the part of their White peers meant dealing with a constant feeling of being "othered" or made to be different. Michelle discussed her experience during her second year in college with White roommates:

> It was really, really hard. Because they grew up in like, somewhere weird, like a weird little town off to the side of [the state]. I don't know what it is but, it was one of those little bitty towns somewhere in [the state]. And so, they had not interacted with Black people at all. They had like a couple mixed people in their high school . . . that was the culture down there. And you know me, I'm like, well you know I'm me.

But, it was weird because they listened to rap music. They listened to rap music [on Black Entertainment Television—BET]. And they would make comments like, "What about the WET?" I'm like, "What's WET?" "White Entertainment Television." I'm like, what, we can't have one channel? So, I was living with this. You know you rarely do see Black people on TV. So, I'm like that is the one channel that has people of color and that's it. And every other channel is . . . [White Entertainment Television.]

In this example, Michelle's roommates were complaining that Black Entertainment Television (BET) should have included more White people, or that there should have been a White Entertainment Television (WET). Michelle's experience with her roommates made her feel different and marginalized in what was supposed to be her home.

This experience provides a good example of the racial separation on campus—an earlier lack of exposure to diversity resulted in ignorance on the part of Michelle's White peers. This ignorance worked to further drive a wedge between racial groups on campus and also created race in a series of stereotypes. Additionally, in this example Michelle emphasized the way the media often misrepresent or fail to represent people of color. On campus, White students often relied on these images (or lack of images) as their primary exposure to people of color, perpetuating stereotypes and generalizations. While the stereotypes were represented in the media, they were reinforced at MU through interactions like this one. Unfortunately, there were few mitigating forces that provided positive cross-racial interactions, further working to isolate the students of color in this case. Weighing the evidence, the women felt isolated both among their Black peers and among their White peers on campus.

In another example, Leila, a sophomore business major whose parents were college-educated recalled a conversation she had with peers in her residence hall:

One time . . . I have Pine Sol in my room. And like whenever I went to the bathroom in the dorms, I never went unless I wiped down the toilets in the stall. So, I had my Pine Sol. So I had it in my hand and this one girl came in and she asked me, she said, "What's the Pine Sol for, oh what's that for? Do you use it in your hair?" She was like, "You put it in your hair?" I was like . . . "What?"

The peer's question to Leila possibly stemmed from a lack of interaction across racial groups on campus. Regardless, Leila took it as yet another instance where she felt an imposition of difference, as if her hair—and ultimately she as a Black woman—were not normal. Leila's White peer was clearly uninformed about

African American hair practices. While they had interacted about a difference in their hair, the interaction was filled with misunderstandings and hurt feelings that only underscored a feeling of isolation on campus for Leila.

It was surprising how few descriptions there were of positive cross-racial interactions on campus, either inside or outside of the classroom. Isis, who graduated during the course of the study, said at the end of one racially mixed sister circle session (where one woman brought a White friend), "We need more opportunities like this . . . in our classes and on campus." However, the majority of the campus conversations on race that emerged in this study, both in and out of the classroom, were filled with discomfort, racism, and a lack of honesty that worked to further alienate students of color. For the African American women, there was a great deal of pain associated with racial discussions. There was a general exhaustion from talking to their White peers on campus about race because there was such a lack of exposure and understanding.[4]

Turquoise, the only first-year graduate student in this study (she began her master's degree during the study and was invited into the study by another participant), also highlighted the separation and feelings of isolation on campus, where Black students and White students were not together socially or academically. She concluded, in reference to her own feeling of isolation:

> When I came here I faced two issues. Being from the South, we mingle and interact with other White people. We have no choice but to talk and mingle with each other. People are just friendly. Blacks talk to Whites, Blacks talk to Blacks, we talk to everybody. And when I came up here, I was telling my mom that, "God mom, I feel so Black in [this state]." Because here you have these cliques of people that you talk to. Blacks talk with Blacks and the Whites talk with Whites. You don't see a lot of intermingling and stuff. So, it was like, wow. It was just different. I was just used to talking with a White person and having a conversation and it was fine. But, it seemed like it was hard to do that here.

The racial separation left Turquoise feeling "so Black," as if she were alone, an indication of the depth of her isolation. For Turquoise and many of the African American women in this study, being Black was a more salient identity on campus because they often felt different or like the "only one." Additionally, she highlighted the way in which the women felt pressured to only speak with people from their own racial group.

Perhaps the lack of positive racial conversations stems partly from the separation of Black and White students that Turquoise mentioned. Since students rarely interacted across racial lines, there may be few opportunities for honest dialogue. Regardless, the imposition for African American women to constantly teach their White peers became a central component of their identities on campus. The racial separation and isolation had serious implications for the Black women. Lisa, a sophomore secondary education major, noted, "I am just so tired of teaching everyone about race," as the primary reason she decided *not* to return to campus for her junior year. Is there a way to intervene or mitigate this exhaustion that Lisa described? Is there a way to lessen the culture shock and isolation experienced by these women in the predominantly White setting?

INTERVENTIONS INTO CULTURE SHOCK?

It has become common knowledge that feelings of isolation and alienation are repeatedly reinforced for students of color at predominantly White colleges or universities (e.g., see Allen, 1992; Feagin, Vera, & Imani, 1996; Loo & Rollison, 1986). Yet perhaps there is some hope that these feelings can be mitigated. For instance, programs geared toward racially underrepresented, low-income, and/ or first-generation college students helped some of the women to navigate these feelings of shock and isolation.

The necessity of early intervention programs for students of color—programs that supported them financially, academically, emotionally, or socially in order to provide access to college—was underscored by these women.[5] Claudia described her time in the Trio Summer Program,[6] a federally funded early intervention program that brings first-generation students to campus before the academic year begins, as being "at home." The Trio Summer Program had helped bridge the gap between home and campus for Claudia and nearly all of the first-generation African American women, providing a new type of "home" on campus.[7] Krystal, a first-year sports marketing major, and Mercedes, a first-year criminal justice major, who both also came to campus with the Trio Summer Program, longed for the "responsibility" and "restrictions" that they had in the summer program, noting that it helped them to do well academically. When asked what they meant by responsibility and restrictions, Mercedes and Krystal mentioned "having study hours," "having meetings with other students of color," and "curfews."

Corroborating the experiences of Claudia, Krystal, and Mercedes was Ryan's insight into her own experience with an early intervention program. Ryan, a first-generation student and a sophomore biochemistry/pre-med major, noted that she would not have been able to attend college, financially or academically, without the assistance of the Upward Bound program. Lisa, a sophomore secondary education major, described a merit-based support program as "helping my transition."[8] The continued support offered by this program included social and financial support through academic tutoring, the provision of a formal mentoring program, and funding for tuition and fees.

THE INTERACTION BETWEEN THE ISOLATION, CULTURE SHOCK, AND THE UNCHOSEN ME

As previously mentioned, culture shock and isolation were described as being experienced by the women as imposed externally (through peers, professors, and the larger campus structure), in reference to the White mainstream. Thus, they are related to the Unchosen Me concept as factors that influence identity for African American women. Both isolation and culture shock were imposed externally on the women as they were compared to the White mainstream campus environment. Identity, in this case, was constructed around "difference," "not fitting into campus," or "being the only one." The sense that they were racially outnumbered, that there were hardly any others like them on campus, could influence the women's acceptance of Unchosen Me aspects of identity—that is, as the women altered their behavior or way of thinking to fit into the predominantly White culture, they may have been more likely to accept unchosen aspects of self. There were few alternatives that appeared viable. Additionally, the sense that they were always different or outnumbered created race in distinct categories that seemingly could not be altered.

The issue of culture shock and isolation helped to evolve the Unchosen Me theoretical concept as *influencing factors* that shape identity. These experiences were imposed on the women externally. They influenced the way in which the women experienced and perceived their time on campus—as constantly different from the mainstream—and ultimately, this altered the women's construction of their identities. Thus, the isolation and culture shock actually became an integral component of the campus culture (fig. 4.1). For example, as the women felt the imposition of difference or of being racially outnumbered, they experienced "shock" and "isolation." These experiences then surrounded all of their subsequent experiences and their identity as a type of isolating haze around the self (fig. 4.1).

CONCLUSION: THE HOMELESSNESS OF CULTURE SHOCK ON CAMPUS

As the African American women navigated the culture shock and isolation associated with transitioning into the predominantly White campus environment,

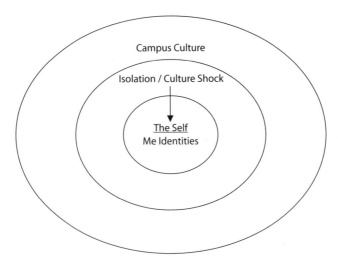

Figure 4.1 The influencing factors of isolation and culture shock

many of them described feeling as if maybe they would fit better back in their home environment. However, the women, particularly first-generation students, often came to the painful realization that insofar as they did adjust to campus life, they no longer felt that they belonged back home, thus creating a sense of homelessness.[9] Race, in this case, was created with Whiteness as the norm or standard, as if those who were unable to fit in this category (i.e., Black women) were continually unable to be included in the mainstream, in what was deemed "normal" on campus.

What perpetuates the experiences of culture shock and isolation that were described so vividly by the African American women in this study? The subsequent chapter focuses on the academic experiences of the African American women, the way they were "spotlighted"—as if they had to speak on behalf of their entire racial group—or were made to feel "invisible"—as if they, their ideas, and their aspirations were unimportant and nonexistent in the predominantly White environment. Hence, the isolation and culture shock were perpetuated through these academic experiences.

CHAPTER FIVE

ACADEMIC PERFORMANCES

Between the Spotlight and Invisibility

> I don't know what the ideal campus culture is, but, whatever
> it is, I don't fit it.
>
> —*Lisa, sophomore secondary education major*

Many of the African American women's campus experiences alternated between being in the spotlight, representing their entire racial group, and feeling
invisible—as if they didn't exist or stood in the wings. This was particularly the
case in academic settings. Seldom was there a time when the women didn't feel
a push and pull between these two extremes. At times, they felt like they were
in the spotlight and invisible simultaneously. Lisa, a sophomore secondary education major captured this feeling:

> Like, how many times have you been in a class and you are like the only minority
> there and like one of two things happen: either one, you are the advocate for your
> race. Or two, you just don't say anything because you decide to set the standard
> another day. There is something that comes to your mind that you really just want
> to say it, but you are like, "whatever" because nobody else cares; people don't care,
> so you just don't say anything.
>
> And you get tired of it too. You just get to the point where you are like whatever.
> And people don't understand that just because you're Black does not mean that you
> represent the (emphasis) Black race. . . .
>
> But, if you don't [speak out], then your voice is just ignored. But, then every
> time you talk it's like you are talking for your race. It's just, a lot of pressure if you

say anything. But then there's pressure if you don't say anything. People continue to have this mentality . . . . It's frustrating. It's frustrating.

Several issues are salient in Lisa's description.[1] The forced choice to either "represent the Black race" or have her "voice just ignored" is couched in her own feeling of isolation since she is the "only minority." This speak-on-behalf-of-your-race-or-remain-silent pressure resulted in frustration. Lisa felt "tired of it." The pressure to speak on behalf of her race was experienced as externally imposed through her peers and professors within the White mainstream of campus. But as she continually experienced it, she began to internalize this pressure and felt as if she needed to put pressure on herself to speak out and represent her racial group well.

Numerous women provided examples similar to Lisa's in which they felt trapped between being a representative for their racial group or remaining silent and invisible.[2] As demonstrated in the last chapter, African American women often experienced isolation and alienation on the predominantly White campus. Here the women provide a deeper explanation for these feelings of isolation and the way that racialized experiences were woven consistently into their college experiences.

These experiences of either being in the spotlight or being invisible were described as existing in academic settings such as the classroom, imposed by both majority and minority groups on campus (peers and professors). As illustrated in table 5.1, the sense of being in the spotlight was experienced as both imposed externally through the mainstream Whiteness of campus (feeling forced into positions to represent one's racial group) and internally through one's minority group (feeling a responsibility to represent one's racial group). Being invisible was imposed through the Whiteness of the mainstream on campus, as if the Whiteness was so overpowering that the women were invisible. The external imposition occurred as the women had experiences in which they were avoided or ignored. Yet the feeling of invisibility was also felt as internally imposed or internalized at times, when the women acted as if they were invisible

TABLE 5.1
The Spotlight-Invisibility Imposition

	Type of Imposition	Source of Imposition
Spotlight	External and Internal	Minority groups and Majority groups
Invisibility	External and Internal	Majority groups

or put themselves into situations where they would not be noticed by others. The spotlight/invisibility dichotomy in many ways foregrounded the women's experience of being in the minority, of being different or somehow never able to fit into the mainstream on campus.

ON BEING IN THE SPOTLIGHT

On the Midwest University campus, the physical marker of difference was so pronounced that the African American women constantly felt like they were different because of their appearance—as if a spotlight was constantly shining on their difference. This feeling of being spotlighted became one reason for the women to change their behaviors and interactions on campus, particularly in academic settings like the classroom. They experienced this as pressure to represent themselves well within this spotlight because there was an implicit assumption that their actions represented *all* others in their racial group.

Leila, a sophomore business major, maintained that being an African American woman on campus meant "You stick out, it's like so obvious." She decided that because she was already in the spotlight due to her race, she needed to present herself well. She explained, "I sit in the front row all the time, you know front and center. I wish I would have known someone else in the class to just be in a group with them." While she wanted to represent herself well, she also felt isolated both because she was different and because she had represented herself as a "good student." Though she wanted to be a good student, this highlighted her already visible difference. Her physical difference felt like an external imposition on her, imposed by the White mainstream on campus. The result of this feeling of difference was a change in her behavior (e.g., sitting in the first row) that was also experienced as an imposition from the majority group, or mainstream because she felt that others around her wanted her to represent her race well. But it was simultaneously experienced as an imposition through the minority groups on campus, because she felt that her actions should represent her racialized group, Black students, well.

It was not uncommon for the women to describe classroom situations where they were unable, even if they put forth what felt like a great deal of effort, to find students with whom to work in small groups in class, as if their visible marker of difference reinforced the sense that they were untouchable—as if they were on stage. At other times, professors and instructors, perhaps subconsciously, shined the spotlight on the women. Semea, a first-generation senior exercise science major, described being in the spotlight as always being noticed by her professors: "I'm in a class right now where I'm the only Black person in there. And like the teacher would call attendance. And she'll go, 'Semea you're here.' And it's like she doesn't even look when she's saying it. Because I'm the only Black person." Semea's account of being in the spotlight intimately linked to her feelings of isolation and feelings of difference at the predominantly White institution. Because she was the "only" Black person in her class, she felt like she was constantly spotlighted.

LaShara, a first-generation junior Legal Studies major, elaborated on Semea's statement: "Right, cause you are the only Black person. So, she doesn't even look." Michelle, a first-generation senior Health and Recreation major concurred and shared her own experience, "I know teachers who only know four peoples' names, mine, and people who are Black. [Making a gesture as if she were the professor, looking down.] 'Michelle, hello!' Because I'm the only minority in this class."

While it could be considered a positive thing that the professors had noticed the women and were attempting to be friendly, the fact that their professors obviously *only* knew the names of the Black students exacerbated the sense for the women that they should represent their race. It felt obvious to the women that the professors only knew their names because they were different from the majority of their peers, underscoring the feeling that they were not the norm within their classrooms. The women felt spotlighted, and this spotlight aggravated their sense that there was an imposition placed on them by their professors to represent their race in the classroom.

The feeling of representing one's race is linked to stereotypes or external pressures: the women felt as if their peers and professors generalized and claimed to already know all about them, as if all African American women are the same. For example, Leila described her struggles with trying to disprove the stereotypes that others, both peers and professors, had of African American students:

[The other students] never listen to me until for some reason [they can see] I'm serious about class or stuff like that. It's not like that with anyone else. No one else . . . it's not like that with anyone else. It's like [that] with all my classes. It's like . . . Have you ever felt like you represent your own race? In a lot of classes, especially [in the business school], it was me and like, two other Black people, out of like 800 students. And the section that I was in, I was the *only* Black person.

For some reason or another, I will be late every once in a while. So, whenever I walk in late, I'll be like "Oh my gosh." I feel like they will be like, "Oh my God, Black people are always late." You know what I mean. So, it's like, okay. I am just being late like every other student is late. And I feel like every time I do that I feel like I have to act so much better than everyone else.

Leila feels that she must *not* act out the stereotypes that she feels others have of Black people—that Black people are always late. In an attempt to dispel potential negative stereotypes that others may have of her because of her skin color, Leila worries about her behavior and constantly feels that she must prove that she is a serious student and that she is unlike the negative racial stereotypes.

Leila feels external pressure to represent her racial group positively because she is in the minority. Additionally, she highlights her isolation, noting that she is the "only Black person" and that "it's not like that with anyone else." Leila altered her behavior, or worried about how her behavior was perceived, linking this to performative roles, or the "performance" of race. Her identity became associated with trying to exhibit what she was *not,* rather than exhibiting who she *was.* In fact, Leila was a very serious student: she graduated from high school at 16 because she took college preparatory classes, and she will graduate from college before she is 21. Leila's individual sense of being isolated or spotlighted was worsened by her age difference in relation to her peers. This pressure to act *against* stereotypes works to create race in stereotypical ways. The women in this study often felt compelled to alter their behavior, meaning that they had to constantly interact with the stereotypes to discredit them, even if these stereotypes did not fit them. This is an example of the way that race-as-stereotypes was created in the classroom.

During class time, while some instructors did attempt to bravely forge into the topic of race, many times there was a lack of sincerity or an obvious discomfort on the part of the instructor that worked to create race in old, unequal ways. This was manifested as a failure to intervene or a telling silence when the students invoked the spotlight through racial stereotyping during class time. Sometimes racial discussions in class only served to perpetuate stereotypes and racism among the students. Mercedes, a first-generation student and a first-year criminal justice major, recalled one such experience in class: "This White lady, she was just intrigued. 'I love listening to your type of people's music.' And she was talking about some church song and I don't even go to church so I don't know what she was talking about." Implicit in the White peer's discussion about "your people's music" are stereotypes that all Black people listen to a particular type of music, that all Black people attend church, and that this music is outside of the mainstream, or not the norm. The instructor in this situation did not attempt to intervene, letting this stereotype remain and thus allowing racial stereotypes to be created in the classroom.

The majority of classroom discussions among mixed racial groups, like the one Mercedes experienced, resulted in stereotypes and a spotlighting of the African American women who were generally in the minority in their classrooms. Tracey, a first-generation sophomore business major shared, "I hate it when people come up to me and ask, 'So, do Black people do this?' I don't know. I can't speak for every Black person. That's what I tell them now. I'm not the spokesperson for everybody." Tracey continued to describe the way that both students and professors asked these questions, spotlighting her during her classes. Leila agreed, describing her peer relationships: "It irritates me when someone knows about five Black friends and they think they know the whole Black race." As Leila indicated, there are many times when African American women on campus felt like they were the representatives of their entire race. Leila's example also implies that there are numerous stereotypes and generalizations that are imposed on minority students. These generalizations and stereotypes have a compounded, cumulative impact because the women's race and the history of racism are also unchosen by the women.

Michelle, who grew up in an urban neighborhood that she described as "dangerous," shared a classroom experience where she was the only African American student in a class and a White peer had spotlighted her by invoking a stereotype:

"Black people are lazy. They are not going to get ahead in this world. That is why they are just sitting here in the same spot." And I'm like, "I've got three jobs while I am in college and I [am] reading all the time." It was so far beyond racist. And they couldn't see it. Not just to say that, people in general are lazy. You know what I'm saying. Not just White people, not just Black people, not just Hispanic people. People in general are lazy. All cultures. For you to think that it is just one population that is lazy.

I guess I just went back and forth with that. I can see how people that have been discriminated against for so long are just like, could just feel like [sighs] there's not a role model around. Like, I guess I could see like growing up in the neighborhood I did and the school I did and just not even considering school. But I did. I was like, there's a lot of stuff out there that I want to do. I heard it all in that class. But I couldn't believe it.

When I asked Michelle if the instructor had challenged the student's assumption that "Black people are lazy," she responded that the instructor had remained silent. In this case, the instructor's silence spoke volumes and served to further alienate Michelle as one of the few students of color in the class. The classroom discussion, like the one Mercedes mentioned, had allowed a negative stereotype to remain. Once again, this classroom discussion served to perpetuate existing stereotypes, simultaneously creating race in stereotypical ways.

Michelle knew what it was like to feel as though "there's not a role model around." While Michelle experienced overt stereotyping in her classes, she also felt the painful lack of Black role models, further alienating her in academic settings. When professors or administrators remained silent during racist or stereotypical comments, this intensified feelings of isolation and alienation for the women.

Michelle felt the pressure to work even harder than her peers because there were not successful persons that looked like her either on or off campus. She went from a neighborhood that lacked positive role models to a campus that had few people of color in leadership positions. The lack of positive role models was a burden that Michelle and other African American women mentioned more than once. In Michelle's case, she had proudly worked to rise above the stereotypes and lack of role models. She graduated during this study and enrolled in a master's program in community health.

However, these negative classroom experiences, the constant spotlight of stereotypes invoked by White peers, and admittedly, by professors' silence, did have a cumulative effect on many of the African American women, further dividing students across racial lines. Claudia, a first-generation senior psychology major concluded:

There were moments in my classes where I wanted to kick [the White students]. I kept wanting to turn around and punch them. But, I'm serious, it takes a lot for me to get like that, you know? But, you know what? When I get to that person, I'm like, "You don't even know what you were taught." So, obviously, those White people or those popular kids, smart kids, that's just how they were taught. Their parents taught them to be that way. You only do what you know.

So, I try to not look at White people and just like hate them for what they are saying. Because ultimately, you are an adult when you're in college. You know what you are doing. But, if you were raised in a pattern where you learned to hate minorities, or ignore them; you are gonna grow up with that same feeling. That will be your attitude. So, I have learned to look past that. White people. I've learned that you have to look past that. That's what you have to do. I think you really have to get there so you can actually ignore some of the ignorance of White people.

Claudia felt frustrated with the stereotyping that she experienced from White students in her classes.[3] It is noteworthy that Claudia associates "popular, smart kids" with "White people" in her statement, reinforcing her felt and unchosen differences. This illustrates the way normalcy and hierarchy were created on campus. Inherent in Claudia's explanation is her own difference or inability to be one of the "popular kids, smart kids" because she is not White. Also, she has developed a coping mechanism: realizing that White people are often going to be ignorant, as a Black woman she faces two impositions—one of having to learn to bear the ignorance of those around her, and one of having to learn to ignore it. This is a sad description of her general expectations for White students—that they will often be ignorant, and that Black women will simply have to look past that ignorance if they don't want to be angry all of the time.

It is noteworthy that the Black women did not mention institutional support structures or people on campus that would help to educate the White students. It was assumed that the African American women, by coming to this White campus, had to bear the burden of dealing with this ignorance on their own. This example uncovers one way that race was created—as White students being "smart," "popular" and perhaps the norm, and as Black students being the ones who must learn to tolerate ignorance.

Claudia, a Puerto Rican senior psychology major who self-identified as both Black and Latina, described the spotlight of being a minority on campus as feeling as if someone was watching her all the time. During a conversation about being spotlighted, she encouraged the other women in her sister circle to be careful to represent themselves well:

I think that is just a part of life. When you are around different people there are certain ways that you act, like if you are in the business world. Or, like if you are with your friends. There are just different roles you have to play. And I just think that if you are at home, you know you can let your hair down and do your thing. And when someone comes to your house they have to accept you as whatever you are. But, if you are out in public . . . there's just some things . . . like you don't know who's watching you. So, you have to just play that role like somebody's watching me so I have to be a little more cautious about what I say or how I act. I think that's just how it is in our society.

For Claudia, feeling as though someone was constantly watching her was an imposition from the mainstream of campus. She felt she had to "play a role" to counter the mainstream expectations of her. Because she was in the minority, Claudia felt that her actions were watched more closely and that others generalized those actions to the Latina and/or Black populations as a whole. This illustrates what it is like to be a minority in the predominantly White setting: as if a spotlight was constantly following her every move, watching to see if she made a mistake. The pressure Claudia felt to represent her racial group was an internalized pressure, and as she spoke to her peers, she encouraged them to follow suit.

It is noteworthy that the African American women did not at any time describe the campus as a place where they felt at home, a space over which they had some sense of ownership, even though there was a recently built Black Culture Center on campus. When asked about this culture center, the students indicated that it was always closed and that it was too far from the center of campus. The women in this study described campus *only* as a "public place" where one had to be "careful" of how one acted, much the way Claudia did above. It is remarkable that they did not refer to finding a home-like space (a place similar to family or where they found comfort) on campus. Even when describing the public space of campus, this was sharply differentiated from the way that they described their hometowns as home-like spaces, even though their hometowns would technically also be considered public places. Perhaps this was because so much of campus (the demographics, the norms, etc.) was different than home for many of the women.

When the spotlight shines, there is a shadow behind it where what is on the other side appears invisible. Being in the spotlight is in part a result of being in the minority on campus: because there are so few African American women, they feel like they are constantly representing their racialized group. Invisibility, on the other hand, is the result of feeling outnumbered, as if the Whiteness of campus is so overpowering that the African American women are pushed into the wings of campus, both literally and metaphorically.

ON BEING INVISIBLE

When the African American women didn't feel like they were put into a spotlight for being in the minority, they were often ignored in the classroom altogether, treated as if they were invisible. They felt as if there was no middle ground. At its extreme, this externally imposed invisibility removed the women's power to determine their own existence on campus, particularly in academic settings.

Leila, in the example above, felt a need to prove herself to her peers and professors, or the mainstream on campus. In Leila's view, White students and the men in her business courses did not experience the same the pressure to prove themselves and their intellect. The message Leila heard from the subtle and overt actions and messages of her peers and professors was that White students and males were considered to be serious students until they proved otherwise, whereas for Leila it was the opposite. She felt she had to adapt her behavior to prove that she was a serious student (through always coming to class on time, sitting up front, trying not to make mistakes), whereas the other (White) students did not have to make this change in their behavior. Until Leila proved that she was a serious student, she felt invisible to her peers and professors, but once she did prove herself, she felt spotlighted. Ultimately, this paradoxical situation creates a feeling that academic experiences are a no-win situation for the women, who often feel caught in a racial script that was already written before they arrived on campus.

Like Leila, many of the women in the study described experiences in which they felt that they had to *demand* to be seen by professors rather than being recognized for who they were (e.g., smart, creative, good students). This is in contrast to the spotlight imposition in which they felt noticed for the wrong reason—just because they appeared different than their peers. For Leila, the feeling of invisibility manifested itself in a need to prove herself to her professors. For some of the other women, like LaShara, this invisibility made her feel like she needed to assert her physical existence in class. LaShara, a junior legal studies major, told a story to her sister circle about a time when she tried to speak up in class:

> In my classes it was only me. Sometimes at first I would see all the students in the class. And I'd sit in the back of the room because we had five like seats. And so all of the students didn't even get to sit in the seats. But, if I ever raised my hand, it would be like nobody noticed. The teachers would be like, "Why isn't nobody saying somethin'?" I would stay after class. And my professor said, "Why aren't you talking?" I would be like this, "I stood up on my chair and I am waving my hand off and you don't notice me because I'm Black and I'm sittin' all the way in the back of the room." The teacher was like, "I just didn't notice."

LaShara stresses the reason that she felt like she was invisible to the professor: she was the only woman of color in the class. Even after she made a scene by standing on her chair, the professor continued to make her feel invisible. While Leila used the invisibility as an opportunity to prove herself, LaShara changed her behavior in the opposite direction. As the class continued, she constantly felt frustrated, and finally she stopped raising her hand and mentally disengaged from the class. Again, the external imposition of invisibility, fostered by the overwhelming numbers of White students in the classroom, led to a change in behavior and to disengagement—not a self-initiated change, but rather a response to the actions that fostered the feeling of invisibility.

Leila considered the way racial issues were discussed in her classes: "I would say that, you know, talking about race, sometimes people are a little bit hesitant. But, I mean, I still think we still need to talk about race." Here Leila implies that failing to discuss race may make race itself seem invisible. Tracey agreed, "I love when people talk about race in class because they open up and you can tell what they are thinking." Tracey intimated that discussions about race may encourage people to be more honest. Assessing her peers' beliefs about race became one way for Tracey to gauge the classroom for inclusion of her and her own beliefs.

Yet at times invisibility was manifested through silences—both the silences of African American women and the silence of instructors during racial discussions. Camiya, a first-generation sophomore undecided major, explained:

> I have a class and it is only me and this other girl [who are Black] and today the teacher was like, "We're gonna talk about race, I'm gonna start," and I could tell that she was just so [emphasis] uncomfortable talkin' about race. And she started out, and she just couldn't [talk about race] . . . We were having this discussion about violence, and there was a White guy standing there and a Black guy came in and she grabbed her purse. And she didn't have any idea of how to talk about it. I didn't say anything . . . cause usually I talk in class, but I just wanted to hear what other people had to say, about race.

In this example, Camiya decided to remain silent, as if invisible, because she didn't want to stand out as the only minority in class, and because she wanted to test the honest opinions of her peers.

While in some situations Camiya and other women decided to remain silent or invisible, this was largely because they felt their true feelings either would not be well received or that they and their opinions would be ignored. So while the women in some ways used invisibility to learn more about their peers' beliefs about race, there was still an imposition of difference that came before this, connecting invisibility itself with imposed norms on campus. However, it is also noteworthy that the instructor failed to realize that the example given in class invoked a stereotype: that Black men are violent. In this case, the instructor's discomfort with racial discussions facilitated a silencing of Camiya and the seemingly invisible normalcy of a racial stereotype. The stereotypical comments of peers and the silence of professors exacerbated the sense that women could not connect with others in the classroom, that they were isolated. But it also *created* race by allowing racial stereotypes to remain unchallenged in the classroom.

While sometimes the women were made to feel invisible simply because they did not look like their classmates, at other times, they felt invisible because the content of their courses did not reflect the places where they planned to work after college or the communities from which they came. It was as if the places themselves, often locations with larger minority populations, were nonexistent in the curriculum. Lisa, a sophomore secondary education major with aspirations to teach in an inner city, mostly Black school in Washington, D.C., noted that in class, most of the time, "the diversity sections of textbooks are skipped" because "the teachers don't think it is important since they think everyone will teach in White suburban schools."[4] Assumptions made by Lisa's instructors that the education majors will only teach White students (perhaps because most of the students are White) failed to recognize Lisa's aspirations to teach diverse, urban populations. She concluded, "Inevitably, we are not learning things that are realistic for where I want to be." Lisa often described class experiences where the curriculum excluded urban settings and minority students and thus excluded her and her aspirations. Failing to teach the "diversity" sections of the curriculum deemphasized and devalued Lisa's interests and ultimately left her feeling personally devalued.

Making her aspiration to teach in an inner city school invisible had serious consequences for Lisa, causing her to question whether or not she should continue with her degree. While she had been an excellent student in high school and early in college, she increasingly began to pull away from college in her sophomore year because she felt her aspiration to teach in an urban setting and the populations she desired to teach were less valued. Lisa accepted that her aspirations were unimportant, and she decided to leave college after the spring semester. Thus, Lisa had internalized this imposed invisibility, and ultimately she made herself physically invisible by leaving the campus.

Another way that invisibility was manifested was through a discrepancy between espoused and the actual institutional mission. Although the Midwest University campus prides itself as being "diverse," the African American women did not have a perception that diversity was really encouraged. Many African

American women were told during recruitment that the campus was welcoming and diverse, but this was not their experience upon arriving to campus. It was as though diversity was an invisible norm of campus that was espoused but not enacted. According to Lisa and many of the women in this study, even when diversity issues were enacted, the efforts were sidelined or sabotaged (e.g., the African American residential learning community with a floor dedicated to African American students described in chapter 4). Lisa struggled with the espoused versus the enacted diversity issue on campus:

> I see a lot of things with conversations about race. A lot of support type programs and stuff. And I think that what happens is that we have all these things for diversity and stuff and we don't really advocate [emphasis] for diversity. And I think a lot of people think that it doesn't feel that good if you aren't a part of the ideal campus culture. You know, we-don't-talk-about-it type of thing. I heard at a talk the other day in a program on European American versus Latino Americans on campus . . . and I just feel like, there is so much fear of diversity. There's a lot here, like even the mission statement. It's just not, I don't know if they support their purpose.
>
> Basically, I just think there is a lot of diversity here and even though there is diversity here, people don't appreciate it. Or, it's here just because it looks good on paper. Like I said, it looks good on paper. Everything on this campus looks good. Like when you see it online and you see it in brochures, it looks good on paper.

Lisa describes two important issues: the unspoken "ideal campus culture" and the lack of consistency between the campus mission for diversity and the enactment of that mission. When asked what she meant by the "ideal campus culture," Lisa responded, "I don't know what it is, but I don't fit it," underscoring her estrangement from the mainstream campus and simultaneously defining her own identities by what she is not. While Lisa couldn't define the "ideal campus culture," she knew that it was not inclusive of her or those like her, as if she was invisible or nonexistent within it.[5] This illustrates the challenge of making cultural changes on campus because it is difficult to articulate what one grasps implicitly. That is, while Lisa articulates not fitting in the campus culture, she is only able to define the "ideal campus culture" implicitly in terms of what it is not (i.e., it is *not* inclusive of her). Hence, making a cultural change on campus becomes difficult because so many aspects of culture are tacit, that is, subconscious.

This relates both to the issue of isolation described earlier and to campus norms where the African American women often felt that they could never be included within the "ideal" or mainstream of campus, which was defined by Whiteness. Lisa refers to the MU institutional mission that maintains that the institution will "embrace diversity in all its dimensions." While the mission embraces diversity, many of the African American women, like Lisa in this example, felt that this is where the campus stopped, never actually *acting on* this mission—ultimately, making the mission of diversity invisible while simultaneously, and perhaps unintentionally, treating a population of students likewise.

THE INTERACTION BETWEEN THE SPOTLIGHT AND INVISIBILITY AND THE UNCHOSEN ME

The constant saliency of race for African American women emerged as a tension: as a minority woman, one will almost always be a "representative" and be in the "spotlight" on a predominantly White campus. If she wasn't in the spotlight, she was "invisible," as if those around her had the power to erase her existence on campus. Even when the women opted to seem invisible through their silence, it is unclear whether this silence was really a choice. The women's stories suggest this was more of an imposition that they *should* remain silent in certain situations in the classroom, or they were ignored, which forced a silence on them. This forced choice between being in the spotlight or being invisible in academic settings did not allow the women much room to simply be themselves: they were always negotiating their identities as representing their race or remaining silent.

The spotlight/invisibility dichotomy primarily occurred in academic settings like classrooms, the curriculum, and study groups, and as a result, academic settings were often experienced as constraining to the women. Both the spotlight and invisibility were experienced as being chosen *for* them and imposed *on* them, and this was disempowering to the women. Even in the instances where the women in some ways decided to remain silent, as they did in some racial discussions in class, the sense that silence was necessary was an imposition on them based on their difference from the White mainstream.

The experience of having to choose between the dichotomous poles of representing one's race or being invisible is related to the formation of identities, particularly the Me aspect of self, because the Me initiates in the social structure. The represent-your-race-or-be-invisible conflict was a factor contributing to the acceptance of Unchosen Me aspects of self because *viable* alternatives were inhibited or hidden within academic settings on campus. While the women did not necessarily choose the imposition of this polarity, they did in fact claim it as part of their experience and ultimately as a factor influencing their identity, academic success, and persistence decisions over and over again. Thus, the women were more likely to reaffirm Unchosen Me aspects of self—aspects of their identities, or their Me parts of self—that were unfitting and inhibiting to their own self expression. In this case, in academic settings, the women would either be spotlighted or invisible—never allowed to just *be* who they felt like being.

This imposed pressure of being spotlighted or invisible led the women to change their behaviors and interactions on campus, factors that facilitated the acceptance of Unchosen Me aspects of self. The change of behavior was evidence of the acceptance of Unchosen Me aspects of identity as the women experienced the imposition of having to act in a particular manner and then changed their behavior in response to this imposition. Sometimes this resulted in positive academic behaviors like Leila's, when she tried harder in class. But other times, as was the case with Lisa, it resulted in disengagement from academics.

The racialized campus experiences illustrated by the women's descriptions were constantly connected to larger social/cultural/identity structures in a way that is consistent with the development of the Unchosen Me theoretical concept. In my discussion of the Unchosen Me, I assert that one's identities (at least the Me aspects of self) arise out of the already stratified social structure and that therefore one's identity is a constant reflection of that stratified social structure.

In a classroom, a Black woman like Lisa wished to speak but worried that others might take whatever she said to be representative of *all* Black students. In principle, a student who felt spotlighted like Lisa *could* have said, "You must not think that what I say is representative of all Blacks—I cannot be sure, but I have the worry that some of you will see me as a representative of all Black people because this is known to be a tendency in human beings." In principle, this sort of talk *could* be chosen. But to actually do it would require enormous confidence, exposure to precedents (i.e., other students speaking out in this way), and quite a few other things (like a professor who would accept this type of assertive behavior) that cannot be expected of most students and that may not have been accepted by her peers or professors. So to be placed in a situation like this is *unchosen*—it is not only the categorical structures that cannot be avoided for the situation to exist but also the extent to which they are sedimented outside the possibilities for easy, natural critique.

The dichotomous imposition of the spotlight/invisibility involves the Unchosen Me theoretical concept because the imposition is nuanced and dynamic. The concept of being in the spotlight was related to behavior, as something that was imposed externally on the women, in relation to the mainstream (White) campus. The concept of invisibility was also in relationship to the mainstream; however, it was both externally and internally imposed on the women. In the example that LaShara gave, where her professor did not to see her physical presence in class even after she repeatedly raised her hand, invisibility was imposed on her externally through the professor, silencing her voice and perspective in the classroom. In Lisa's example, where the group she wanted to teach was ignored in her teacher training curriculum, invisibility was imposed on her both externally and internally. Her professor, by ignoring diversity in the curriculum, imposed invisibility externally. But Lisa internalized this and ultimately decided to leave her degree program because she began to feel invisible internally, as if she did not belong on campus.

At the heart of the spotlight/invisibility dichotomy is the issue of recognition. The women were *over*-recognized and spotlighted, *not*-recognized and invisible, or completely *mis*-recognized by the perceived pressure to either represent one's race or remain silent. Yet in academic settings, the African American women did not feel that they were simply recognized for who they were—they did not get to determine their own sense of recognition from their peers and professors. The issue of recognition also links to the creation of race and gender. If one can only be recognized through particular behaviors—and even then, if one is misrecognized—this can work to create race in stereotypical, unequal ways.

CONCLUSION: THE ISOLATION OF THE LIGHT AND THE SHADOWS

The spotlight and invisibility, two opposing sides of the same coin (fig. 5.1), were experienced primarily in academic settings such as the lecture halls, classrooms, and small groups on campus. Unlike those in majority groups on campus (White students), the African American women were pressured to perform academically amidst the light and the shadows—as if they were on stage in the spotlight or behind the spotlight and invisible within the shadows. The performance aspect of these academic settings provides an example of one of the ways that race was created on campus. In this case, race in the classroom was continually created as performative: represent-your-race-or-remain-invisible. This was created explicitly by the actions of professors and peers, and implicitly by what was and was not included in the general curriculum.

The act of being spotlighted yet simultaneously invisible perpetuated the feelings of isolation and culture shock expressed in chapter 4. It was as if the isolation and culture shock exacerbated the feelings of being spotlighted or invisible

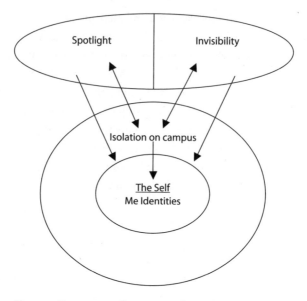

Figure 5.1 Race as a performance and reaction in academic settings

for African American women. Yet, simultaneously, the way the women were made to feel spotlighted or invisible in academic settings created deeper feelings of isolation (fig. 5.1). Race, in this case, became like a reactionary and performative role—not necessarily a role that the women *chose,* but one in which they felt suddenly *placed* by their peers and professors within their classrooms and lecture halls—a performative role for which they did not have a script but felt it necessary to act anyway.

This is not to undermine the agency of the women. Yet, regardless of their agency, they were interacting in a setting—in this case an academic setting—that already had well-established rules of engagement, along with well-established scripts, for the creation of race. These "rules" placed the women in a catch-22 between being spotlighted, which for them felt like the need to represent their racialized group, or being invisible, which had the consequence of placing them and perhaps their racialized group into a position of silence or nonexistence.

The next chapter focuses on the way race was created in social settings at Midwest University through peer interactions. Not unlike a dichotomy of either being spotlighted or being invisible in the classroom, in social settings, the African American women felt pulled between being perceived by their peers as "too White" on the one hand or "too Black" on the other.

CHAPTER SIX

"TOO WHITE" OR "TOO GHETTO"?

The Racial Tug-of-war for Black Women

I feel like being Black is imposed on me. [Midwest
University] makes assumptions about me because I'm
Black.

—*Michelle, first-generation senior health
and recreation major*

Michelle, quoted above, was not alone in her sentiment about the imposition
of race. Indeed, as demonstrated in chapter 5, Black women repeatedly encountered the imposition of being "spotlighted" or having their identity erased, feeling as if they were "invisible" on campus. Ultimately, "being Black" was something that African American women on campus at Midwest University felt was
an unchosen, or imposed characteristic. While they may have attempted to claim
their Black identity for themselves, within the predominantly White setting they
often found that their racial classifications were already chosen *for* them. This
lack of choice, or imposition of an Unchosen Me, occurred in multiple ways,
whether through the assumption that one needed to either speak on behalf of
her race or remain silent, or in the tension between being perceived as either
"too White"[1] or "too Black" / "too ghetto" as described in this chapter.

The Black women at Midwest University felt as though they were the rope in a
tug-of-war between their Black peers, families, or past communities and the predominantly White campus environment. Being Black was constructed differently
in different contexts on campus. They perceived themselves as barely keeping

their balance, as needing to remain in between the two sides, desiring not to "sell out" by "acting too White"[2] but also not wanting to become "too ghetto" by "acting too Black."[3] This tug-of-war phenomenon, the attempt to refrain from being perceived as either "too Black" or "too White," fostered a sense that the women's racial classifications were determined *for* them, or external to them through the institution and their peers. It was as if society, White peers, and their Black peers were pulling them in opposite directions. Yet the racial classifications were often based on superficial stereotypes. The women's Blackness, or racial category, was external to them, or experienced as an Unchosen Me, because they usually felt as if they were blocked from choosing their own racial group, or from what it meant to belong to a particular racial group. In addition, they often felt pressure to act in particular ways, to alter their behavior, and this also fostered an Unchosen Me for the women. The consequences of this process of racial categorization were many. Perhaps the most insidious was the painful loss of self—a loss that led many of the women to disengage from campus life, to resent the campus, or to leave the campus altogether.

The tension between being "too White" and being "too Black" or "too ghetto" highlights both *between-group tensions*—that is, between the Black women and their predominantly White peers, faculty, and administrators— and *within-group tensions* among those in the African American or Black group or community on and off campus. The between-group and within-group tensions provide evidence of the interaction of race as an ongoing process between the Black women and those with whom they came in contact—in this case, peers. The "too White" or "too ghetto" dichotomy was related to performative roles or the actions / observable behaviors of the women. In other words, the constant tugging between the two identity impositions affected how the women acted, spoke, dressed, and thought. It also influenced their sense of belonging within a particular racial group and within the campus environment more generally.

The sister circle data demonstrate that the messages and boundaries around the concepts of being "too White" or "too ghetto" were externally imposed on the women by those around them, by popular culture or media, and by the larger society in general. This is not to say that each end of the dichotomy emerged in the same way. The "too White" concept was experienced as an external imposition. Minority peers, families, or past communities (hometowns) were perceived as the sources of this imposition. White majority groups on campus were both an additional source and reinforcers of this imposition, but with a different power reference. For instance, White groups (i.e., peers, friends, faculty, and

TABLE 6.1
Race as an Imposition for Black Women on a College Campus

	Type of Imposition	Source of Imposition
"Too White"	External	Minority groups and Majority groups
"Too Black" / "Too Ghetto"	External	Minority groups

administrators) had the power to determine whether a Black woman was "White enough" to gain full membership in the White racialized group.

On the other side of this dichotomy, the "too ghetto" or "too Black" concept was also experienced as an external imposition by the women in this study. Yet this concept was perceived as being imposed by the minority group—as a need to represent the minority group well. Indeed, one major reason for this reinforcement from the minority group was related to the interaction between this group and the larger social structure that often privileges White people, White-centric ways of behaving, or the general concept of Whiteness. But for the purposes of this discussion, I focus on the way the women described the "too Black" concept as largely experienced as being reinforced only by the minority group.

External impositions in many ways represent one's interaction with the larger social structure. However, because the women in this study experienced these external impositions as also coming from peers, this represents a simultaneous interaction with others and with the social structure. I summarize both the way that the Unchosen Me imposition is experienced (externally, rather than internally), and the sources or groups from whom the imposition came and was reinforced (majority and/or minority peers) in table 6.1. Groups, in this case, refer to all those with whom African American women came in contact: peers, friends, families, administrators, and faculty.

"TOO WHITE" / "NOT BLACK ENOUGH"

One of the dominant experiences with which the women grappled in nearly all of the sister circles was being told by others that they were "too White" or "not Black enough." This idea of being "too White" was imposed differently by the White majority group and the Black minority group on campus. The "too White" concept appeared in both the women's observable behaviors and tastes, in reference to both White and minority peers, as if being "too White" meant that one was *acting* in a particular way (i.e., having particular tastes in music, clothing, or activities). The women indicated that this imposition was reinforced both on and off campus.

"Too White": Imposition by the Majority Group

Many of the women said that worrying about being perceived as being "too White" was something they had navigated for the majority of their lives. Indeed, this struggle continued and intensified on campus with both their White and minority peers. White peers imposed being "White" on Black women, defining the African American women's racial identity *for* them, dangling in front of them the possibility of inclusion in the White racial category, although full inclusion would never be possible. In this way, being "too White" was an Unchosen Me. This was experienced by the African American women as a sense of loss, as if their White peers had the power to take or steal their self-identified racial classification or identity.

Tina remembers her White peers on campus telling her, "I don't consider you to be Black. I consider you to be White. You are not like the rest of the Black people." Tina's White peers determined her racial category as "not Black" or as "White" even though she self-identified as African American. The power of her White peers, who represented the White mainstream on campus, to change Tina's race *for* her is evidence of the external imposition of racial categories on campus, of an Unchosen Me. But delving deeper, Tina experienced this as a loss of self—as if her White peers had the power to take and redefine her identity and as if her own racial group was invisible because of the pervasiveness and power of Whiteness on campus. Tina's statement also implies a judgment or racial ranking from her White peer: that it is *better* to be White and not "like the rest of the Black people." While Tina's White peers may have been attempting to include her in some way, Tina was left feeling distrust for White students, making the campus seem less welcoming to her. She often talked about feeling left out on campus.

Tina provided another example of a time when her White peers had defined her as "White." She remembered hearing from White men on campus: "They'll be like, 'You don't have the attitude. You are like the average White girl.' They was like, 'You don't have that attitude, that edge because you grew up around White people.' It's like all Black women got an attitude." The assumptions about differences between Black and White women here are striking. Tina's White peers assumed that to be a Black woman means to "have an attitude," to be difficult to get along with, or to act aggressively—all which have negative connotations in the way that they are defined. The alternative is passivity, which was largely framed as something that described White women. There is an additional assumption that White women are easy to be around and/or less assertive.

These assumptions relegate Tina to the difficult position of either choosing to be aggressive and Black or choosing to be passive and White—neither of which is an acceptable course of action for her.

Tina's White peers redefined her racial classification as "White" because she did not fit the stereotypes that they had for Black women. Her White peers, perhaps because they were in the majority on campus, acted as if they had the power to define her racial identity *for* her without her consent and without her input. This also illustrates the way that normalcy was defined in racial terms. In this case, the "average White girl" was not assertive, reinforcing Whiteness/passivity for women as the norm. In determining that Tina is "like an average White girl," her White peers stole her racial identity and created her identity in a way that fit on the predominantly White campus, even though it did not fit Tina.

Many of the Black women suffered from the stereotype that Black women are overly aggressive. This left many of them struggling to determine when to assert themselves. For some of them, this meant that they would refrain from speaking or participating in classes for fear of being perceived as too aggressive. Yet, as I demonstrated previously, this silence in classes was often perceived by professors as a lack of interest in coursework.

The "too White" category, when imposed by majority peers, was an example of between-group tensions. This category highlights the implicit power structures on campus that often privilege the category of Whiteness (ways of behaving, knowing, speaking, or being that are linked to White people or norms), and that, in effect, privilege White students. But this also represents a misunderstanding and potential area of ignorance between White and Black students. Stereotypes are invoked in this case, perhaps in absence of meaningful between-group interactions.

"Too White": Imposition from the Minority Group

Being "too White" was not only imposed through the majority White groups on campus but it was also imposed, although in a different way, by minority groups. Among students of color, this struggle was often couched in terms of wanting to resist mainstream culture or intentionally leave their mark (i.e., an understanding of their own culture) on the psyches of others. In this way, the concept of acting "too White" was in part linked to the women's resistance of the White mainstream on campus.

Tina noted the burden of trying not to be perceived as "too White" by her African American peers: "It's like you have to be something else. People will always want you to be something you're not. People will talk about you and they will say, 'She's not really all the way Black or she's not Black enough.'" The "not Black enough" concept is a way that racial groups emerged as bounded on campus. While the African American students comprised less than 4% of the campus, *belonging* within that group and being allowed to claim an *identity* as a group member meant acting, dressing, speaking, or thinking in particular ways. This highlights the within-group tensions among African American women or in the minority group itself.

As the women described times when they were either being called or calling someone else "too White" or "not Black enough," this was experienced as being imposed through minority peers, as being related to behavior and perceptions that those from their own minority group had of their behavior. In addition, this links to the roles associated with the *performance* of race. The women often felt that they had to act, dress, or speak in a particular, pre-defined way in order to belong in their self-identified racial group on campus. They experienced this pressure to behave in a certain manner as an imposition—something that they would not choose if it were not for the negative connotation and solitude of being perceived as "too White."

Brandi, who grew up in a midwestern metropolitan area, described the way in which not being Black enough was linked to behavior: "I know it's hard 'cause like, some have the image that it's hard to be not as Black as somebody if you don't like talk a certain way, if you don't like, do certain stuff." Being perceived as Black enough by her Black peers meant behaving in the ways prescribed to her through her minority peer group, although it was difficult for Brandi to explain at first. This could perhaps be an indication of the pervasive, yet subtle, nature of the "too White" phenomenon and the creation of race more generally. Many of the women shared Brandi's initial challenge in defining the concept: they referred to it often but had difficulty calling out its meaning.

I would often try to encourage the women in the study to begin to define the concept, asking them what is means to be "too White," or how they would know if someone was "too White." Brandi responded, trying to explain one way that she altered her behavior so as *not* to be perceived as "too White": "A store I would never go to would be like Abercrombie and Fitch. [Others in her sister circle laugh and groan.] Because, I mean, I don't think they represent . . . They don't represent anything other than White people. Like, as far as their advertising or anything. Or, anybody working there." In this case, for Brandi, attempting to be "Black enough" means particular shopping habits, associating this concept with behavior. Also, she is concerned about who the business represents, both in the products they sell and in the people employed in the stores. Shopping habits and styles of dress were often cited as examples of being "too White."

As the issue of acting "too White" continually became a topic of discussion, the definition of what it means to be Black emerged simultaneously. Musical tastes and ways of dressing were described repeatedly as a way to perform race, a way to behave "Black" or "White." Michelle, who grew up in a predominantly Black urban area, related the issue of being called "too White" to her time on campus, explaining her frustration with this issue:

> I feel like, I came to college and it's reverse racism. You don't have to worry too much about the White people because they already feel like their ancestors have done something wrong. Times have changed, times have changed so much. You might get the one person who's like, "Well I don't like Black people," but, then you have a bunch of other people ganging up on him saying, "That is so old, nobody does that anymore." And I feel like I am more accepted by the White people than I am [by] the Black people. Because they're like, well, she doesn't dress a certain way, or . . . "Why are you listening to that type of music?" You can't be eclectic. You gotta listen to rap. You have to listen to R&B. You develop more problems with the Black people because you are not Black enough.

Michelle pointed out the way in which the pressure, the imposition that one is "not Black enough," fostered particular ways of dressing and musical tastes. In Michelle's example, she felt unaccepted and limited by her African American peers, evidence of the way in which this imposition is experienced as an external pressure imposed by minority peers.

This is also an example of within-group tensions inside the African American minority group. Michelle struggled with wanting to be "Black enough," although her own musical tastes and clothing styles were at times outside of the boundaries of what her African American racial group on campus defined as being "Black enough." When Michelle was not around her Black peers, I observed her enjoying country and western music rather than R&B or rap. Perhaps the tight boundaries around so-called Black musical tastes were a way to assert Blackness on a predominantly White campus, as if unifying the group around musical tastes would create a stronger Black presence. For Michelle, although she was highly involved on campus as the president of her historically Black sorority and a leader in a mentoring organization, she still voiced resentment for her campus experience. She often talked about her time on campus as "painful."

Isis discussed the way the "too White" phenomenon leads to assumptions. She struggled with the assumptions being made about her, and her own assumption about what it means to be Black and what it means to be White. From her conclusions, musical choices and the ability to dance were integral aspects of the performance of race:

> "You dance because you Black." Like, I like to dance, but I can't dance just because [emphasis] I'm Black. You know what I'm saying? We got a little more rhythm, honestly we do. When I see [White people] dance, though, I make fun of them, and we need to get you some dancing help, honestly. But, they thought it was just because I was Black. Basically it's just the assumptions. You don't expect it. Like you are expected to listen to hip hop. So, everybody's got their assumptions.

She continued her description of people's racialized assumptions:

> I was walking out of the library and there was a car going by and I couldn't see who was in it, but I could hear the music. They were listening to 'Lil John. So, I was like "yeah, this is bad." I looked around, and it was a car full of White girls. Oooweee! [In a high-pitched voice]. I was thinkin' that I was about to see somebody cute! Not that they weren't cute, I'll give them that. You don't expect them to be listenin' to that.

While Isis dislikes the assumptions made about her that she can dance, she made her own assumption that Black people have "a little more rhythm." In her first example, where others assumed that she liked to dance, she provided an example of what her White peers expected of her because she is Black. In the second example, where she was surprised to see White *women* listening to hip hop music, when she had expected Black men, she provided an example of what she anticipated from her White peers. This demonstrates both the separation of White and Black students on campus and the way that racial group membership is bounded by one's tastes and behaviors—creating race as tightly bounded and based on taste and behavior. Isis's statement illustrates both between-group tensions (what behavior is expected in order to differentiate groups) and within-group tensions (what behavior is necessary to belong within the minority group).

For Multiracial women, a dual imposition or a sense of racial homelessness emerged in which they were not White enough to be associated with the "White" mainstream on campus, yet they were "too White" to be completely accepted by their minority peers. Renee, a Multiracial woman whose mother is White and father is Black, grew up in a mid-sized midwestern town. She remembers dealing with the "too White" issue in her hometown and continuing to navigate this issue on campus:

Definitely, I think I grew up culturally White. But it's because I wasn't really raised around Black people, like I didn't have any Black friends and my dad didn't have any close family around. Even though he was around my whole life, I was mostly around White people. And so I had this imposed Black culture on me. So, I had things imposed on me that I didn't even know that were cultural things. White people expected me to act a certain way. There were things that Black people expected me to know and expected me to be a certain way and I'm not. Like, identity is so weird. I am culturally White.[4]

Renee, who self-identifies as biracial, as "Black" but "culturally White," struggled with her identities relative to race because of the assumptions others made about her. She made a clear delineation between her past, being "culturally White," and her present, feeling an "imposed Black culture." Her identities are dichotomous, "culturally White" yet also desiring to be "Black enough." She attempted to exhibit behaviors associated with being either Black or White, depending on the context. It is remarkable that she admits that "Black culture is imposed" on her both through her White and Black peers. This is consistent with Michelle's statement above. As she indicated that she was expected to know or act in particular ways solely based on her physical appearance, she provided evidence of an external imposition, imposed through both her minority and White peers, to behave or associate her tastes within racialized boundaries.[5]

Isis responded to Renee's story, admitting, "Like, I'll tell you about you, Renee. When I first met you, I could figure that you were culturally White. Like, I don't know how you figure the race of people. Because I would have asked you questions that I would ask any normal White person . . . stuff that I thought they would know." In this example, Isis perpetuated the imposition of racial classifications as she considered Renee "culturally White." Note that Isis would have asked Renee different questions after deciding that she was "culturally White," determining her racial classification *for* her and indicating that Renee did not fully belong to the Black racial group on campus. This is an example of a direct creation of race through an interaction between peers.

Renee remembered her first year on campus: "It was the first time that I had been around a lot [of Black people]." While her physical appearance disallowed her from being classified as "White" by her White peers, it was a new and uncomfortable experience for her to be around African American students. In Renee's work study job, she worked for an African American woman who did not think she was Black enough. Renee recalled, "Like [my boss] said that I was a 'White girl' and that I was her 'project' to make me Black. I think that is not a good attitude to have." This is an example of a time when Renee felt that having a Black identity or acting a particular way to be "Black enough" was imposed on her on campus. It was especially difficult for Renee to navigate this imposition because it was coming from her supervisor at work, and thus there was a power differential in their relationship.

Throughout the sister circles, Renee mentioned numerous times when she had been considered "White" by African American students because of the way she talked, dressed, and behaved. However, Renee mentioned that White students without question considered her to be "Black" because of her appearance. As a physically identifiable minority, she navigated the perceptions that others imposed on her based on her racial classification. Again, this contradiction exemplifies the way racial categories were often determined for a person without that person's consent, or even involvement, in the decision. For Multiracial women, there was a unique experience of never being able to fit into either racial group. Renee graduated with a degree in art during the course of the study. She did come back to visit the group with which she had been involved, and she continued to discuss this racialized tug-of-war even after she left the campus, indicating that it continued off campus as well.

Lisa, a Dominican/Multiracial woman who self-identifies as Black and Latina, grew up in an urban setting. She admitted her own tendency to measure people as "not Black enough," explaining her culture shock in moving to the Midwest from the East Coast: "Black people here don't know how to be Black people. The culture is totally different." For Lisa, there was a particular set of attitudes and behaviors associated with being "Black," and she did not believe that African Americans in the Midwest exhibited them. When asked for some examples of these behaviors that were "not Black enough," she cited not knowing about "go-go music," knowledge of Black history, and styles of dress. Lisa continually struggled with the "too White" issue, often bouncing from one racially oriented group to another on campus (e.g., the Latina student organization, the African American student organization) but never really feeling like she fit with any particular group.

Ways of dressing and material items were related to the concept of not being Black enough, as a visible marker of racial identity. Some women, like Monica, a Black woman whose parents were college-educated, discussed wearing flip flops as being "a White thing to do." Renee commented, "It's sort of funny, culturally, because like I wear urban styles sometimes when I go out. My friends are totally used to that. Not like close friends, but other people, think that I'm like coming out and being myself and being really Black. And I'm like, this is so weird, like you could wear these clothes. I don't know. It's just a weird thing. They think that I'm just lettin' go and being myself. Like, usually I am just Whiter." Renee realized that her White friends considered her to be Black, but she never felt "Black enough" when she was around other African American students. The forced choice between being White or being Black did not allow her to fully express or freely develop her own identity. Thus, she often felt caught between either "acting Black" or "acting White" as an effort to fit in; depending on what was expected of her in a particular situation. Renee's example is a striking instance of when the boundaries around racial groups on campus were difficult to permeate; she found it difficult to find racialized reference groups through which to be recognized on campus. She did associate with other visual arts majors on campus (mostly White) and seemed to find some recognition there.

Of course, the "too White" / "not Black enough" concept, imposed by both White majority and Black minority peers, is only one side of the force pulling the rope away from the center line in the tug-of-war that was race for Black women on campus. The other pull on the rope is the pressure that women feel not to be perceived as "too Black" or "too ghetto."

"TOO BLACK" / "TOO GHETTO"

Being perceived as "too Black" or "too ghetto" is the other end of the tug-of-war from being seen as "too White" or "not Black enough." Being "too Black" or "too ghetto" refers to experiences in which people in a particular racial group act in a way that is perceived as unbecoming of the racial group. Like being "too White," this was defined in terms of performative roles or behavior—in this case, the perceived need to represent one's racial group in a positive manner. This phenomenon was experienced as imposed externally on the women by their minority peers, families, or home communities. This issue was highlighted for the women because they were in the minority on campus. Here the concept of desiring not to be perceived as "too Black" refers to within-group tensions inside the Black minority group. However, this is arguably an implicit indication of between-group tensions because the concept was primarily associated with representing the racial group well to majority groups.

Not unlike acting "too White," acting "too Black" often meant speaking or behaving in particular ways, or the avoidance of speaking or acting in certain other ways. For instance, Krystal, a first-year sports marketing major, indicated that acting Black meant speaking a certain way, a way she largely rejected. She remembered some of her African American friends on campus encouraging her to lower her voice: "They said, 'You are going to have to make your voice a little deeper, it is just too high pitched.'" If Krystal failed to lower her voice to meet the standards imposed on her through her minority peers, she ran the risk of being "too White."

Yet Krystal's long-time close friend Mercedes delved deeper into this issue, raising another intricacy, "It is not deep enough to be ghetto; for somebody to take her serious." Mercedes ultimately reinforced what Krystal's peers had reminded her—she would not be taken seriously by other Black peers if her voice was too high-pitched. Yet Mercedes' response indicated her desire to *not* be associated with things she considered "ghetto," linking the word "ghetto" to being "too Black." While Krystal did seemingly desire to be "Black enough," she was also experiencing pressure from her close friend Mercedes not to be "too Black" or "too ghetto." This delicate balance was one about which Krystal felt both confused and frustrated because there was not a clear way for her to choose an option that did not place her on the poles of being either "too Black" or "too White."

The "too ghetto" or "too Black" notion was described as being related to speech patterns as in the example above, but it was also associated with behaving in ways that legitimated stereotypes or negative attitudes toward minority students. For example, Mercedes and Krystal, both first-year students, lived on campus in an African American living-learning community, a floor in a residence hall targeted at providing a place for African American students to live together at MU. They spoke quite negatively about their experiences within this community, concluding that the residence hall community reinforced stereotypes and negative images of Black students. Mercedes concluded that the living-learning community was "ghetto": "It wasn't what it was all cracked up to be. They claimed that you are gonna live with a lot of Black people and so . . . people who do not have closed minds, but small-minded where they don't feel comfortable around too many White people? It was great for them, you know, because they can stay in their area where they can act like they want to act." While the residential learning community was perhaps intended to bring African American students together to provide them a sense of community, Mercedes maintained that this goal was not met:

> But the [learning community] floor has too many bad things going for it. And where I say that Black people really act their color . . . on our floor. The police are always over here. Something is always happening. Something is always broken. And the attributes that Black people have . . . that's why. Because of stuff like that that has been going on. And they feel like we are all around black people so it's all cool.

No it's not cool! Not all black people live like that. Not all Black people want to hear music at three, four, in the morning. Or want to be loud all the time; you know what I'm saying. But, that's where they get some of that stuff from and they think that people are racist. No, it's just the way you act. And they see the way you act.

This program showed me what I don't wanna be. It's a prime example of what I don't want to be. It's ghetto. It's ghetto.

Mercedes blamed the Black students in her residence hall for the stereotypes that were perpetuated about them, noting that these stereotypes occurred because of Black students' behavior, saying that they "act their color." Mercedes wanted to disassociate herself from what she saw as being "ghetto," linking Blackness with being "too ghetto."

As Mercedes explains her experience in the African American learning community, her reference group shifts: in one case, she is relating back to Black peers on her residence hall floor; while in the other case, when she is critical of Black students in the living community, her reference group is the White mainstream on campus. Mercedes' description differs from the many examples in this chapter in which African American students described racist stereotyping (imposed by the majority group) that they experienced from White peers and professors on campus.

Both Krystal and Mercedes indicated that living on the African American floor made them feel "ghetto-ized" or restricted from campus activities. While they initially did make the decision to live in this community, they were unaware of the negative aspects of the program until living there. Mercedes explained what she meant: "It's ghetto. It's breaked down. It's rundown. It's trashy. Nobody wants to come over there. If you want to get in trouble and get into a fight, that's where you go. If you want to see somebody, it's drama, somebody in a towel. Anything that you portray for Black people, that's what it is [emphasis]." Adding to this negative portrayal of the African American learning community, Mercedes considered the future consequences of this program: "After a while, we don't have any respect or whatever. And that's why people may see [the campus] as unwelcoming. Because they try to clump groups of Black people. Stay away from that! That's not gonna do anything but get you in trouble."

Again, she associated "ghetto" with behavior and particular environmental/ physical conditions, with acting "too Black" or acting in stereotypical ways. In this example, Mercedes indicated that the behavior of students in the residential learning community perpetuated negative stereotypes about African American students, creating race, perhaps unintentionally, in stereotypical ways. The placement of the physical structure of the residence hall was on the fringes of campus. Mercedes alluded to that placement when she said that people don't want to "come over here." Students' desire not to come to the residence hall could be related both to the remote physical location and also to the behaviors occurring there. Because of the experience Mercedes and Krystal had in the living-learning community, they felt they had been segregated or ghetto-ized by this program, and in the process they had been surrounded by the stereotypes that they wished to avoid.

Mercedes, who grew up in a predominantly Black neighborhood, maintained a strong desire to distance herself from things that were "too Black" or "too ghetto," discussing her desire to be around White students so as not to be "too ghetto," adding, "I would rather hang with White people than hang with Black people any day." Her desire to disassociate from other Black students on campus was unique compared to most of the women in the study, as if somehow she could only belong in the predominantly White environment if she lessened her Blackness. Yet she could not become fully associated with Whiteness either. Toward the end of the study, Mercedes began to speak differently about other Black students. This was in large part due to her joining a Black, Greek-lettered organization where she had positive relationships with other African American students.[6] Krystal, however, continued to struggle with being considered either "too White" or "too ghetto." She told me many times in individual interviews away from the sister circle that she was considering transferring to a historically Black college or university. She had not made her decision at the conclusion of the study.[7]

"TOO WHITE" / "NOT BLACK ENOUGH," "TOO BLACK" / "TOO GHETTO," AND THE UNCHOSEN ME

Racial categories and racial group belonging were experienced as bounded. The rules of belonging within a racial group were often experienced as dichotomous, as though the women had to navigate between wanting to *not* be perceived as "too White" (through their minority and majority peers) or "too ghetto" (through their minority peers). This fierce dichotomy felt immovable, with no middle ground, leaving the women often fighting to maintain their balance in a tug-of-war between unwritten and always changing rules.

The forced dichotomy of racial identification could perpetuate the existence of power disparities because of the lack of alternatives or choices within view for the African American women. When given only two options, the women felt pressured to accept a racial classification that didn't fully represent them: the Unchosen Me. One thing was eminently clear: they did not want to be identified with either extreme. Of course the salience of these concepts may be stronger in particular situations. The women's presence on a predominantly White campus where they were in the minority may have contributed to the prominence of these issues.

The phenomenon of "too White" or "too ghetto" was related to the performative roles or behaviors of the women. Thus, the women could easily point to someone who was *acting* "too White" or "too ghetto," even though it was hard to articulate the exact definitions. Like former Supreme Court Justice Potter Stewart's famous definition of obscenity, "I know it when I see it,"[8] the concepts of being "too White" or "too ghetto" were tough to define, but the women knew the behaviors when they saw them.

Additionally, this notion of being "too White" or "too ghetto" was situational. The women experienced the imposition of this dichotomy as coming from different groups in different contexts: sometimes this dichotomy was experienced as an imposition from the mainstream White presence on campus, and sometimes it was felt to come from the minority groups on campus, indicating that it is related to both within-group and between-group tensions.

The dichotomy between acting "too White" or "too ghetto" provides evidence consistent with the Unchosen Me theoretical concept because it was created through interaction (between one's self, others, and society) and the bounded nature of racial group belongingness, and because it emerged as lacking viable alternatives or options. It was as if the women's actions could only be recognized and evaluated through a preset system of racialized categories about which they had no choice.

The Unchosen Me, as it relates to race, has much to do with categorical frameworks that one cannot easily escape. Thus, the women at Midwest University did not experience the imposition of a single category (race), but a *system* of categories related to race and the boundaries of these categories. It was difficult for the women to bring critique to these categories because they are so complex and normalized.

In my development of the Unchosen Me concept, I highlight Mead's (1934/ 1967) notion of identity development, which holds that the "Me" aspect of self must be socially recognizable. Thus, one can only make a claim to identity insofar as it is recognized in social settings. On campus, and arguably in several other settings, race is evaluated and interpreted in fixed, bounded ways that are difficult to alter. As such, actions are recognized in race-related ways, with little room for gaining identity recognition that differs from these fixed ways. In sum, acts are recognized, but often *not* in accordance with the meaning the actor wishes them to deliver. The data here indicate that with regard to racial classifications and racial group belonging, only particular claims, performative roles, or behaviors are socially acceptable or recognizable. Hence, *misrecognition* often takes place. Indeed, when acts are not "socially recognized," they may actually be *misrecognized,* that is, thought to mean something about the actor that she did not intend or does not embrace about herself.

Only two socially recognized options for racial identification emerged: "too White" or "too ghetto" / "too Black." Yet both of these so-called options meant that a woman would be marginalized by a racial group. This is a factor associated with the acceptance of Unchosen Me aspects of self because there were few viable options for racially related claims / performative roles that would be recognized and evaluated in the way that the actor intended or desired on campus.

Race, and the boundaries that surround belonging within a racial group were defined *for* African American women on campus via both their White and minority peers. Again, this relates to the Unchosen Me in that they were disallowed or disempowered from determining and choosing their own racial classifications. Or, if the women did attempt to choose an alternative identity associated with race, there were negative consequences, such as being unaccepted by either racial group. For example, Tina was told that she is "like an average White girl." In this example, her White peer defined her race *for* her, both normalizing Whiteness and indicating that Tina cannot identify her own race. The power here happens *through* others (White others in this case) who do not understand their privileged positioning and who then use cultural values/norms that they take to be common sense or universally true to invoke norms in their interactions on campus. Even if the intention was to be inclusive (as was the case with the African American residential learning community), many of these intentions were not *experienced* as inclusive by the African American women.

The altering of behavior that resulted from the pressure *not* to act "too White" or "too ghetto" related to the Unchosen Me theoretical concept. The women often described feeling as if they had to act, dress, or speak in a particular manner so as not to be called "too White" by their Black peers, or so that they would be "Black enough" (but not "too Black") for both their White and Black peers. Michelle's example, where she felt pressure to listen to R&B or hip hop music illustrates this: while she admitted to liking other types of music and listened to country music privately, she often listened to R&B or hip hop when among Black peers as a strategy to disassociate herself from being perceived by them as "too White." The alteration of behavior is a factor that could facilitate the acceptance of Unchosen Me aspects of identity. Acting in particular ways repeatedly for the strategic reason of being perceived in a favorable way by others could eventually alter one's self perceptions, and in this case, this alteration of self perceptions would likely be detrimental.

The "too White" or "too ghetto" dichotomy helped to evolve and change the development of the Unchosen Me concept by providing evidence of the nuanced and situational emergence of impositions on campus. This dichotomy demonstrated the pragmatic or action-oriented nature of the Unchosen Me, illustrating the bounded character of racial groups on campus. The "too White" and "too ghetto" phenomena were experienced as externally imposed through both the White mainstream on campus and the minority groups. This imposition was experienced differently, depending on the context or situation. For instance, in some contexts, the women felt pressure to not behave as "too Black" as a way to represent their Black peers, or their entire racial group, in a positive light. At other times, they felt pressure to *not* behave as "too White" or "not Black enough" in order to fit into the bounds of the minority racial group.

While the spotlight/invisibility dichotomy (chapter 5) relates to particular situations on campus and preconceived stereotypes, the "too White"/"too ghetto" polarity relates to the way one's identities are manifested within these situations through action. In other words, the judgment of whether someone is "too White" or "too ghetto" is based on the behaviors of the women. This encouraged the women to alter their behavior because of the lack of options given to them by others, which is consistent with the Unchosen Me. Even so, the specific link to action helps to evolve the Unchosen Me theoretical concept. While the women could likely identify actions associated with either pole ("too White"/"too ghetto"), it was difficult for them to articulate this dichotomy in words, further indicating the pragmatic, action-oriented nature of this phenomenon.

Finally, racial categories and racial group belonging were bounded on campus. Thus, even though one might self-identify with a particular racial group, one's belonging in that group was dependent on one's behavior *and* the way it was perceived by one's peers within a particular racial group. In my initial conception of the Unchosen Me, I did not consider the boundaries around racial groups. Hence, the "too White"/"too ghetto" dichotomy added complexity to my development of the concept, highlighting group-defined boundaries around identity. In other words, one's racialized group could bound the available identities, and this could facilitate one's acceptance of Unchosen Me aspects of self because of the lack of viable options. To be in a particular racial group, one must act in a particular way even though one does not specifically decide these boundaries, nor does one decide whether the actions within these boundaries will be socially recognized.

The racialized aspects of identity were a contentious issue for the African American women at MU. While they struggled to identify their own uniqueness during their time in college, they felt the imposition of constantly having to choose between dualities—between being in the spotlight or being invisible, between being "too White" or "too ghetto." Thus, the women often experienced a great personal burden of enacting the racialized tug-of-war on campus— ultimately, an unchosen burden. This burden was too great for some, and they left the institution (e.g., Lisa and Ariel).

ACTING WHITE OR RESISTING WHITENESS?

I did not enter into this study seeking to engage in literature about the "acting White" phenomenon (see Appendix D).[9] However, the issue of being perceived as "too White" was broached by the women in nearly every sister circle during the study. Regardless of the questions I would ask during our many sister circle meetings, the women's discussion often veered in the direction of the tug-of-war between acting "too White" or "too ghetto." As the women took greater ownership over their sister circles, they often initiated dialogue on the topic, emphasizing the high importance of this issue for the African American women.

The times when the "too White" phenomenon was imposed on the Black women by their majority peers (by calling a Black woman "White") provide an example of the ongoing interaction of racial categorization. As White peers determined that a Black woman was "White," this reinforced the power of Whiteness as the norm. But more than that, the White privilege of the students in these examples provided insight into a power structure whereby the White peers felt empowered, whether knowingly or unknowingly, to determine the racial categories for their Black peers. The limitations of White peers in speaking about complex matters of race in a sophisticated manner turned something that could have been intended as welcoming and real into something limiting and imposing, ultimately creating race in unequal ways. Even if the African American women were deemed "White" momentarily, they would never gain full membership in the White racialized category. In this instance, the brief and partial inclusion of Black women into the White racialized category actually reinforced the boundaries around Whiteness (and race more generally), allowing White people to include or exclude others at will. This inclusion or exclusion is itself an interaction, demonstrating the White peers' interaction with a system that privileges their racialized group.

At other times, when the "too White" concept was imposed on the women by their Black peers, this was a way to place boundaries around what it meant to be "Black" on campus. Arguably, this could have been an attempt by Black peers to resist the predominance of Whiteness on campus—a way to encourage one another to be embrace their differences from White peers and White norms. Yet the embracing of Blackness, or the resistance to Whiteness, only went so far. The women experienced an imposition from their Black peer group to *not* be perceived as "too Black," meaning that they should not associate too much with this group or with stereotypes of Blackness, but they should represent their racialized group in a positive light.

Race was experienced as an interactive process. The Black women interacted with their own sense of self (identities) and with other minority peers, majority peers, and the larger campus environment. Ultimately, race itself can be seen as an interaction in these examples. Figure 6.1 illustrates the complexity of the interaction of race that Black women experienced within the predominantly White setting.

Of course, the interaction of race is more complex and nuanced than a figure can represent. The figure represents the *process* of the interaction between the Black women and their peers, the institution, and the social structure. It provides an illustration of the simultaneous tensions experienced by Black women on campus: between oneself, one's minority peers, one's majority peers, the

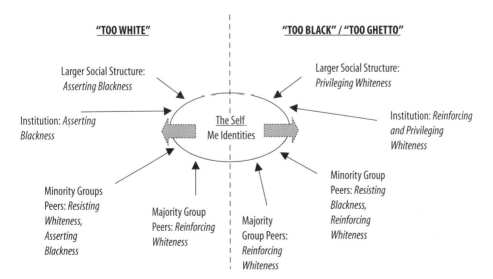

Figure 6.1 Race as an interactive performance for Black women

institution (faculty, administrators, policies, and practices), and the larger social structure.

The women's stories suggest that they experienced impositions from all of the above-mentioned groups or structures. As they interacted, they perceived a need to signal in a way that reinforced White privilege as the norm, resisted Whiteness, and/or asserted Blackness. Perhaps the major imposition was that the women perceived a need to signal all of these things simultaneously. This resulted in an Unchosen Me aspect of identity whereby the women were disallowed from choosing the campus structure of which they were a part (or from which they were excluded), the system of rewards that privileged some behaviors over others, or the interactions necessary to maintaining the "too White" / "too Black" dichotomy. While the women could have interacted to create race differently than presented here, this may not have been recognized or may have been misrecognized, perpetuating stereotypes. Thus, the women experienced race as largely an Unchosen Me aspect of self. This is not to say that there is no room for resistance. In fact, the women in this study did at times resist this Unchosen Me, or the prescribed interaction of race. However, it was remarkable how prevalent the impositions were for African American women. While some women discussed a desire to resist, they often lacked groups with whom to be socially recognized while they resisted. Some women mentioned the sister circles as a place where they could resist, but more spaces are needed for resistance to be encouraged.

CONCLUSION: BOUNDARY MAINTENANCE THROUGH THE UNCHOSEN ME

At stake with the "too White" / "too ghetto" dichotomy is what it means to belong within a particular racial group. As the Black women felt pressure to act in particular ways in order to be perceived as neither "too White" nor "too ghetto," this created and maintained the necessary characteristics that one must possess in order to gain or maintain racial group membership. Yet the women were largely disallowed from choosing to which group they could gain *full* membership. Even the Multiracial women who self-identified as partially White could never be full members of the White racial group. Thus, the interaction of race—between oneself, one's peers, an institution, and the larger social structure—is in itself a prescripted interaction. The students—both Black and White—used these scripts to create race on campus. Perhaps resistance could be located in a re-writing of these scripts, these interactions, in a pushing of the boundaries around racial categories. But here the pre-scripted interactions left the women continually pulled in an unchosen tug-of-war, perpetually feeling that the balance was shifting, moving from one side of the dichotomy to the other, giving them the sense that they could never be at rest.

CHAPTER SEVEN

LEARNING TO BE A "GOOD WOMAN"

Interpreting Womanhood through Race

It's like as a Black woman we got a double whammy.
Because to be a woman that is one thing, and then be a
Black [emphasis] woman on top of it. I feel like to overturn
that, you do have to be a little bit more than everybody else.
—*Michelle, first-generation senior health
and recreation major*

Race was gendered, and gender was racialized, as African American women negotiated the predominantly White campus. The categories of race and gender—and arguably class as well, given that the majority of the women self-identified as low-income and/or first-generation college students—intersect so completely that it was not possible for the women to explore their gendered experiences without linking these experiences to race. Michelle's assertion that as a Black woman she must work harder than others because she has a "double whammy" refers to a sense that she must grapple simultaneously with impositions due to her race *and* her sex. The "double whammy" of Black womanhood is not necessarily new. But remarkably, it is still alive and well on predominantly White campuses today.

Gender was depicted by the women in this study within the boundaries of a continuum between being a "good woman" and a "bad woman," referencing particular gender-related norms on campus.[1] Being a "good woman" meant demonstrating particular traits: silence, passivity, and caring. These characteristics

TABLE 7.1
Learning to be a "Good Woman" on Campus

	Type of Imposition	Source of Imposition
Learning to be a "good woman" on campus	Internal and External	Majority groups and Minority groups
Silencing the strength: A "good woman" is silent, passive, and caring	Internal and External	Majority groups and Minority groups (secondary source)
Learning to be a "good wife": Romantic relationships on campus	Internal and External	Majority groups and Minority groups

were at times directly contradictory to the individualistic structures of formal higher education, where judgments of one's intellect are often related to one's ability to assertively voice opinions. Thus, African American women experienced gender as negotiating between their desire to be accepted as a "good woman" both by their peers on campus and by the larger society, yet also grappling with their own sometimes conflicting notions of strength and womanhood. Here, I explore the way women learned to be a "good woman" on campus, particularly exploring the issue of silencing that occurred as women learned this lesson. Then, we listen in as the women grapple with their notions of being a "good wife" and the way this influences their romantic relationships on campus. Table 7.1 provides a depiction of the way these gendered norms were experienced as imposed on the women.

LEARNING TO BE A "GOOD WOMAN" ON CAMPUS

Learning to be a "good woman" was experienced as imposed both internally and externally. Up to this point, the "mainstream" has referred to the White predominance on campus. In this chapter, the mainstream refers both to the White predominance on campus and to the way in which many social institutions, including education, were historically (and are perhaps currently) constructed for White *males*. The "maleness" on campus, or the subtle and overt privileging of males/men and those ways of thinking or being associated with being male, worked to create a definition of womanhood. Specifically, the maleness of campus created a notion of "good"/"bad" womanhood in much the same way that Whiteness perpetuated a construction of race around being "too White" or "too Black." The notion of "good" womanhood was associated with displaying particular traits that were largely decided *for* the women by others (e.g., peers, family, the larger institution).[2] Silence and passivity were often put into direct conflict with demonstrating intelligence on campus. Caring was indirectly contradictory to being smart, in that the women sometimes felt pressured to spend more time caring for others (e.g., family, friends, all others before oneself) than they did on their studies. In some instances, the time consumed by caring for others tended to distract from academics. The bounded space surrounding the ideal of a "good woman" was initiated within and linked to the women's backgrounds (i.e., families, previous educational experiences). But the boundaries surrounding gender were reinforced through campus experiences, through interactions with peers, professors, and administrators.

Silencing the Strength: A Good Woman Is Silent, Passive, and Caring

The silencing of African American women on campus was both overt and covert. At times the silencing occurred as Black women were ignored or assumed to be less valued or less intelligent by their White peers and professors.[3]

Silencing in the Classroom

Leila, a sophomore business major, provided a good example of the way that silence was perpetuated in the classroom, describing her experience of being simultaneously silenced and ignored in class and then punished for not speaking:

> Oh my God! I would never be the one shouting harassment or anything [said as a question]? It probably wasn't something personal or anything, but I feel like [the professor] was picking on me. Okay, I am the only Black woman in the class. And I had my hand up. She was just like, "Great." And I was like, I had my hand up here. She was like, "Okay, you have something to say." And I was like, "Don't do that." And then another time about two weeks later or something, I had my hand up again, and after class she was like, "You need to speak up more in class."

In this situation, Leila openly expressed a desire to contribute in class. However, she was not called on by her White professor, and this silenced her opinion. Then she was reprimanded for being silent, even though her silence was chosen *for* her through the neglect of the professor. This is also evidence of the intersection between race and gender: although both Leila and her professor were women, Leila experienced differential treatment, and it seemed as if the only possible reason was because she was African American and perhaps also because she was female. While she seemingly backs off from calling this a racist experience, her linking it with "harassment" makes it seem like she does in fact feel like this was related to her racial category, coupled with her gender.

Offering another academic experience where she was silenced, Leila described a time when she felt inferior and stereotyped by her peers as less intelligent:

> Like, in the Business School . . . you know, there are a lot of, you know, White males there. I remember like even in the job interview stuff, like we had this company presentation. But, it was like a group of us there. I was the only Black female there. I was the only female. There were no females at all. No Blacks at all. It was like, nothing. I felt kind of odd because they were all males.
>
> I was kind of ignored a little bit. It was kind of like . . . whenever there was a question or something like that. You know, anything that I said or anything like that . . . it was a little bit. It was like, I don't know . . . I felt like being a female also, you know? It was like, cause I feel like men always have that unconscious thing like, "Okay . . . females are just *way* inferior." You know what I mean? Even if they don't show that . . . or even if they don't think that, I feel like they unconsciously act like that. It is hard to feel competent with them like that.

Leila experienced an imposition that she, as a Black female, was made to feel inferior to her White male peers. This highlights the intersection of race and gender and also the way race and gender were created in the classroom in ways that disempowered Blackness and femaleness. She experienced this as a climate where she was stereotyped as less intelligent both as a woman and as racial minority; and this environment was not conducive to allowing her to "feel competent," potentially affecting her academic performance, but at the very least, affecting her ability to enjoy her class. Arguably, this could also influence her career aspirations.

While Leila did often speak up in this group project, she always felt the imposition of others' judgments and stereotypes of her. Leila indicated that she *felt* incompetent "even if they don't show that . . . or even if they don't think that." This suggests that she had internalized the classroom interactions that created race and gender in unequal ways. The silencing, and her interpretation of it, is reinforced by the isolation of being the only woman and the only African American student in her group. The silencing also creates gender or womanhood in a veil of silence.

Leila continued to reflect on her experiences in class, providing another example of the gendered socialization on campus, a time when she and her female peers didn't know an answer:

So, I was like, "I don't know how to do it; we'll just have to ask around or something." They were like, "Oh my gosh, I don't understand." And like one of them was like, "Why don't we have a guy in this group?" I was like, "What the hell? You should be happy that [stutters] we were a group of all females. It's very different. Because usually that doesn't happen. So, you should be trying to represent or something. We are females and we are doing it!" It's like, she wanted to have a guy [emphasis] in this group.

In this example, the women actually felt and acted inferior and less capable because they were female, perpetuating the stereotype that women are inferior to men or somehow less capable intellectually. This internalization of feeling inferior enacted that which the women felt was espoused implicitly and explicitly around them.[4] This is an example of the way the women internalized the external impositions in such a way that they eventually began placing the same impositions on other women through their interactions, creating gender in a way that was constrained. Or it could be evidence of the way women themselves place boundaries around what it means to be a "good woman," creating and interacting with it as being in conflict with characteristics implicitly associated with maleness: being intelligent, competent, or able to speak one's opinion. Leila also discussed the pressure that she feels to "represent" all women, both because she is a woman and an African American female student. While Leila may have felt a sense of pride in being a woman, desiring to demonstrate her strength and intellect, this ultimately conflicted with being a "good woman" because gender was being created as associated with intellectual inferiority. Hypothetically, Leila could choose to assert her intelligence, but she risks being unrecognized or misrecognized by here female (White, in this case) peers.

Even as Leila's examples provided a way that silencing was imposed by her White peers and professors in the classroom, at times the silencing occurred through pressures to appear passive, weak, or not bold/non-aggressive.

"I'm not as bold as I used to be": The Silencing of Strength and the Strength of Silencing

The majority of the African American women identified in some way with being "strong" as a woman. During one of the activities within the sister circles, I asked the women to respond to the question, Who am I? in whatever way they saw as appropriate (e.g., drawing pictures, listing characteristics, writing an essay). The majority of the women responded to this activity by listing adjectives or characteristics with which they associated. Many of them responded by listing "strong" as one of their identities. Others listed synonyms associated with strength, such as "assertive," "aggressive," "independent," or "bold." For example, Ryan, a first-generation sophomore, read her list of identity characteristics: "I put strong, determined . . . dependable, a mother, a daughter, a sister, a 'sista,' a lover, a fighter, explorer for truth in all situations, mysterious, un-moldable, liquid, dreamer." Many of these characteristics were associated with strength in some way. Ryan continued, describing strength in relation to being a "sista":

> A "sister" is relation, blood, kin of some sort, maybe not blood like foster sister, something legal, documented, something like that. A "sista" [emphasis] is somebody you can depend on, basically blood but not really. It's like as close as you can be without actually being of relation or also I find myself using it as a representative of certain group of people, specifically Blacks sometimes, but then other times it's a friend of mine.
>
> A lot of my closest friends I would say are my sistas. A lot of strong, political leaders I would say are sistas. Instead of saying those are some strong women, I would say that. They don't even have to necessarily have to be Black in my mind. I could say Hillary Clinton is a sista just because she has been through a lot but she is a survivor. It is a word that just holds a lot of strong traits.

In this case, a "sista" is associated with a trustworthy, strong woman—a role model or friend, a "survivor," in Ryan's description. Also, the notion of being a "sista" is framed in a way that associates caring for others with strength. In this case, Ryan defined strength-through-caring in positive terms. Yet she was one of the only women in the study to describe strength in this way.

The women simultaneously self-identified with characteristics associated with strength and saw this strength as a potential liability in college. For instance, Sheree, a first-generation junior, characterized herself as "independent." Yet, when she talked about being "independent," she said it was a "negative characteristic to have on campus." While Sheree self-identifies as independent, she also sees this as a potential barrier to academic and social success. When asked why she saw independence as a "negative characteristic," Sheree reflected that she felt it would keep her from "belonging" both among her peers and in academic settings.

Sometimes women were silenced by subtle and overt messages that they are less intelligent than men, while at other times female peers perpetuated the silencing themselves, as if they have internalized the silencing to such an extent that they began to impose it on one another. One way that the silencing of women's assertiveness occurred was through messages from both peers and mainstream cultural sources that exhibiting certain traits (e.g., assertiveness, aggressiveness, boldness) would be unacceptable if one desired to be a "good" woman. When the women exhibited these characteristics, it led people to assume that they were too aggressive, meaning that they were not performing "femaleness" properly. For African American women, this silencing occurred as they were told by the media, peers, and professors that they had an "attitude problem," a derogation of their race and gender identities.

Keisha, a first-generation sophomore, remembered that when she first arrived on campus, "A lot more people started saying I had an attitude problem. Like a lot of my friends." When asked what her peers meant by "attitude problem," she responded, "They think I'm smart and they don't like it. But a lot of times I [was] playing. It's just that they really don't like that, so they take it seriously." Here Keisha is told by peers that she has an "attitude problem" because she is seen as "smart." Keisha's friends were primarily other students of color. In this example, Keisha experienced the pressure to be a good, *less*-intelligent woman as being imposed on her externally through her Black peers.[5]

Perhaps Keisha's African American peers had internalized the campus norms and messages regarding the traits one must possess to be a "good" woman, and they subsequently imposed these norms onto Keisha. Or, conceivably, Keisha's peers were concerned that her behavior was not illustrative of their group—that she was somehow not representing them well. Admittedly, it is possible that Keisha's peers were envious of her academic abilities. Yet the "good woman" norm, in this case, was put in direct opposition to intelligence and to notions of strength, creating femaleness through weakness and intellectual inferiority. Relating this to Leila's assertion that she and her peers should "represent," this is an indication that there are few viable options for the women: they can be a good woman, exhibiting the traits of silence, caring for all others over themselves, and passivity; or they can be strong, assertive, and caring for both others and themselves. Yet, according to the women, only the first notion of womanhood was recognized or encouraged on campus.

Continuing the women's stories about notions of their strength and "goodness," Krystal, a first-year student, asserted that she was "bold." When asked what she meant by bold, she responded, "I put bold because they told me I'm outspoken. But I can't help it. I just can't help it. I say what's on my mind." Here, it is almost as if Krystal is apologetic for being bold, but she "just can't help it." By "they," she is referring to her peers on campus.

Mercedes, responding to Krystal's notion of being bold, considered the ways that she had changed since coming to college: "Sometimes I stop myself because

I do start to say something, and I'm like 'never mind.' I'm not as bold as I used to be but I still say things." While Mercedes used to feel that "bold" would characterize her, since coming to campus she has begun to disassociate with boldness, simultaneously disassociating with speaking her opinion—self-monitoring in a way that often silenced her strength. What occurred to encourage Mercedes and women like her to be less bold / more passive? When asked why she was "not as bold," she was not able to answer, implying that it was perhaps a subtle process that had occurred. She could tell that she had changed, but it was difficult to pinpoint exactly when or how the change had occurred. This shift away from boldness could ultimately chip away at Mercedes' and other women's self esteem, becoming a damaging influence on their identities. Arguably, this could also influence academic achievement for these women.

As Michelle concluded, "It's like as a Black woman we got a double whammy. Because to be a woman that is one thing, and then be a Black [emphasis] woman on top of it. I feel like to overturn that, you do have to be a little bit more than everybody else." This "double whammy" resulted in a sense that one must work harder, Michelle argued: "You know what I'm saying, be on top of yourself, and being assertive and aggressive. Because I feel like if you're not, then you won't get the opportunity to be in leadership roles or stuff like that. And I think you need to be firm at the same time." Michelle had gathered in her four years at MU that the only women who were allowed to be in leadership roles were those with assertive and aggressive characteristics. Thus, while the women often felt sanctioned or chastised for being bold, assertive, aggressive, or strong, there was also a contradiction here, a sense that strength was necessary in order to be in leadership roles or, ultimately, to be successful on campus, for Black women in particular.

A Good Woman Cares for Everyone Else before Herself

Among many of the Black women at MU, there was a stated need to care for their families, friends, or those around them. At times this imposition of caring became a distraction for the women or acted in opposition to the competitive and individualistic environment in college. Many of the women expressed frustration with having to "take care of my family," as if it distracted them from school. Ryan, who often worked to make women in her sister circle comfortable, noted, "I rarely think of things for myself." Explaining that she typically put her own needs last, Ryan asserted that the needs of others should come before her own, suggesting that her needs are less important than the needs of others. Like Ryan, other women often talked about the importance of caring for others first, placing their own needs and desires last.

At times the emphasis on caring was detrimental to the women in academic settings, because they spent so much time, energy, or resources caring for others that there was little left over for their studies or to meet their material needs (e.g., food). Mercedes admitted, "I send my financial aid refund checks home." She gave the school funds to her family, but then confessed, "I am almost out of meal points for the semester." At MU students purchased a particular number of points for their meals in the cafeteria. Once the points were gone, they could either purchase more points or, in the case of Mercedes when she did not have the money to purchase more points, they would go without. She said this in March with nearly eight weeks left in the semester.

At other times the notion of caring was enacted through a sense of uplift, a feeling of responsibility to one's community. Ryan reported that she would often visit her home community to speak at high schools there: "I try to find a high school that's struggling and encourage them to show somebody that they can make it to college." She felt proud that she would often attempt to "change [high school students'] viewpoint or change the way that people look at college life." Ryan's statement indicated that her degree was not only for her own mobility but for the uplift of her community.

The desire to encourage other children in their communities to pursue college was a common trend among the women. Ryan expanded on the notion of uplift: "You don't have a group that does it, you have a representative. So if one person [goes to college], then everybody gets credit."

While Ryan's notion of uplift and caring seems more positive, she still admitted, "It's really pressure, so much pressure." Here, Ryan confessed that while she desired to care for her family and community by giving her education back, that this did create an added "pressure" for her. In some ways, this sense of giving back was an imposed, or Unchosen Me form of identity for Ryan. The "pressure" she described indicates that perhaps she did not really choose this for herself, but rather felt compelled to give back because it was expected of her.

Learning to Be a "Good Wife": Romantic Relationships on Campus

The pressure to exhibit silence, passivity, and caring that the women encountered among their peers and in the classroom was often reified in their discussions about romantic relationships. Overwhelmingly, the women described traditional, heterosexual gender roles in their romantic relationships, both outwardly and implicitly. There was a tension between the learned, socially imposed roles of what it meant to be in a romantic relationship and what the women

really wanted or were learning in college. Oftentimes the learned roles for romantic relationships (e.g., caring for one's man, doing domestic chores like cooking and cleaning as the woman's responsibility) came into direct conflict with
what the women wanted professionally and academically.

A "Good Wife" Is a Traditional Wife

The women at MU described the notions of womanhood that they were taught
on campus and those that they had observed while considering their future
roles. Their vision of marriage often came from their families, but as they talked
with one another, they reinforced and put their own boundaries around the
gender roles that were initiated in their families.

Tina, a first-generation senior psychology major, stated that in the future she
would like to be a "good wife." When asked what she meant by a "good wife," she
responded, "I would say that to be a good wife, I would want to be like a traditional wife." This was a conflict for Tina and many of the women because being
a "traditional wife" often would mean not working outside the home, yet the
women were working toward degrees so that they *could* work outside of the home.
If they envisioned themselves continuing to work after marriage, the women
struggled with how they would be able to balance their careers with their role as
a "traditional wife."

Many of these roles were defined by the women's families. Tina expanded on
her notion of being a "traditional wife," remembering her role as a female child
in her family: "I still remember, it'd be like six o'clock in the morning on a Satur-
day and me and my sister [would] be cleanin' and my brother would be out there
sleeping until about 2 o'clock. Oh, they'll come home and go to sleep and don't
wash the dishes. They'll wake me up at 2 o'clock in the morning to do them
[laughing]." Tina's desire to be a "traditional wife" could relate back to her familial
patterns that dictated that it was the woman's responsibility to complete domestic
chores. Although she was in college, she felt that one of her future jobs would be
to cook and clean for her husband, just like she used to do for her brother.

Isis, also a senior, first-generation student, responded to Tina's statement, summarizing her own vision of a good marriage and initiating a dialogue about the
percentages that men and women should work in the home: "I don't think that
the wife should do everything. But, I think it should be more like 70-30. The
woman should do more of the taking care of the kids and the cleaning. As long
as the husband was like, going to work and doing what they should be doing.
Even if I was working, I probably wouldn't work as much if I was married. Like,
I think he would be the breadwinner and I would be doing the stuff with the kids

and stuff like that." Isis elaborated on her vision of a "traditional wife," adding that this relationship had socially constructed expectations for the man as well as the woman. In this case, the man in the relationship had a responsibility to be the primary breadwinner for the family, to make money, while the woman had the responsibility for the domestic chores and childrearing.

However, there was some disagreement about the roles that women should play in the home. Claudia, a first-generation senior countered Isis's percentages, offering:

> Now, see I think that's different. Like, I think when there's kids, it needs to be 50-50. Like, because when I was growing up . . . my mom used to stay home with us. She still had a part-time job. But she did stay home with us. And my dad worked all the time. He brought the money in. But we never got to see my dad like that. So, we remember when he went on vacation [emphasis] with us and stuff like that, but there were times when we did something bad and he came home and talked about it. Because by the time he came we were asleep. So, you know, I think that for me it's important because I guess that I was raised like that. To have a relationship with your dad whether you are a boy or a girl. But, you have that good relationship with your father [emphasis].

Claudia's experience provided an example of the unintended consequences of the traditional gender roles in marriage—that the father would not have a meaningful relationship with his children. While she did think that the relationship should be more equal, she struggled with how this would play out.

Isis explained herself, noting that she felt her ideal of marriage to be the right thing: "I don't mean it like that. Like, with my parents, my father worked the most. But, like, I got to see my dad. Like he came home and, I was like five. So, I'm not saying 'oh he shouldn't be with the kids.' I'm just talking about just general stuff. Just like cleanin' up and cookin'. Like when he comes home, like the food should be cooked." While Isis agreed with Claudia that the father should have a relationship with his children, she ultimately still held fast to her opinion that the woman should take responsibility for the majority of the household chores.

Renee challenged the notion that women should complete all domestic chores, highlighting the potential conflict: "You've been working all day too though . . . right? Taking care of the kids . . . you will be working more [emphasis] than him." Renee's statement provided an example of the continual struggle that many women experienced as they attempted to balance the gender roles that were presented to them by their families with their own, perhaps contradictory, desires to be respected by men and to work outside of the home. Looking to the future, they anticipated that creating such a balance would be a struggle. Renee's comment may also be linked to class differences related to notions of womanhood. Her parents were college-educated, and she self-identified as middle class. Perhaps this in part accounts for the difference in her opinion.

Claudia reflected that one's exposure to gender roles affects one's notion of the appropriate assignment of responsibilities, noting that she was not bothered by her role:

> I think that depends on how you were raised too though. Because like my mom, she always had somethin' cooked for my dad. And my grandma was always that way too. Like, all the boys always got fed . . . like even my uncles, my grandma's sons, they always got fed first. It was all about the man first. Yeah, that's how she was. But I can see that I got that in me. Like, with my boyfriend, I always gotta make sure, "Did you eat? Did you eat? Are you hungry?" Like, I always gotta do that. And even when we got to my house, my mom'll be like, "Okay you serve him." Like when I'm at home I have to serve him his plate. You know, to eat. So, I think that was kind of instilled in me because it doesn't even bother me that I have to serve him.

As Claudia related her own relationship with her boyfriend to her families' gendered roles, she provides an example of the way gender roles are passed on from one generation to the next. Because she observed and expected to emulate particular gender roles, namely, that women should serve their men, she saw this as normal and as a behavior that she needed to continue. Here, Claudia's description links not only to past socialization but also to her future expectations of women's roles. But there is also a link to how she sees herself as a daughter or part of her family—as if enacting a particular gender role is important in carrying on her family norms or expectations. In addition, the notion of making food "for" a man relates to the idea of caring for others (male others in this case) before oneself.

Michelle, one of the few women in the sister circles who self-identified as a feminist, challenged the women in her circle by commenting, "I think that it goes both ways. I don't want a dude who when I get home is like, 'You should cook supper.'" Yet when it came to children, she did feel that the woman should play the primary childcare role, "I mean if I had kids, I would probably work less." In general, the women struggled with what seemed like a forced polarity: a woman can not be a good mother or wife and work full-time. Many women admitted that they did not *want* to stay home with their children, but that they felt they *should,* emphasizing the imposition of their gender socialization, or the unchosen nature of their gendered roles. When pushed for the reason that women should stay home with children, the women did not indicate a clear answer, further demonstrating the way that Unchosen Me aspects of identity can be manifested—one knows what one "should" do, but it is not always clear why. This is one way that gendered/racial norms are created.

Isis agreed that she wanted to stay home with her children rather than working outside of the home. She considered this decision as something that a woman must accept as her only option. This lack of options could be an imposed role: "I decided if I'm working and I have kids, I'm gonna work even more [inside the home]. You know? It's just like, if you have kids, you wanna stay home with your kids anyway. So, it's like it doesn't matter if you take the time off and stay at home. After a while it's just something you get used to, you know? Like, this is what I can do."

It is remarkable that Isis considered her future gender role as "something you get used to." She did not consider it appropriate to question this role. The inability to question or the lack of viable alternatives that she admitted with her statement that "this is what I can do" is an example of an imposed Unchosen Me characteristic or role. Isis may or may not actually *want* to stay home with her kids, but she felt like she could settle in and "get used to" the role if needed because it is the only role she saw as available to her in the future. This represents the bounding and restricting of women's life chances that led them to feel pressured to accept Unchosen Me characteristics within the boundaries of being a "good woman": a good woman stays home with her children and looks after her man. But this involves an additional assumption that the man is not very involved in the day-to-day child rearing process because he is expected to provide for his family.

With all the discussion of romantic relationships, marriage, and motherhood, it was interesting to consider the way the Midwest University women described their relationships with Black men. In general, they highlighted a tension between Black and White women for the attention of Black men on campus.

"Black boys could not control the Black woman": Competition for Black Men on Campus

Some African American women expressed anger or frustration at the seeming increase of interracial relationships on campus because they felt that White women were "stealing" the dwindling numbers of African American men on campus. Some felt that White women were simultaneously fearful of and attracted to Black men. Leila reflected, "I would think that probably not all of them, I think that there are some White females who have not had experience around Black males, or Blacks in general, would probably be afraid of Black men.

They usually are." This notion of an unexamined fear of Black men on the part of White women is an example of one way that race and gender can be created in stereotypical ways.

Tracey, a sophomore business major, countered, "There are also some White women who are intrigued by Black men." Leila responded, "I think it's both though. I really do. I think they're afraid, but sexually, they are intrigued." Tracey continued, "But at the same time, they are attracted to them." This dialogue between Leila and Tracey calls attention to the perception that many of the African American women had of White women: that they wanted to flirt with the potential danger of dating Black men, perpetuating the stereotype that Black men are somehow inherently dangerous or taboo and yet (or therefore), sexually attractive. In this example, Tracey and Leila implied a desire to protect the men in their racial group from racial stereotypes. They provided an example of the way that their African American brothers are bounded or separated. Interracial dating was considered abnormal or against cultural norms and unacceptable in this example and in most descriptions by the women in this study.

Camiya, a first-generation sophomore, added another layer to the discussion, offering that one reason Black men didn't date Black women is because Black women are "too assertive": "It goes both ways. My friends . . . I had a lot of White girlfriends in high school and they all dated Black boys, all of them. And it's so interesting because the Black men couldn't . . . I'm not sayin' never, but most Black boys could not [emphasis] control the Black woman. But, in situations with my [White] friends, they did everything for their boyfriends." As Camiya described the reasons she feels that Black men were attracted to White women, she wavered between what it might mean to be a "good *Black* woman": aggressive or passive. Yet the message was clear that African American women faced the consequence of losing African American men to White women if they were too assertive or not willing to cater to the desires of Black men. In turn, there was also an implication that White women are often more passive than Black women and more often willing—as Camiya suggests—to do everything (e.g., domestic chores, favors, etc.). The implicit message is that to "keep a man," a woman, especially a Black woman, would need to be more passive, again alluding to the notion that a "good woman" is passive.

There is also an implicit reference to the strength of Black women as Camiya noted that Black men may not be able to control Black women. Previously, Michelle maintained that to be a successful Black woman meant that one needed to be "firm" or "assertive." Yet Camiya indicated that on campus, assertiveness could be unattractive to Black men. This also links to the domestic roles that the women described, maintaining the men as the breadwinners and the women as homemakers and caretakers. Perhaps in this case, the Black women's development as "assertive" was *not* generated in relation to an approving (or disapproving) Black male audience. Or perhaps Black men, in their interaction with the White-centered mainstream on campus, at times identified with and saw as attractive what the Black women described as the White-centered notions of femininity (i.e., silence, passivity). This tension became complex for Black women as they navigated their emergent desire to have relationships with African American males and also to maintain their assertive identities.

The discussion continued with further dialogue about what it was that the Black men saw in the White women that they perhaps didn't see in Black women. Leila summarized: "So, I think that Black people, or a lot of Black males, that's the main reason that they tell me that they go to [White] frat parties. They always expect to find someone to at least do something. They will find one [White woman] that they will be able to have sex with after the frat party is over. The Black guys I know, because I've been to Black frat parties here, and they are pretty cool. But, they don't do it like that." Leila infers that Black men may want to date White women because they are, in their estimation, more sexually promiscuous than Black women. Also illustrated by Leila's description is the racial separation between student organizations on campus, a difference between White and Black fraternity parties. White fraternity parties, for instance, serve the purpose of matching people up for the purpose of having sex, while Black fraternity parties do not, at least in Leila's experience.

Camiya added: "This weekend, there was an all-Black party at the Union. But all the Black basketball players and football players were at this party. And I was like, oh my God, I cannot believe that they are at this party. Because they do not come to Black parties. We do not flock to them. Because I admire basketball players, but I do not flock to you. You're not makin' any money. You don't pay for anything." In her view, White women were particularly attracted to Black male athletes. Through her description, Camiya implies that Black women must be strong, independent, and *not* sexually promiscuous, while concurrently, there is a sense that Black men desired women with the opposite qualities.

Tracey agreed, saying, "But White girls will do it. They will do it." Camiya continued, "I see a basketball player with a White woman, and I think, he's havin' sex with her." Camiya's response illustrates some of the tension, perceived competition, and possible misunderstandings between Black and White women on campus.

In the examples above, there is a cross-over and an intersection between race and gender and the way that these categories are imposed on the women. Being a Black woman was associated with features commonly associated in positive ways with masculinity: active, assertive, aggressive. Being a White woman, on the other hand, was associated with characteristics that were portrayed as appealing to men (particularly Black men) and commonly associated with femininity: passivity, docility, doting. The Black woman was portrayed, through a contrast with White women, as sexually controlled, while the White woman was portrayed as sexually promiscuous. Little room was left for ambiguity. It is as if a Black woman could not choose to behave in both feminine and masculine ways. They felt pressure to represent their racial group in ways that would be accepted on the campus (passive, silent, caring) and yet represent their racial group in ways that would perhaps be accepted *within* the group, given their common references to strength (active, assertive, smart).

BEING BLACK AND FEMALE ON CAMPUS: THE INTERACTION BETWEEN THE UNCHOSEN ME AND GENDER NORMS

Being an African American *woman* especially compounded the feeling of being different at MU. On campus, many of the women discussed a need to work harder than their peers, particularly their White peers. Thus, while the women felt pressure to be "assertive and aggressive" as a means to be successful and to overturn racial stereotypes inside and outside of the classroom, they simultaneously felt pressure to be passive and silent so as not to be accused of having an "attitude problem" as evidenced above by Keisha's statement. Add to this confusing continuum the perceived necessity to care for others and the women's perceptions of romantic relationships, and being Black and female became a nuanced, complicated, multi-messaged experience. The women experienced *simultaneous* and *conflicting* pressures about what it meant to be a "good woman" in this predominantly White setting.

While the women in this study often voiced a desire to move beyond conventional female roles and norms, they struggled with the impositions of peer, family, societal, and eventually internal messages regarding what it meant to be a "good woman." In the main, for African American women, being a good woman meant exhibiting particular traits of silence, passivity, and caring for others before oneself. These characteristics were experienced by the women as both external and internal impositions. Initially they were external, learned from media,

peers, family, or acquaintances. But eventually these gendered norms were internalized, and the women often began imposing the norms on one another. This
exposes the interaction between self, others, and society and the way these interactions can lead to impositions that create race and gender in unequal ways.

As the women described the traits associated with being a good woman,
these descriptions became associated with being a good *White* woman. The African American women experienced these gendered norms as imposed externally through the White male and female mainstream. At times they experienced gendered norms as being mediated through Black males on campus: as
Black males chose to date White women, the African American women interpreted this as a message about what the Black men wanted in a woman—or what
the Black women were *not*, as in the conversation between Tracey and Camiya
above. Thus, the African American women were constantly compared to the
White-woman standard of what it meant to be "good." Many of the experiences
described by African American women were about being sanctioned or reprimanded for exhibiting characteristics that were outside the boundaries of being
a good woman, but perhaps the African American women were sanctioned because they were exhibiting characteristics other than those for *White* women.

At times the intersection of race and gender resulted in discord between Black
women and White women on campus. For example, in the discussion between
Leila and Tracey, the perceived norms for Black women and White women differed, ultimately putting Black women and White women (figuratively speaking)
into competition with each other for the attention of Black men.

The traits of silence and caring involved in being a good woman may inherently conflict with the structure of formal higher education, which is highly individualistic and in which judgments are made based on one's ability to voice
opinions. One manifestation of this conflict was evidence that while the women
were encouraged by their peers and professors to be silent, they were also sometimes penalized for it. As the women were forced to choose to be passive, silent,
and caring, they often had to sacrifice other behaviors that would be rewarded
on campus (voicing opinions, being assertive, and being individualistic). This
could have a serious influence on academic performances.

At other times, the intersection of race and gender could suggest that if African American women did not have to contend with the White-centric notions of
the "good woman," they might choose a womanhood that was associated with
strength, power, and assertiveness. While the women struggled with feeling
sanctioned by their professors (see chapter 5), White peers, and even by each
other for being "too assertive" or "too bold," they still often encouraged strength

in each other. Perhaps there was a tension between notions of "good *White* womanhood" (silence, passivity, caring only for others) and "good *Black* womanhood" (strength, assertiveness, boldness, caring for oneself and others in place of oneself), although often these were conflated or confused as the women grappled with their own gendered roles. Although these perceived conflicting pressures were perhaps on a continuum, the women in this study experienced them as imposing polarities that were simultaneously and inextricably racialized and gendered (fig. 7.1).

The notion of "good" womanhood relates to the Unchosen Me through its link to recognition. Being a "good woman" is linked to recognition in that the women were only able to be recognized socially if they demonstrated behaviors or traits associated with being a good woman—passivity, silence, caring—even if those characteristics were contrary to their own notions of strength. Or they were *misrecognized* (i.e., misinterpreted) for exhibiting characteristics outside of these bounded norms, evaluated through White-centered notions of femininity, and consequently sanctioned. For example, Leila was silent in class, although not exactly by choice. Yet her silence was reprimanded by the same professor who ignored her and therefore imposed the silence on her. Or Black women felt that to be successful on campus, one had to be assertive, as in Michelle's example, even if this meant that they would be sanctioned in other ways. This assertiveness is potentially at odds with the ability of Black women to have romantic relationships with Black men, as evidenced by the conversation between Tracey and Leila.

With the Unchosen Me concept, I argue that one only has access to choices of identity insofar as the identity will be recognized by others. Thus, as the women

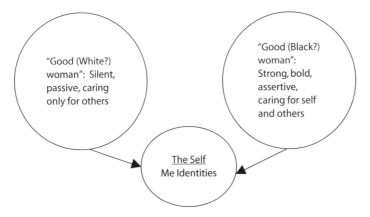

Figure 7.1 The self and learning to be a "good woman" on campus

were presented with what it means to be a good woman, they realized that if they exhibited traits outside the bounds of passivity, silence, and caring, they would be unrecognized, *misrecognized,* and often sanctioned by those around them. Accordingly, the women accepted Unchosen Me aspects of self because there were no other viable options. Or, they chose *not* to accept these characteristics and risked being sanctioned due to systematic misrecognition.

This helps to evolve the Unchosen Me in its link to behavior and traits. The traits of being a good woman are directly linked to one's behavior—the acting out of those traits. In my original conception of the Unchosen Me, I considered alterations to one's behavior as facilitating one's acceptance of Unchosen Me aspects of self. But the acting out of traits adds a deeper understanding of the way that behavior can link to identities, and particularly to *unchosen* aspects of identity.

CONCLUSION: GENDERED RACE, RACIALIZED GENDER

Gender and race become inextricably linked through notions of womanhood and particularly through notions of "goodness" in that womanhood. Ultimately, through their descriptions, the Black women created the boundaries around gender, or the possible roles that they could play as women, at least on this particular predominantly White campus. But not to be forgotten is the crosscutting boundary of race with gender. That is to say, because of their racialized (perhaps even unchosen) category as African American or Black, the women encountered particular gendered prescriptions that were intended solely for them based on their race *and* gender categories simultaneously. Hence, gender was ultimately unchosen in many of the same ways as was race. Alternatively, they also encountered boundaries around what they should *not* be as Black women. In due course, the women were pushed and pulled between strength and passivity, silence and assertiveness, caring only for others and self-care, yet another unchosen game of raced and gendered tug-of-war.

The process of learning to be a "good woman" on campus is both racialized and gendered, although this may often be a very subtle process of boundary-making and creating particular available identities. What should a woman make of her experience on campus if goodness is described in a way that is ultimately not inclusive of her and ultimately limits her chances for success? If the dominant gendered norms or roles are really associated with *White* womanhood, where does this leave the Black women who attempt to see themselves reflected in the gendered (and racialized) categories of campus? Must they adopt these often disempowering notions of White womanhood? If they don't, will they be sanctioned, reprimanded, or perhaps worse, misrecognized or unrecognized entirely? Or can they, through their own resistance, *re-create* notions of womanhood in their own image?

CHAPTER EIGHT

THE UNCHOSEN ME AND THE INTERACTIONS THAT CREATE RACE AND GENDER

One ever feels [her] two-ness . . . two souls, two thoughts, two unreconciled strivings; two warring ideals in one dark body whose dogged strength alone keeps it from being torn asunder. This history of the American Negro is the history of this strife—this longing to attain self-conscious [womanhood], to merge [her] double self into a better and truer self. In this merging [she] wishes neither of the older selves [to] be lost.   —*W.E.B. Du Bois, 1903/2003*

Over a century ago, W.E.B. Du Bois (1903/2003) coined the phrase "double con-sciousness" to describe the tension that many African Americans felt in Ameri-can society. Du Bois argued that many African Americans had to remember and enact cultural mores and norms from two cultures—their own and the main-stream Eurocentric culture—acting differently in each culture. Yet this was of-ten a painful process in which one felt that previous selves were lost or that one's dual selves could never merge.

This struggle persists in higher education as African American women navigate the differences between their cultural backgrounds and their cul-tural lives on campus.[1] But the "two-ness" that the women described here reveals more than their own identity struggle. It uncovers the continual *interaction* that creates race and gender in unequal ways in everyday life. As the African American women explained, their cultural backgrounds were experienced as less valued than those of the (White) mainstream campus.

The women described a series of dual tensions between their past and present, their pre-college and during-college identities, being in the spotlight or being invisible, being perceived as either "too White" or "too ghetto," and being perceived as either a "good woman" or a "bad woman." These "double consciousnesses" led the women to alter their behaviors and interactions on campus, factors that facilitated the acceptance of Unchosen Me aspects of self, ultimately revealing the interactions that create race and gender in everyday life. This careful negotiation between dualities fostered the "isolation" that many of the African American women reported feeling as minorities within the predominantly White institution.

RECONSIDERING RACE AND GENDER AS INTERACTIONS

The inequalities associated with being Black and female are alive and well in higher learning and certainly in the larger society today. As I discussed at the beginning of this book, race (and arguably gender) is studied most often from an input (e.g., biological determinism, the idea that a particular racial membership will lead to particular life chances) or an outcome (e.g., victimization, racism, discrimination) perspective (Banton, 1998). Research from these perspectives considers race in higher education in familiar ways. From an input perspective, African Americans are less likely to enroll in and graduate from college (Pathways to College Network, 2003). Or, from an outcome perspective, there is evidence that African Americans continue to face wealth disparities after college as compared to Whites, often because of implicit structural racism (Shapiro, 2004). Gender has been studied in similar ways, asserting a biological difference between sexes that will affect life chances or intellectual capability (an input perspective), or, considering persistent gender disparities in occupational attainment, income, and educational attainment, particularly at the terminal degree level, as due to explicit and implicit sexism (an output perspective) (Glazer-Raymo, 1999). Yet questions remain that these perspectives cannot tackle. Why do these racial and gender inequalities persist? How do race and gender continue to be created in the same unequal ways over and over again? Within the context of this study, what can predominantly White postsecondary institutions do to help ameliorate inequalities related to race and gender on college campuses?

In this book, the Unchosen Me concept provided a way to explore experiences of the social structure, as expressly related to race and gender, through interactions. This identity concept, rooted in interactions between self, others, and society, can be used, as it was here, as a vehicle to discover the interactional nature of race and gender that most often goes unidentified. From this perspective, the Unchosen Me importantly illustrates aspects of identities that are socially imposed. The everyday, natural accounts of women's experiences told through the stories of African American women in this book indicate that race is *created* through interactions between one's self, others, and society. These interactions were demonstrated most often through discussions about impositions on identity and a perception of being forced to choose between seemingly dichotomous and often unfitting polarities (being in the spotlight or being invisible, being perceived as "too White" or "too Black," being perceived as a "good woman" or a "bad woman").

The dualities, or forced polarities, of race and gender that were offered by the women in this book created a constant, albeit contradictory, pressure on the women. There was a façade of choice, but choice was actually quite constrained. Ultimately, the contradictory dualities create race and gender in a series of tensions that arise from that which is mainstream (i.e., White, male) coming in contact with that which is still outside of the mainstream (i.e., Black, female). Yet, in the interactions presented here, this series of tensions reified or *created* race and gender in familiarly unequal ways.

This study adds three major contributions to thinking about race and gender: (1) it helps to elucidate the *types* of dual/multiple identities that African American women experience; (2) without taking away the women's agency, it highlights the frustrating and potentially harmful *imposition* of these identities on the women in this study; and (3) it discusses how identity as a form of *interaction* can inform the interaction of race and gender within society as a whole. To understand these tensions in more depth, the interaction (between self, others, and society) of being in the minority on campus must be further examined.

The Interactions of Being in the Minority on Campus

Being a minority woman in a predominantly White setting was a burden that the women at Midwest University carried with them throughout their college experience.[2] Minority status within the overwhelming Whiteness of the campus manifested itself in different ways in various contexts for different participants. This merits a reflection on the culture shock and isolation women felt; the imposition of race experienced by the women; the way race and gender were integrally linked; the description (or lack thereof) of class on campus, which was compounded by race and gender; and the effect of all of these experiences on the women's persistence in their degree programs.

Culture Shock and Isolation

As described in chapter 4, culture shock and isolation formed a nearly impermeable haze through which the Black women experienced the predominantly White campus. The isolation that the women felt followed them all the way through their campus experience. The three women who graduated during the data collection process (Michelle, Isis, and Claudia) still described feeling "isolation," even as they prepared to leave campus or to attend graduate programs. There is growing evidence that students of color generally face isolation and alienation at predominantly White institutions (Allen, 1992; Davis et al., 2004; Feagin, Vera, & Imani, 1996; Loo & Rollison, 1986; Nilsson et al., 1999). The women's experiences help to build on this rich tradition to better understand the way that isolation affects the identity of Black women as impositions on identity and as a constant shadow over their experiences.

In some studies, the women's perceptions of isolation may have been considered a result of their lack of "integration" on campus (e.g., Tinto, 1993, 2000). However, the three women who graduated during the study, for example, were involved in Black Greek-letter organizations, mentoring programs, internships, work study, and the Black Student Union. It is notable that they were primarily involved in organizations with others of their racial group. Perhaps these organizations decreased their sense of isolation and culture shock in the predominantly White environment. But despite the support that these interactions and efforts may have given these women, they still admitted to a feeling of isolation related to being in the minority on campus. Feagin, Vera, and Imani (1996) argue that "integration" has been designed primarily as a "one-way assimilation process in which Black students are forced to adapt to White views, norms, and practices" (p. xi). The findings here concur with this position, adding evidence to the ways this one-way process occurs as impositions on identity that ultimately create race and gender in familiar, yet unequal, ways.

The Imposition of Race

In large part, the concept of identity, particularly with regard to racial categories, was experienced by the African American women as something that was imposed, or as not a meaningful choice. As discussed in chapter 5, the women experienced invisibility as imposed on them by their White peers and professors. It

was as if others—namely, *White* others—had the power to invalidate their existence, to make them invisible. On the other hand, the women felt that others on
campus (White peers and professors as well as those from racial minority groups)
had the power to define existence *for* them, based on their race (spotlighting).
Forced to either speak on behalf of their entire race or be silent/invisible, the
women felt as if others had the power to determine *for* them the way in which
they were allowed to exist on campus. Lisa, in chapter 5, described her exhaustion
in the classroom, feeling pressure if she *did* speak for her entire racial group (as
if spotlighted to say the right thing, to represent her group well) and pressure if
she did *not* speak (as if that made her and her racialized group invisible).

The imposition of race was largely enforced through recognition or a lack
thereof. As the women navigated the predominantly White campus environment,
they reported multiple experiences when they felt unrecognized or misrecognized
by peers, professors, and administrators. For instance, Isis, in chapter 6, gave the
example of being told, "You are Black, so you must like to dance and listen to hip
hop," making her feel misrecognized for her own musical tastes or interests. Often this was as if the ownership of the women's identity either was taken from
them or was created as not belonging to them. For example, Claudia, in chapter 6,
was told by a White peer, "You are not like an average Black girl." A White peer, in
this case, determines identity *for* Claudia.

The recognition within peer relationships, both positive and negative, had
a significant impact on the success of the women in this study. The Black Student Union, a positive example, was the center of many of the African American
women's social and academic lives on campus—a place where the women felt
their identities were often recognized by their peers. Numerous participants
talked about this organization as one of the primary places where they received
the type of emotional and academic support that they needed in the predominantly White setting. In a related example, after Mercedes joined a Black Greek-
letter organization, she became more satisfied with her college experience.

Also linked to the issue of recognition within peer groups was the women's
self-identification with their racial group. The women were either not recognized or were misrecognized if they didn't exhibit particular racialized behaviors, creating a sense that they could not *choose* their own racial identification. If
a woman behaved in a way that seemed too similar to the White mainstream or
her White peers on campus, she was labeled as "too White" by her Black peers;
yet if she associated too closely with the minority group and particularly with the
stereotypes of that group, she was labeled as "too Black" or "too ghetto" by both

her minority and majority peers (chapter 6). In this way, a woman's racialized existence on campus was imposed on her and the power to self-define her own racialized identities within that existence was external to her.

The dichotomy between being perceived as "too White" or "too ghetto" highlighted both within-group tensions and between-group tensions. As the women within the minority group imposed racial perceptions on one another, this highlighted within-group tensions. But this was also an example of the tug-of-war discussed in chapter 6, between their own racial group norms and boundaries, the racial norms and Whiteness of campus, and the larger social structures. As White peers imposed the "too White" concept on Black women (naming Black women White for particular reasons), this emphasized the between-group tension on campus. In this case, the between-group interaction privileged the White students in a way that allowed them to claim racial categories *for* the African American women, simultaneously reinforcing and creating race in ways that are unequal for Black women.

Often, racialized and gendered experiences and the impositions of what it meant to belong to a particular group in terms of one's identities were intimately linked to behavior. This is consistent with sociological literature linking the creation of gender and racial categories to action. In "Doing Gender" (West & Zimmerman, 1987) and in "Doing Difference" (West & Fenstermaker, 1995), gender and difference (e.g., race or class) are discovered to be linked to interactions and behavior. Implied is the pragmatic or action-oriented nature of race, class, and gender on campus—as if one could literally *act out* a particular race, class, and gender script or category. Yet this acting out ultimately became an interaction between one's self, others, and the larger society that reinforced the creation of race and gender inequality in this case. The women behaved in various ways, at times simultaneously, in order to either associate or disassociate with particular racialized and gendered categories.

One way that race was performed was in terms of representing one's racial group. Many of the women felt pressure to represent their racial group and to demonstrate to others that those in their racial group could successfully enter and finish college. This pressure was a huge burden for many of the women—a pressure that they often did not choose. Example after example indicated that this was externally imposed on the women by their peers and professors, and eventually, the women began to internalize this pressure and impose it on one another. Ultimately, the women were often left with the unchosen decision to either represent their entire race or remain silent. The Unchosen Me, as it developed here, indicated that there is no middle ground; the women described this as a forced choice between extremes when neither polarity felt like a fit for the individual.

At other times, the women attempted to disassociate from their racial group or from being in the minority. This was represented by the "too Black" notion, whereby women didn't want to associate *too much* with their racial group. Perhaps the women, particularly first-generation women, had unrealistic expectations for the way their families could support them. Also related to the disassociation of self to one's past or past culture, there was a self-imposed "get over it" mentality that the women described. Instead of wallowing in their misery, they coped by telling themselves they didn't need negative people in their lives, by surrounding themselves with positive influences, and by forming relationships with others like themselves.

While some of the women felt that they needed to disassociate from all things that linked them to being a minority, others disassociated from the Whiteness on campus. For example, the desire to not be perceived by their peers as "too White" was in many ways a disassociation from a larger idea of Whiteness. Accordingly, the women actively sought out others with whom to commune on campus—others who felt the same sense of being a minority in the overwhelmingly White atmosphere. This disassociation largely became an effort in resistance to the White-centric environment.

Related to the "too White"/"too Black" concept from chapter 6, Fordham & Ogbu (1986) first developed the concept of "acting White" from Signithia Fordham's ethnographic study of African American adolescent males in a metropolitan high school. John Ogbu, as her dissertation advisor, coauthored with Fordham to help her work be published while she was still a graduate student, although he has often received a majority of the credit for this work (Fordham 2008). In this landmark study, Fordham and Ogbu suggested that "acting White" was linked to an oppositional (to Whiteness) peer culture whereby the adolescent African American males at times associated "acting White" with doing well academically. Fordham later indicated that this was in large part because academics were historically the possession of White people (Fordham, 2008). Yet "acting White" still implied an anti-intellectual peer culture among Black youth.

The evidence presented in this book both challenges and builds on the "acting White" phenomenon by adding African American female perspectives on the acting White issue; by providing the young adult, college-aged notion of "too White," which highlights the "burden" aspect of Fordham's initial concept; and by presenting evidence that "acting White" is perhaps less associated with anti-intellectualism than with a resistance to Whiteness, at least for African American college-enrolled women. Finally, in this study, the "too White" issue was compared to an opposite pole of being "too Black," or associating too much with Blackness, a dichotomy that was not in the original conception.[3]

Among young adult (ages 18–22) African American college women, this phenomenon was both a reinforcement of and a resistance to Whiteness. But it was not an anti-intellectual peer culture as the "acting White" concept might suggest. The African American women used the word "too White" to refer to actions, thoughts, speech patterns, shopping habits, or tastes in music that were associated with being White. Noteworthy is the fact that the women did not define being "too White" as being smart or achieving well academically. Among their peers, at times they resisted being "too White," or encouraged each other to resist being perceived as "too White," but it was more of a way to resist the Whiteness of the campus. Indeed, by asserting their Blackness, or their non-Whiteness, the women were resisting that which was perceived as privileging Whiteness. Yet, arguably, the continual need to compare oneself to that which is White could be interpreted as reinforcing existing power structures on campus. Perhaps the desire by Black women to be well represented, and to represent their racial group well, could be a step *toward* intellectualism and positive group representations. In other words, this could be evidence of a *positive* peer culture,[4] at least in part, that encourages the women to do well in college and discourages them from living out the negative stereotypes of their racial group. Yet, even if the concept is no longer linked to intellectualism, it is still connected to the larger norms and values of the campus and those of the larger (stratified) social structure.

In short, the data in this study provide nuance and complexity to Fordham's (2008) "acting White" concept. I argue that in this case the "too White" / "too Black" concept was related to an interaction between Black women, their peers, and the larger social structure: both as a reinforcement of and resistance to Whiteness or the system of privilege that advantages White people or Euro-centered cultural norms, speech patterns, or norms of behavior. While the women here did not use the word "burden," their stories suggest that the continuum between being "too White" or "too Black" is a heavy weight that they are compelled to carry in college, using words like "pain" to describe this experience. Fordham (2008) is concerned that many adaptations of the "acting White" concept have erased this notion of burden—ignoring the way this concept was developed to connote the suffering that Black male adolescents experienced in school. Indeed, the Black college women in this study stressed the sense of suffering—a burden—as they interacted with a racialized system on campus (and in the society writ large) that privileged White people and Whiteness.

Different from the initial "acting White" concept was the comparison of being "too White" to being "too ghetto" or "too Black"[5] that was both explicitly made and inferred by the Black women in this study. As a woman attempted to *not* be perceived as "too White," she also felt it necessary to not associate too much with Blackness and be perceived as "too Black" or "too ghetto." The "too ghetto" concept was related to the racial minority group's perceived need to represent the group well. The issue of representing inherent in the "too Black" concept is also bounded by White privilege and racial norms—working to create race in ways that privilege White groups over non-White groups. This was an effort to disassociate oneself from negative stereotypes of Blackness. While the women attempted to disassociate from being "too White," they also disassociated from being "too Black," reinforcing the need to represent their racial group well. In effect, this could reinforce the continual White / Non-White comparison, holding Whiteness as the standard or the norm. More work is needed to understand the dichotomous nature of acting "too White" and/or "acting Black."

Ultimately, the "acting White" concept needs to be further evaluated among different ages and genders with careful attention to the initial meaning of the concept as an explanation for the way people in a racial minority group confront a racialized system that ultimately treats them as invisible.[6] This data may actually relate well to Fordham's (2008) intent for the "acting White" concept to be a relational confrontation of a society that privileges Whiteness. This data provides evidences of the nuance and complexity of this interaction between African Americans, others, and social institutions. In this case, the dichotomy between being perceived as "too White" or "too ghetto" highlighted both within-group and between-group tensions. As the women within the minority group imposed this on one another, this highlighted within-group tensions. But this was also an example of the tug-of-war discussed in chapter 6, between their own racial group norms and boundaries, and the racial norms and Whiteness of campus or the larger social structures. As White peers imposed the "too White" concept on Black women (i.e., naming Black women White for particular reasons), this emphasized the between-group tension between racial groups on campus. In this case, the between-group interaction privileged the White students in a way that allowed them to reclaim racial categories *for* the African American women, simultaneously reinforcing and creating race in ways that are unequal to Black women.

Racialized Gender, Gendered Race

For African American women, the categories of race and gender were inextricably linked. Gender was also linked to identity issues and was largely framed outside of one's ability to freely choose one's sense of self. Race was gendered—often completely ignoring the voices of Black women. Likewise, gender was racialized—generally framed in ways that create notions of womanhood related to *White* women. Hence the "double whammy" notion that Michelle described in chapter 7, where she said that Black women had to contend, and perhaps be content with race and gender inequalities, and the interactions that created these inequalities, simultaneously and constantly. It was as if others had the power to choose the women's gender-related identities, or, as if only certain identities were even available (recognized by others) when it came to gender.

The women at Midwest University were heavily influenced by strong gender socialization both on and off campus, by an often implicit notion of "good womanhood" (i.e., silence, passivity, and always caring for others above oneself). Yet this idea of womanhood often did not fit the gender socialization that they encountered from their mothers, female role models, or from each other in peer groups. The notion of "good womanhood" was largely framed in terms of what it meant to be a good *White* woman, leaving the Black women to navigate this notion of womanhood that may or may not have fit their own, potentially more empowering, ideals for womanhood.

The framework of "good (White?) womanhood" was often in direct conflict with the requirements for being a "good student." Women felt pressured to be silent and passive and often faced severe sanctions from their peers, faculty, and/ or families if they attempted to move beyond these boundaries. They reported numerous times when they were sanctioned for being "too assertive" or "too bold," yet they also indicated that the way to succeed as a woman in the larger society was to "be assertive" or to "be firm." Hence, the women were left feeling as if they had to decide between a notion of good *Black* womanhood framed in more positive terms of boldness, assertion, and caring for both others and oneself that may benefit them in college, and good *White* womanhood as silence, passivity, and caring only for others. Yet only the version of good *White* womanhood was recognized or rewarded on campus.

This intersection of race and gender, the way that they are inextricably linked, has been explored by Black and Latina feminist scholars (Hill Collins, 2000; hooks, 2000; Hurtado, 1996; Zinn & Dill, 1999). Aside from these studies, often race and gender are seemingly separated, demonstrating privilege structures in society: race studies may implicitly exclude women of color, and studies of gender are framed as an issue of White women. Similarly, feminist theories have been critiqued for only representing White women, again, placing White womanhood as the norm (hooks, 2000; Hurtado, 1996).[7]

For the women in this study, race and gender completely intersected. Yet they felt disallowed from self-defining knowledge or their own identities relative to race or gender. The women's stories here shed light on the interactions between self, others, and society that work to create gender and race in these oppressive ways. An understanding of this interaction could help to reshape the way that race and gender are considered, potentially moving toward a *re-creation* of these concepts. This notion of re-creation relative to race and gender may offer a way to navigate the pressures of the Unchosen Me.

Class as the Big Taboo?

The majority of the women in this study were not only Black women in a predominantly White setting, but they also self-identified as low-income and were first-generation college students on a campus where it seemed as if most students were middle class. Class seemed to be an issue that was always there but rarely discussed. The women only talked about class issues when they knew that they were in groups with others from similar socioeconomic backgrounds.

Otherwise, class was a big taboo, even though the campus was socioeconomically stratified in many ways. For example, the price to live in residence halls on campus differed from hall to hall; thus, students lived in residence halls with people from like socioeconomic backgrounds. This is one way that institutions, perhaps unintentionally, create stratification based on class (or even race and gender, depending on who primarily lives in each hall). Another example of socioeconomic status is that demonstrated through the ownership of material items such as the newest cell phones, iPods, Coach or Gucci purses, and name-brand clothing. Some of the women from lower socioeconomic backgrounds reported working two or three part-time jobs just to have these high-status items. It was as if having these things somehow might make them fit into the mainstream on campus.

Finances were a continued stressor and barrier to earning degrees for these women. Nearly all of them worked at least 20–30 hours per week in multiple jobs in order to pay for college and living expenses. Some of them worked more than 40 hours per week, just trying to make enough money to finance their educational and living expenses. Given that paying for education and living expenses was so difficult, it is interesting that many of these same women still maintained the importance of buying high-status material items. The need to work to pay for college kept many of the women from becoming involved on campus in the way that they would have liked. In particular, the women felt that they *needed* to work to pay living expenses and tuition: it was not a choice. This suggests that more need-based financial aid is needed. Even if students are able to secure financial aid to pay for tuition, they often did not receive enough aid to pay for their living expenses. Most of the women who worked more than 20 hours per week did it because they needed money for food and rent. These women indicated that this made studying and doing other activities on campus quite difficult.

Consistent with other findings (Norvilitis, Szablicki, & Wilson, 2003), credit card debt was a significant issue for all of the women. One woman, Isis, actually considered leaving school to pay off her credit card debt. Many of the first-generation women admitted that they had to pay for tuition, housing, and their books with credit cards. Other women bought high-status items on their credit cards as a way to fit into the campus culture.

Race, Gender, and College Student Persistence

The majority of the college student persistence literature stresses the importance of students' social and academic integration into institutions, maintaining that highly integrated students are more likely to persist in degree programs (Astin, 1996; Beil et al., 1999; Guifridda, 2003; Kuh et. al, 2000; Schwartz & Washington, 2002; Tinto, 1975, 1993, 1997, 2000). The academic-social integration model has implications for the identity of college students because it maintains the importance of integration into the existing institutions of higher education. The underlying assumption is that a *student* must adapt her identity to fit into the institution rather than placing the burden of change and inclusion of underrepresented students on the institution.

The women's experiences add to the critiques of the academic-social integration model (Braxton, 2000; Howard-Hamilton, 1997; Rendòn, Jalomo, & Nora 2000; Taylor & Miller, 2002; Tierney, 1992, 1999, 2000; Torres, 2003), underscoring the importance of including the perspectives of minorities. This book provides an alternative to the academic-social integration model, suggesting that at times underrepresented students are integrated, but there is often a severe sense of personal loss in this integration. Lisa, for instance, was technically integrated into the institution: she was involved in an honors program aimed at serving minority students, and she was involved in organizations in the School of Education. Yet she ultimately left the institution because the personal cost of integrating—the loss of her sense of self—was too high. The question remains: Is there a way to encourage integration without assuming assimilation? Why should some students (namely, students of color) pay a higher personal cost to earn their degrees?

Summary

In sum, the women in this study experienced the burden of impositions on their identity, and these impositions created race and gender in familiarly unequal ways at Midwest University. On top of typical stressors in college (e.g., living on one's own, making friends, learning new academic materials), the women faced the challenge of negotiating between identity dichotomies that were imposed on them or chosen *for* them. These dichotomies—between past/present, "too White" / "too ghetto," "good woman" / "bad woman," and speaking-for-one's-race or remaining-silent—fostered a sense in the women of color that they had to significantly change themselves in order to be successful in the predominantly White environment. These changes to one's self or one's identities often came at a high price to the women, ultimately creating a sense of loss, frustration, and isolation, or an impression that one must accept unchosen aspects of self in order to be successful in college.

THE EVOLUTION OF THE UNCHOSEN ME CONCEPT

The Unchosen Me concept exemplifies identities as interactions between one's self, others, and the larger society. Through this concept, I assert the importance of both internal and external volition within identities. Identity is fashioned from available intersubjective (or mutually shared) material or milieu. The milieu is the boundaries of a field from which identities are possible. One has the agency to act within these boundaries, and at some level, to resist or choose identities. But ultimately, identity development itself is bounded or confined to the available field of identities—those that are recognized by others—making resistance or choice less available.

The initial development of the theory was concerned with the way that identity characteristics can be socially imposed. This theory was an attempt to provide an identity concept that took into account the existing inequalities in the social structure and the way these inequalities may influence one's perception of choice regarding identity. This theoretical concept *could* have been rejected had the women's experiences not been well represented by this theory. However, in this case, the Unchosen Me evolved and changed as outlined below.

Factors Related to the Acceptance
of Unchosen Me Aspects of Identity

Initially, in chapter 2, I provided a figure to illustrate the development of the Unchosen Me theoretical concept (see fig. 2.3). This figure demonstrated a larger, macro-level description of the concept, conceiving of identities as being influenced by existing privilege and opportunity structures. The dotted lines in figure 2.3 denote feedback loops whereby choice, or lack of choice, affects one's perception of privilege and opportunity structures.

The women in this study explained impositions on identity in dualities (e.g., "too White" vs. "too ghetto," "good woman" vs. "bad woman"). These dualities linked to the Unchosen Me because there were often not other identifiable options from which to choose. Additionally, the women did not experience the power to choose the dualities in the first place: they were experienced as imposed, as the only viable or available options. They felt pressured to choose between polarities, neither of which fit them. The women's stories added nuances and complexity to the Unchosen Me theoretical concept. Figure 8.1 provides a visual representation of the way the imposed dualities that the women described were factors that influenced the acceptance of Unchosen Me aspects of self.

One important evolution of the Unchosen Me theoretical concept resulting from this study was regarding choice of identity. Rather than having a clear *choice* of identities, the idea shifts to consider the *boundaries of cultural milieu* within which and from which identities can be constructed. Given this new perspective on identity, even those identity claims that are new or creative will preserve the boundaries of the cultural milieu or the underlying structures (i.e., cultural structures, implicit institutional and interpersonal structures, structures of meaning and intelligibility). The structure of the cultural milieu, then, is the medium and outcome of action. It is bounded; consequently, outcomes are going to basically retain the underlying social structures that were uncovered in this project. But this new perspective on identity also allows for creativity and resistance—for example, acting just "so" between "too Black" and "too White." Accordingly, in a way, identities emerged in this study as unlimited, but bounded. That is, one has the agency to be creative and unique in a way; yet there are boundaries around this uniqueness whereby one will be unrecognized or misrecognized socially if one falls outside these bounds. It is my hope that eventually, if one kept presenting one's own uniqueness within these boundaries, the boundaries would shift to allow for these creative identities to be recognized.

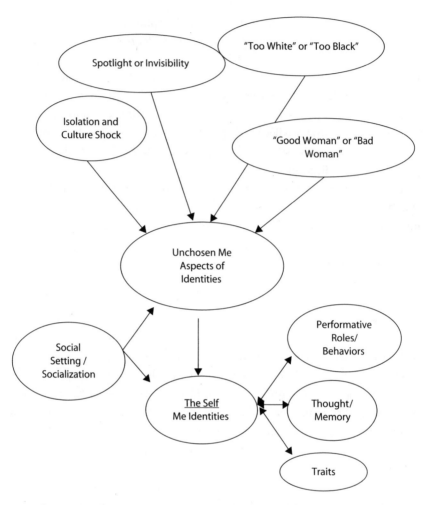

Figure 8.1 Factors influencing the acceptance of the Unchosen Me

Figure 8.1 illustrates the boundaries of cultural milieu, the way that both the external categories (e.g., context, performative roles, memory/thought, etc.) that are representations of one's identities to others and the internal dichotomies of identity (e.g., "too White" / "too ghetto"; "good woman" / "bad woman," etc.) relate to the acceptance of Unchosen Me aspects of self. As evidenced in the figure, the acceptance of Unchosen Me aspects of identities is influenced simultaneously by internal pressures (i.e., the dualities such as spotlight/invisibility, "too White" / "too Black," "good woman" / "bad woman") and external pressures (i.e., social settings, socialization more generally). Once one accepts Unchosen Me's, this alters one's performative roles/behaviors, one's thought or memory, and the traits that one exhibits. Yet performative roles/behaviors, thought and memory, and traits can also influence the Me aspects of one's self or Me identities as represented by the dual arrows in the figure. For instance, a particular performative role, often unchosen in some sense (i.e., only certain roles might seem available), may affect one's available Me's.

There were nuances of identity impositions, such as the way in which the imposition was experienced by the women in the study (externally or internally) and regarding the reference group from whom the imposition stemmed (majority or minority groups).

The Nuances of Identity Imposition and the Creation of Race and Gender

Impositions or pressures on identity through the Unchosen Me concept are one way that inequalities in the social structure can be identified. As the women in this study described impositions on their identity, they simultaneously provided insight into the way that race and gender are created in unequal ways within the social structure. These identity impositions were experienced as internally or externally imposed (or at times, as both externally and internally imposed). Table 8.1 provides a summary of the influences on identities and links them to the type of imposition and source of imposition as the women described it.

Impositions on identity facilitated the acceptance of Unchosen Me aspects of identity. These impositions were nuanced in terms of the reference groups

TABLE 8.1
Identity Impositions for African American Women

	Type of Imposition	Source of Imposition
Culture shock and isolation	External	Majority groups
Spotlight	External and Internal	Minority groups and Majority groups
Invisibility	External and Internal	Majority groups
"Too White"	External	Minority groups and Majority groups
"Too Black" / "Too Ghetto"	External	Minority groups
Learning to be a "good woman" on campus	Internal and External	Majority groups and Minority groups
Silencing the strength: A "good woman" is silent, passive, and caring	Internal and External	Majority groups and Minority groups (secondary source)
Learning to be a "good wife": Romantic relationships on campus	Internal and External	Majority groups and Minority groups

(mainstream, minority, or both) that were doing the imposing and the way the imposition was experienced (internally, externally, or both). Sometimes the women noted that they experienced particular impositions as external to them or imposed on them by peers, families, professors, or the larger social structure (e.g., Michelle's comment that "being Black is imposed on me"). Often these external impositions became internalized or self-imposed. As the women internalized notions of intelligence, for instance, they began to self-impose these norms (e.g., "Men are smarter").

The reference group of the imposition was also nuanced. Sometimes the women experienced the imposition as being through or in reference to the White mainstream on campus (e.g., creating isolation or culture shock or the feeling of being invisible). At other times, the women felt impositions from minority groups or in reference to minority groups (e.g., Don't act "too ghetto"). The experiences of the impositions differed slightly, depending on the way the participants connected campus experiences to other beliefs that they held. However, it is worth noting that the range of variations was not great. The variations of interpretations still took place within the same structures of dichotomous relations ("too White" / "too ghetto," spotlight/invisibility, "good woman" / "bad woman", etc.). By structure, I am referring to cultural, explicit, and implicit structures of meaning and intelligibility.

Related to table 8.1, which outlines the type of identity impositions and the source of those impositions, in figure 8.2, I provide a visual representation of the various influences on identity related to these impositions: social structure and social stratification, individual background issues, and social experiences (e.g., campus experiences). The self would be affected by these influences on identity and the impositions on identity simultaneously. Recall that this notion of identity initiates in the social structure. One's experiences within this social structure and the existing social stratification facilitate the process of Me construction. Accordingly, social experiences such as campus experiences in this case were often influenced both by the social structure or existing social stratification in society and by a person's past experiences. The concentric circles in figure 8.2 illustrate the connection between the social structure/stratification, past experiences, and campus experiences, mapping the nuanced impositions on identity to provide a representation of the way that impositions on identity were experienced by women in this study.

If figure 8.2 were more three dimensional, the identity impositions would lie on top of the existing concentric circles (of social structure, past experiences, and social experiences such as campus experiences). This is meant to suggest

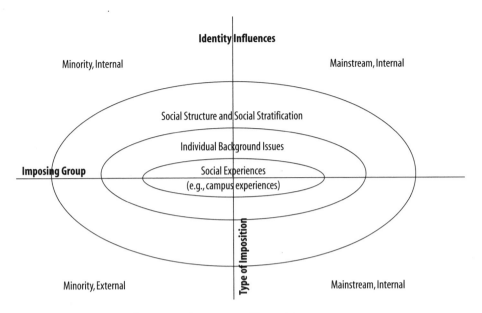

Figure 8.2 Identity influences and categories of imposition

that as one interacts on campus, *all* of these things are called into the foreground in different ways in a variety of settings. For example, one's past experiences may be more salient than the social structure in some settings. Of course, a figure cannot represent all the possible nuances of identity imposition; it is only a tool for better understanding the way the emergent nuances of imposed identity relate to the existing Me part of self and to one's existing experiences.

While the self is not visually represented in figure 8.2, this process, the influences on identity (social structure, background and campus experiences) would holistically and continually affect the way one experienced one's identities, particularly related to the Unchosen Me or imposed aspect of identities. Consequently, based on the nuances of identity impositions that emerged from the women's stories, the Unchosen Me concept evolved as exemplified in figure 8.3. The new conception, based on the data in this book, includes the social structure, social stratification, family backgrounds, and previous social experiences in the concept.

The social structure and stratification within that social structure are primary to institutional and cultural issues. This is represented by concentric circles: one's family background and previous social experiences arise as already within institutional and cultural norms and values. These institutional and cultural norms/values arise out of an existing, stratified, social structure. Yet institutional

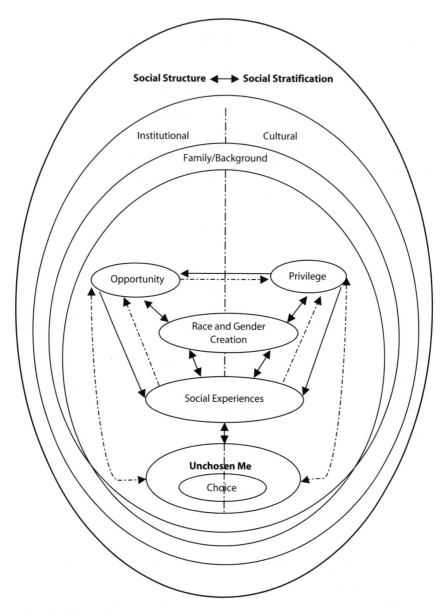

Figure 8.3 The Unchosen Me: the intersection of social stratification, opportunity, privilege, and choice

and cultural norms/values do influence the social structure and stratification, leaving room for agency and change as represented by the double arrow in the figure. Institutional and cultural norms and values represent two sides of one issue: the way in which already existing inequalities become embedded within cultural constructs and institutions (demonstrated in the figure by a line separating institutions and culture). Additionally, this line is meant to represent opportunity as embedded within institutions and privilege as embedded in cultural norms and values. Finally, the creation of race and gender is located in the center of the figure, influenced by opportunity structures, privilege structures, and Unchosen Me aspects of identity. The way in which race and gender are created in social experiences (e.g., campus experiences) then begins to influence opportunity, privilege, and the choices of identity or general choices (e.g., choice to persist in college) one sees as available. Ultimately, race and gender are created within existing social inequality, deeply influencing individual choice and identity. Figure 8.3 allows for a deeper explanation of the intersections between social stratification, opportunity, privilege, and choice.

The Unchosen Me and Structural Symbolic Interactionism

Stryker's (1980) structural symbolic interactionism provided a groundbreaking notion of the Me that allowed for an empirical test of this theoretical concept. However, I begin to part ways with Stryker regarding the issues of identity salience and role choice, the instrumental, external nature of his theory, and the assumption of identity stability.

Stryker's (1980) conception of identity links role choice to identity salience: one's commitment to a group leads to the salience of a particular identity, and that leads toward one's acceptance of a role. Through the Unchosen Me theoretical concept, I question the notion of "choice" in the development of the Me part of self, asserting that at times one is coerced, forced, or persuaded to accept identity characteristics or roles as a way to be socially recognized. If there are few viable alternatives, I argue, then choice is constrained to the point where *aspects* of one's identity are ultimately unchosen. The stories of the women in this study problematize salience, in that salience was often violated. That is, the African American women were often not allowed to reify the Me that they wished to exhibit because of the campus norms and structures, coupled with the expectations of self, others, and society. The women often claimed a particular Me aspect of their identities in order to navigate the predominantly White campus. I argue within this data that: (1) one may knowingly choose a non-salient Me in order to get the action consequences one desires (e.g., passing a class, getting a degree), yet even in so doing, it is unlikely that one will feel less isolated; (2) one may internalize a Me that does become something desired but that is in conflict with other possible Me's (e.g., no longer consistent with past cultural norms or behaviors); or (3) one could reject the non-salient Me and possibly be unsuccessful. In this last case, the Me does not feel right to the person even though the Me is internalized to the point of having some salience. Hence, I am suggesting that there are *salience conflicts* that merit further attention. This delves deeper into cultural power and the potential unequal costs to self. Likewise, one may exhibit a particular role, but I challenge the assumption that one is inherently free to choose this role due to a social structure that privileges some roles over others.

Secondly, Stryker's (1980) notion of identity does not allow for considerations of power and inequality within the social structure. Rather, the theory is primarily instrumental, identifying the motives and reasons behind the performance of particular identities. I suggest that a conception of identity must be more than instrumental. Through the Unchosen Me, I attempt to allow for a consideration of power and the way that communicative action (interactions between self, others, and society), oriented toward understanding (rather than simply that which is motivated toward a particular goal), influence identities.

Stryker (1980, 2000) maintained that the Me part of one's self could be studied by looking at one's commitment to a particular identity, the salience of these identities in various contexts, and one's choice of roles. This notion of identity focuses on an explanation of the external conditions of identity. I focused here on both the external *and* the internal aspects of identity: identity as it relates to that which is constitutive or internal to volition or choice with factors external to volition. That is to say, through the Unchosen Me, I explored the ways in which identity internally and externally allowed or disallowed choices. Many of the women's descriptions of identity impositions referred to performative roles or behavior, where a woman felt inclined to act in a particular way with regard to racialized, class-based (although this was often tacitly, not explicitly mentioned), or gendered categories on campus. The gendered issues were primarily related to particular traits that the women were pressured to exhibit, for example. The illustration of these traits again links to behavior or action as the women felt an imposition to act out these traits whether or not they were naturally inclined or culturally supported characteristics. While Stryker's three parts of the Me (commitment, identity salience, and role choice) may still be present, this study indicates that regarding impositions on the Me parts of self, there are other issues to consider such as memory/thought, performative roles, and traits.

In addition, Stryker's (1980) structural symbolic interactionism primarily remains in the positive pole of identity, investigating the "what I am" aspect of self, empirically testing the Me. I examine the interaction between the Me, "what I am," and the negative pole of identity, the Not-me, or "what am I not." This, in some ways links the Me to the I concepts of self. Mead specifies that in some way the I aspect of self is the sense that "I am not this, not that." So the Not-me is one way to connect the Me and the I aspect of self.[8]

Finally, with the development of the Unchosen Me concept, I call into question Stryker's relatively stable notion of identity, proposing that one's identity is dynamic, in a constant state of flux that is both situation and interaction (between self, others, and society) dependent.

TRANSFORMING THE INTERACTIONS THAT CREATE RACE AND GENDER: SHIFTING TOWARD RE-CREATION

In many ways this book centers on the problem of identity impositions, specifically, the way that these impositions are manifested in higher education to influence the success of African American women. How can the topic be shifted, then, *From Oppression to Grace*, as the title of an edited volume about Black women's journeys in academia (Berry & Mizelle, 2006) suggests? The verbiage of imposition and the Unchosen Me seems to imply that one does not have choice when it comes to identity. What about agency? Is there a way that these impositions on identity that ultimately work to create race and gender in unequal way can be resisted?

Naming the Problem: The Need to Study the Interaction of Race and Gender

The Unchosen Me connotes the boundaries around a field from which identities are possible or from which identities are made less possible. The women in this study felt pressure to accept imposed identity characteristics, often because they were unrecognized or misrecognized for accepting alternative identities, or because there were not viable options of identities in view. However, at some level they still maintained their agency to resist these impositions. The discomfort that the women expressed as they described the imposed identities could be considered a form of resistance. Likewise, consciousness-raising efforts, much like what occurred during the sister circles, could be a useful tool in fostering resistance to the impositions on identity. The issue of resistance merits further attention in future work.

I am not attempting to simply describe the *problem* that is the Unchosen Me or impositions on one's identities. I am arguing here that this knowledge in itself creates a responsibility in scholars, students, faculty, administrators, and those outside of the institution of higher learning to begin to change the factors that cause these impositions. This knowledge poses a responsibility to actually pierce inequality related to race and gender—calling for a *re-creation* of these concepts.

Naming the problem can foster efforts to solve that problem. That is, the various identity impositions presented here shed light on the ways in which race and gender are continually created in unequal ways through interactions between self, others, and society. Illustrations of these interactions can provide an opportunity for beginning to re-create race and gender—to transform the racial and gender inequality that is perpetuated in everyday life. The knowledge that African American women experience college as a series of seemingly endless dichotomous, if not extremely painful, polarities allows for thinking to begin on ways to *re-create* this process in ways that provide more viable alternatives. The knowledge that students often feel spotlighted or made to feel invisible in the classroom can be an impetus for change for professors. Or, knowing that in peer groups Black women felt that they had to keep from being perceived as either "too White" or "too Black" can provide an incentive to carefully evaluate peer groups on a college campus or in other settings to identify ways that perhaps these groups could be altered.

As for the study of race and gender, I am suggesting that these concepts need to be studied in ways that are not only input- or outcome-based. Rather, these concepts should be considered as the ongoing, everyday interactions that they are. One deals with race and gender, and interactions between self, others, and society related to these categories, on a daily basis, and this in itself can clarify what is known about these issues.

Toward a Sociological Perspective of College Student Identity

This project advocated shifting from a psychological notion of college student identity to a sociological perspective, emphasizing the social structure and inequality within it.[9] While the psychological perspective on identity has greatly advanced work on college student identity development, a more balanced approach is needed, namely, sociological perspectives on identity that highlight social-structural problems (i.e., inequality, stratification), particularly for the study of underrepresented student identities.[10]

The psychological perspective of identity generally maintains a series of stages through which a person will progress, often in a linear fashion, while the sociological perspective maintains a more fluid, continuous notion of identity.[11] The sole use of psychologically based theories without a sociological perspective may disallow for experiences that do not match a linear progression. In this case, the women's depictions of identity did not fall into a linear set of stages. Rather, the women continually felt pressured to choose between multiple dualities throughout their time on campus, usually because of their minority status.

Additionally, many psychologically rooted, stage-based theories problematize particular aspects of or stages within the identity process, often placing value on one's development or progress through the stages. Because the possibilities are limited to particular stages, this may limit what can be found within the data. Many of the women in this study, for example, would have been placed in early stages or would have been considered to not be progressing through the stages.[12] The sociological perspective does not assert a particular process through which one must advance. Rather, the sociological perspective provides a type of identity that is holistic (meaning that one's identities are evaluated simultaneously) and fluid, whereby one's own processes are valued, whatever they might be. While the stage-theory literature is a rich line of research, stage theories run the risk of labeling and limiting people and potentially causing harm (e.g., through stereotyping), which is one of the primary reasons that I avoided the use of such theories in my study.

The singular notion of identity within the psychological tradition can be limiting, considering the way in which women here described their identity in dual, or multiple ways. The focus on cognitions or mental processes in the psychological perspective shifts the focus away from the social structure and toward individuals. Using a sociological notion of identity, I asserted that identities initiate in the social structure and therefore, as one develops identities, one is also interacting with the existing inequality in the social structure. This interaction-based concept of identities, using a multiple-identities perspective, allowed for a reconsideration of the larger concepts of race and gender as ongoing interactions between self, others, and society.

With respect to the rich tradition of psychologically based theories, my theoretical development and data analysis call for a consideration of a continuous development of self whereby one constantly interacts with the social structure, not in predictable, ordered stages, but in a way that gains recognition of oneself by others and by one's self. The Unchosen Me is continuously an issue, although sometimes it may be more or less of an issue, depending on the context. (For example, one may not feel the pressure of unchosen identity characteristics when one is with a like-group or when one feels fully understood by others).

The impositions on identity, or the Unchosen Me aspects of self arise because of concern with how others perceive one (the interaction between self and others) as people attempt to gain recognition from others and are often misrecognized or not recognized. This also allows for an illustration of one's perceptions of the social structure related to race and gender (the interaction between self and society). A fully autonomous person is freer of the need to have others perceive him or her in certain ways. But few people are *fully* autonomous, and very autonomous people are likely to experience a good match between an inner sense of their identity and the way that others perceive them. One can think of famous exceptions, people who never felt understood by others but still proved themselves to be very autonomous, but those are rare cases. Identity impositions concern whether or not the conditions needed to develop into an autonomous and self-possessed person are met.

The stories of the women in this study indicate that race and gender—through the study of identity as the interaction between self, others, and society—are being created in unequal ways within higher education. The up side, then, is that growing knowledge of the way race and gender are created could lead to a *re-creation* of the way that race and gender are considered that also has implications for institutions of higher education and society at large. Realizing that the idea of a transformation of the ongoing interactions that continue to create race and gender in unequal ways can in some ways feel abstract, I provide some concrete suggestions for change, particularly related to higher education.

Support Structures: The Practical Side of Things

More institutional support structures are necessary for African American women. But these support structures need to be somehow incorporated into the mainstream of campus rather than on the fringes of campus to keep students from feeling "ghetto-ized." This is not to undermine the importance of offering spaces—both physical and figurative—for students of color to be with other students of color (e.g., culture centers, organizations primarily associated with minority students). But the campus—and the nation, for that matter— send a powerful message about what is important, about whether or not diversity is truly *valued*, through the allocation of resources. This suggests that there is a need for more resources to be spent on support programs for students of color and for the resources to be spent in the right places.[13]

Institutional Support Structures

The majority of the women, like Isis, noted that the sister circles, which met for a long period of time (9 months), were one of the first opportunities that they had on campus for honest and meaningful interracial contact and interaction. Most of the instances of interracial communication that were described in this study, both inside and outside of the classroom, were negative and detrimental to the women of color involved. The interracial communication could occur in the classroom, but it is vital that professors and instructors are trained in ways to approach the topic of race so that the conversation isn't detrimental. This is a vital aspect of the students' educational process. It should be nearly impossible for a student to leave a large public institution like MU without having had the opportunity to think critically about issues of race, class, and gender. Administrators, student affairs practitioners, and faculty members at predominantly White institutions need to give serious consideration to the tone of interracial contact at the institution.[14] More opportunities for honest dialogue, questioning, and interaction are needed.

While the majority of the racial conversations in this study were negative, there were attempts on the campus of MU to create positive discussions on race at the undergraduate level. For example, a program called Dialogue on Race,[15] facilitated through the Housing Department on campus, allows for Multiracial groups to discuss issues of race. This program in particular has received national attention, and there is evidence that it is received very positively by both White students and students of color. However, as the data here suggests, there is a great need for more frequent, intentional, and structured opportunities to discuss race on campus.

Campus-based policies need to be evaluated to consider their impact by race and gender. For instance, how are students chosen for honors programs, campus-based awards, or for campus-based resources (e.g., student organization resources)? If there are few honors students who are from underrepresented groups, why might this be the case? None of the women in this study were in the university honors program. This was not due to a lack of ability, because some of the women were involved in an academic merit-based program that was his-torically for students of color (5 women). But there was a huge disparity in the types of funding provided for the campus-based honors program and the aca-demic merit-based program for students of color. When asked why they weren't in the honors program, the women generally said that they didn't see it as "for" them, or they didn't see it as welcoming to them. This highlights potential prob-lems in recruitment efforts within the honors program and also in the practice of programs like this on campus.

As with race and gender, Midwest University and other institutions need to consider ways that the campus is stratified socioeconomically. The residence hall example, where some halls are more expensive than others, provides an illustration. Perhaps the housing department could consider ways in which the residence halls could be more mixed socioeconomically. As one solution, students could receive housing scholarships to live in the higher-priced residence halls. Or the residence hall expenses could be equalized so that all halls would cost the same amount.

In general, the women in this study did not understand how to budget their finances. For example, Krystal spent her entire student loan check in the first two weeks of the semester and was left paying the rest of her semester expenditures on a credit card. That this was not an unusual case, suggests the need for campus-based programs to address credit card debt and budgeting issues for students. These women would have benefited greatly from information about the way that debt could affect their financial future and from financial management tips, preferably early in their college careers. This type of support could be offered by student affairs practitioners, particularly in residence halls, careers centers, or student activities offices.

Related to finances, MU and other similar institutions need to seriously consider low-interest rate loans or full scholarships for underrepresented students. The need to work nearly full-time greatly influenced the women's academic and social experiences on campus. If they had not had to work as much, they likely would have been more involved on campus and perhaps they would have felt differently about their experience.

African American women and other students of color need to be involved in the policy-making decisions on campus, particularly for programs that are geared toward supporting them. There is a need for students of color to be brought to the table to discuss institutional policies related to diversity and support programs for underrepresented students. For example, one of the University of California campuses has initiated a campus-based program to support the enrollment and college success of low-income students in which low-income students were included in the policy-making process and the implementation of that policy (Tierney & Jun, 2001). It is no surprise that this program is achieving great success.

Administrators, faculty, and staff need to be educated about phenomena such as those described in this study so that they can better understand some of the issues that students of color, particularly women, face in a predominantly White setting. Upper-level administrators can lead the way in creating an environment that fosters inclusion, maintaining no tolerance for those who attempt to make the campus less safe for students of color. More resources must be allocated to the hiring of minority faculty, staff, and administrators on campuses so that students of color have role models in leadership positions that look like them. The hiring of faculty, staff, and student affairs practitioners who do not have this sensitivity should be questioned. A campus audit relative to diversity issues would be useful in identifying areas for growth and change on campus.

Perhaps the most influential group on any campus is the faculty. All students come in contact with faculty during their time in college. Thus, faculty could be trained and perhaps even audited on issues of diversity. For this to work well, it would need to be organic and initiated by faculty. That is, faculty would need to identify the best ways to train and evaluate one another in the tradition of faculty governance or tenure and promotion or a buy-in from them would be less likely. If credit were given for exemplary work on inclusivity or with diversity issues within tenure and promotion processes, for example, this might be more success-ful. Faculty training could occur during faculty orientation, and then subsequent follow-up training could be offered at various points during a faculty member's career (either every few years or at tenure and promotion points).

Another implication related to resource allocation is that of space. Students of color need both figurative and literal space to exist on campus. The physical space for students of color on the MU campus was lacking. Many of the women de-scribed a lack of physical space where they felt safe or where they felt like they could exist and simply be themselves. Claudia, for example, indicated that she was "always watched," as if the entire campus was a public space where she felt put in the spotlight to represent her racial group. There were numerous culture centers on campus, but they were primarily on the fringes rather than in central locations. The Black Student Union building, a newly renovated structure, did not have restaurants, was often locked, and was far from many of the academic buildings. Culture centers, Black student unions, and allocated physical space in the primary campus union are examples of the types of physical space that could be consid-ered. These physical spaces need to be in central locations—sending a message that the students of color are accepted centrally into the campus environment.

In addition, there is a need for *liminal* space on campus. By that I mean the space-in-between, the middle space where women can simply be themselves rather than feeling a need to represent their race. The women in this study de-scribed their experience in a series of imposed dualities in which they felt as if they had to choose between polarities—between being "too White" or "too ghetto," representing their race or being silent, and so forth. Serious thought is needed regarding the campus climate related to race and gender and the types of liminal space that could be offered. There must be a way for Black women to simply be themselves without having to constantly feel pressured to choose between two ends of a polarity when neither pole suits them.

Student organizations often offered the liminal space, or the space in between the dualities in a figurative sense. For instance, the Black Student Union organization, a student government for African American students, was the center of many of the African American women's social and academic lives on campus. Numerous women talked about this organization as one of the primary places where they received the type of emotional and academic support that they needed in the predominantly White setting. In another example, when Mercedes joined a Greek-letter organization, she became more satisfied with her college experience. Again, this Greek-letter organization was not necessarily a physical space, but it was a figurative space where she felt accepted.

Related to discussion over both physical and liminal space, peer relationships have the power to influence students' decision-making processes regarding their satisfaction with college and their persistence in degree programs. The women in this study were particularly affected by student organizations that were related to their racial/ethnic groups. Leila, like many of the women of the study, found a place to fit on campus through the Black Student Union. Yet these organizations often have trouble finding larger campus support. Campus administrators could use this data as evidence supporting these organizations.

Peer relationships can also reinforce stereotypes and be a detriment to educational success, as indicated by Krystal and Mercedes in their discussion about the African American residential living-learning community. Their negative experience was largely related to the fact that this residence hall was on the fringes of campus and that the facility was run-down. As the students initially moved into the hall, they interpreted a powerful message from the placement of this community—that they, as African American students, were on the fringes of the White mainstream. The lack of resources that were allocated to this program also sent a message that this community and the students within it were unimportant to the larger campus. Again, the campus sends a powerful message about priorities through the allocation of resources. If the campus truly supports diversity, more resources will be needed for programs like this.

Finally, more work is needed to include families in the women's college experiences. Many of the women mentioned feeling unsupported by their families. Yet, if the campus were to offer family/friend training workshops, brochures, or communication to include families, particularly those of first-generation college students, perhaps families/friends would find ways to offer emotional support to their students.

Local Support Structures

College towns like Brady, the home city of Midwest University, are often predominantly White, like their local universities. Faculty, staff, and administrators from the institutions have a responsibility as community members to lead the community in creating an environment that is welcoming to underrepresented groups. The women in this case experienced "culture shock" both on and off campus. They even found it difficult to buy appropriate hair products in town. Institutions like Midwest University should dialogue with their local communities about making the community environment more welcoming to students of color. If faculty/staff from MU were to talk with local business owners about the specific needs of underrepresented students, perhaps the businesses would see the value in offering these products and services.

National and Statewide Support Structures

In times of threatened funding for need-based financial aid programs, many of the women in this study (18 women) were involved in a statewide early intervention program (starting in fifth grade) that offered need-based financial support for college. These findings corroborate the findings of other studies, indicating the importance of early intervention programs in providing access and fostering student success for underrepresented students (Musoba, 2004; St. John et. al, 2003; Tierney & Jun, 2001).

Federally funded on-campus support structures also had a significant impact on the women in this study. Mercedes noted that "without Upward Bound, I would not have been here." Students in both Trio Summer Program and Upward Bound indicated that these programs were *the* primary factor that prepared them academically and socially for college.[16] During college, many of the women continued to receive their primary academic and social support from these programs, or from the leaders of these programs. Yet despite evidence that these programs are helping underrepresented students to gain access to higher education and persist through degree programs, funding for many of these programs, particularly Upward Bound, which provides the most extensive academic and financial support, has declined in recent years (Kuenzi, 2005).

There is also a need for institutionalized mentoring programs. Many of the women (18 women) were involved in a campus-based mentoring program that matched underrepresented student with faculty and staff of color. While this program was not federally funded, it would have helped if it had been governmentally supported at the federal or state levels. During the course of the data collection process, this organization nearly lost its funding because campus resources were so tight.

Future Research

As I have suggested here, the women's stories often border on resistance. That is, there are times when the women in this study implicitly expressed a desire to resist the Unchosen Me, even if they did not actively do so. The sister circles at times provided a space for resistance and a re-creation of race and gender in new ways. Future work should consider ways that African American women resist the Unchosen Me, re-creating race and gender in new ways, and still remain successful in education.

There are a variety of ways in which this empirical work could be expanded to include different demographics of students and students at different types of institutions. It would be interesting to compare the results of this study at a large, public, Research Extensive university to other institution types (e.g., historically Black colleges and universities, private institutions, women's colleges).

Male students would provide a good addition to this line of research. Gender issues in particular, would probably be quite different for male students. Would male students of color experience the Unchosen Me in the same way that it emerged for female students? Most likely, male students of color would have similar racialized experiences but would not experience the gendered impositions that the female students in this study reported.

Another way to expand research about the Unchosen Me would be to study policies for evidence of impositions on identity. For instance, in what ways would affirmative action impose on the identity of students? Other policies, like financial aid policies, could be researched to evaluate potential impositions. Or, one could conduct quantitative analysis because it would be generalizable to larger populations. Because identity characteristics, particularly imposed identity characteristics, are not directly measurable, one might need to employ advanced statistical techniques such as structural equation modeling, which estimates qualitative causal assumptions, to be able to measure something that is, at this point, difficult to quantify.

The "too White" or "too ghetto" phenomena that the women described here needs further exploration. While there has been literature regarding "acting

White," in this research the concept of acting "too White" emerged differently because of the participants (young adult, college-enrolled women rather than adolescent boys). The "acting White" concept needs to be further evaluated among different ages and genders. Additionally, contrasting the "acting White" idea with a dialectical concept—the idea of being perceived as "too Black" or "too ghetto"—could provide a way to deepen the "acting White" discussion.

Future studies using long-term focus groups like the sister circles in this study could further reveal the potential of using this method as an empower-ment tool for underrepresented students. The sister circles in this case were one way that the women found to resist imposed identities during their time in col-lege. The use and study of this methodology could actively lead toward resistance and, subsequently, more equal *re-creations* of race, gender, and identity. Addi-tionally, more work is needed to better explain the way that the demographic compositions of groups can shift group dynamics and the level of disclosure. Finally, more research is needed to understand the potential racial difference in attitudes toward the research process.

CONCLUSION

How great a personal cost is too much to pay for a college degree? Some students, namely, students of color, continue to pay a higher personal price. Even after they gain access and matriculate, they experience impositions on their identity in the predominantly White environment. These identity impositions can provide in-sight into the way that race and gender are created in unequal ways. Illuminating this interaction that creates race and gender could allow for *re-creations* of race and gender—resistance of the inequality that is often associated with these cate-gories. How can race and gender be re-created in more equal ways that do not perpetuate an unchosen sense of "two-ness"? This question remains.

Participants in the Study

TABLE A.1
Demographics of Participants

	Number of Participants
Race/ethnicity	
African American	26
Black Latina	3
Multiracial	1
Year in college	
First-year	6
Sophomore	8
Junior	6
Senior	9
First-year Graduate	1
Major by college	
Arts and Sciences (AS)	13
Education (E)	4
University Division / Undecided (U)	5
Business, Marketing and Management (BMM)	6
Health and Recreation (HR)	2
First-generation student	
First-generation	24
Parents had college degrees	6

TABLE A.2
Participant Information

Pseudonym	Sister Circle	Race/Ethnicity	Year in college	Major	First-generation?
Lisa	1	Dominican / Black Latina	Sophomore	Secondary Education	No
Brandi	1	African American	Sophomore	Biochemistry	No
Monica	1	African American	Sophomore	Sociology	No
Ariel*	1/5	African American	Freshman	Undecided	Yes
Mercedes	2	African American	Freshman	Criminal Justice	Yes
Krystal	2	African American	Freshman	Sports Marketing	Yes

Pseudonym	Sister Circle	Race/Ethnicity	Year in college	Major	First-generation?
Serena	2	African American	Freshman	Education	Yes
Leila	3	African American	Sophomore	Business	No
Camiya	3	African American	Sophomore	Undecided	Yes
Tracey	3	African American	Sophomore	Business	Yes
Turquoise	4	African American	Master's	Recreation	Yes
Renee	4	Multiracial/ Black	Senior	Art History	No
Michelle	4	African American	Senior	Health and Recreation	Yes
Keisha	4	African American	Sophomore	Business	Yes
LaShara	4	African American	Junior	Legal Studies	Yes
Sheree	4	African American	Freshman	Undecided	Yes
Maria	4	Black Latina	Freshman	Undecided	Yes
Claudia*	4/7	Puerto Rican/ Black Latina	Senior	Psychology	Yes
Tina*	4/7	African American	Senior	Psychology	Yes
Isis*	4/7	African American	Senior	Non-profit Management	Yes
Semea*	4/7	African American	Senior	Exercise Science	Yes
Ryan	5/8	African American	Sophomore	Biochemistry/Pre-med	Yes
Jennifer	7	African American	Senior	Biology	Yes
Jarena	7	African American	Senior	Apparel Merchandising	Yes
Maya	7	African American	Junior	Marketing	Yes
Camille	7	African American	Junior	Biology	No
Carmen	7	African American	Junior	Public Policy	Yes
Elaine	8	African American	Senior	Early Childhood Education	Yes
Daphene	8	African American	Junior	Elementary Education	Yes
Talia	8	African American	Junior	Undecided	Yes

*The participant was involved in more than one focus group/Sister Circle.
**Sister Circles 6 and 9 were composed of all White women and therefore were not included here.
***Sister Circle 5 included two White women who are not included here.

Data Analysis and Validation

To make clear the sometimes implicit concept of identity, I employed a variety of research techniques. While identity can be tested empirically in a quantitative way, the primary research questions in this study were most meaningfully examined using techniques from ethnographic research methods. Ethnographic methods, over a prolonged period of time, allow for the researcher to use multiple techniques such as observation, dialogue, and writing analysis. In particular, I examined the socialized, role-taking, observable aspect of identity called the "Me" in Mead's conception of identity (Mead 1934/1962). Critical research methods are particularly useful for topics such as the subject matter of interest here: race and gender interactions that impose identity. The notion of imposed identity implies disadvantage or oppression because of the imposition. Critical inquiry works to uncover oppression as a way to ameliorate inequality (Carspecken, 1996).

HABERMAS'S VALIDITY CLAIMS AS A FOUNDATION FOR RESEARCH

Jürgen Habermas's (1984, 1987) three validity claims provide useful tools for the analysis of research. In this section, I consider Habermas' three validity claims (subjective, objective, and normative-evaluative) and their use in qualitative inquiry, particularly in the data analysis of this study.

Validity claims are "equivalent to the assertion that the conditions for the validity of an utterance are fulfilled" (Habermas, 1984, p. 38). Habermas separates these validity claims into three ontological categories that he argues are referenced in every speech act in everyday communication: objective, subjective, and normative (1987, p. 120). Table B.1 offers a summary of these validity claims (Habermas, 1984, 1987; Carspecken, 1996, 1999).

Through understanding the role of validity claims in everyday communication, we can formulate the "special requirements that a social researcher conducting formal inquiries into social processes must employ to produce a trustworthy account" (Carspecken, 1996, p. 58; Carspecken, 1999). In this research, I used Carspecken's (1996) ethnographic methodology that builds on Habermas's (1984, 1987) notion of validity claims to explore the meaning behind participants' statements. Examples of the use of these validity claims in data analysis are included in Appendix C.

TABLE B.1
Three Validity Claims: The Three Worlds

Validity Claim	Type of Access	How to Validate	"World"
Objective	Multiple access	Through repetition to find the same	The world
Subjective	Privileged access	Through honesty, sincerity of claim	My world
Normative	Shared access	Cultural, social, difficult to validate	Our world

Source: Adapted from Habermas, 1984, 1987; Carspecken, 1996, 1999.

RESEARCH QUESTIONS

The overarching research question for this study was: How are race and gender created through interactions between self, others, and society? I chose to study the interactions that create race and gender through an examination of an interaction-based notion of identity (defining identity as the interaction between self, others, and society) that explicitly allows for considerations of identity impositions (the Unchosen Me). Therefore, the investigation into how race and gender are created on a college campus led to other specific questions, including:

1. Do policies and practices within higher education facilitate institutionally imposed identity / Unchosen Me characteristics that are racially, gender, or socioeconomically biased?
2. If identity is imposed, how does imposed identity affect students' transitions into and through college, their college experiences, and their retention in degree programs?
3. How do institutional structures affect student transitions, success and retention? What, if anything, do the students perceive the institution to be doing to mold itself to their needs? What are student perceptions of early intervention programs, financial aid programs, and/or social support programs created for minority student groups?
4. What is the campus climate like for students from underrepresented groups? Is the campus perceived as welcoming to students who are the minority on campus? What policies and practices make the campus seem more/less welcoming to students?

DATA ANALYSIS

All data were transcribed verbatim, including laughs and other sounds made during the sessions. My primary tool of data analysis was coding. What follows are concepts that I used to add depth to inform my coding analysis (see Appendix C for examples of analysis).

All forms of analysis were rooted in critical ethnographic methods as developed by Carspecken (1996). I analyzed the data as follows: (1) meaning field analysis, (2) hermeneutic-reconstructive analysis, (3) coding, and (4) the duality of identity, or imposed identity analysis. At the larger level, I attempted to find broad general patterns, conducting what Carspecken (1996) calls systems analysis. Lastly, at the end of this section, I explain the relationship between theory, the theoretical concept that I developed (the Unchosen Me), and the data in this project.

Meaning Field Analysis

The first technique that I employed in my analysis of the data was meaning field analysis. This allowed for a "range of possible interpretations," making tacit meaning more tangible (Carspecken, 1996, p. 96). It helped to clarify initial impressions of meaning from observations and to lay the groundwork for reconstructive horizon analysis.

A meaning field is defined as the range of possible meanings or interpretations for an act (Carspecken, 1996). This is the "uncertainty principle of meanings," or that meanings are always experienced as possibilities within a field of other possibilities (p. 96). The meaning field ranges from the "tacit" to the "discursive," referencing the ambiguities of meaning with statements such as *and, or,* and *and/or* (p. 96). While this may initially seem to be a heuristic, or a shortcut to the intended meaning of an act, in fact, meaning fields allow one to fully understand the act, delving deeper into the tacit meaning before beginning to code the data.

The concept of meaning fields belongs in social theory because it is more than an analytic tool; it attempts to elucidate both overt and covert categories of meaning, both of which are inherently linked to socialized norms, beliefs, and attitudes in everyday life. Meaning fields allow for interpretations of meaning that make explicit that which is already being experienced. Thus, meaning fields are connected with social life, not just research methodology. This is important as one begins to consider the ways in which the micro-level data connect to macro-level concepts (i.e., the larger social structure, social stratification, larger inequalities).

One example of a meaning field constructed around a statement regarding race would be the commonly used statement, "Black people are better athletes." The meaning field (MF below) could be as follows:

> **MF:** "Black people are better athletes than people of other racial groups" AND "Whites / other racial groups are not good athletes" AND/OR "I am not as good an athlete as a black person" AND/OR "There is a biological difference between racial groups" AND/OR "Black people don't try as hard because being athletic comes naturally" AND/OR "Blacks are not good at non-athletic things."

As evidenced in the example, the meaning field analysis allows a researcher to understand the full range of possible meanings for a statement, connecting these statements with *and* or *and/or* to link them together. Meaning fields also allow one to better understand the way in which the meaning is bounded. Given the above example, the statement "Blacks are better athletes" is bounded, meaning that it could not mean something like, "Light bulbs are bright." Or, even more related, the statement "Blacks are better athletes" would not mean "Black people like to drive fancy cars" or something like that. Meaning fields allow a researcher to understand the full range of possible and less possible meanings for a statement.

After the meaning field analysis, I conducted reconstructive horizon analysis on the data that takes the meaning field analysis one step deeper to understand the "horizon" of possible meaning behind a participant's statement.

Reconstructive Horizon Analysis

I conducted reconstructive horizon analysis on the data as another way to provide insight into the coding. Acts or speech acts are classified as being overt, "foregrounded" or tacit, "backgrounded" (Carspecken, 1996, p. 105). I was particularly interested in identity claims, or the "mix of normative-evaluative and subjective" claims (p. 104).

Habermas presents three "worlds," or validity claims as discussed above, to describe actor-world relationships of action that are oriented to mutual understanding: the objective world, the social world, and the subjective world (1987, p. 120). The speaker takes up a "pragmatic relation" to these worlds such that "what the speech act refers to appears to the speaker as something objective, normative, or subjective" (p. 120). Habermas argues that all three "worlds" are referenced in a single speech act: "Communicative action relies on a cooperative process of interpretation in which participants relate simultaneously to something in the objective, the social, and the subjective worlds, even when they *thematically stress only one* of the three components" (p. 120). Habermas continues to explain that every utterance is a test: "[T]he definition of the situation implicitly proposed by the speaker is either confirmed, modified, partly suspended, or placed in question" (p. 121).

Building on Habermas's (1987) validity claims, Carspecken (1996) developed the concept of reconstructive pragmatic horizon analysis that uses the speech act to understand the objective, subjective, normative-evaluative, and identity claims of communicative acts. All three "worlds" or validity claims are referenced in each speech act. This analysis technique illuminates these claims, making them explicit and allowing the layers of meaning, both subtle and overt, to be considered. Also by linking Carspecken's (1996) pragmatic horizon analysis to Habermas (1984, 1987), communicative action, rather than perception, is considered to be the most primary in experience.

Carspecken (1996) used the concept of horizons, coupled with Habermas's (1987) validity claims, to develop the "pragmatic horizon analysis" (p. 103). This approach varies from the constructivist multiple realities approach to analysis through the use of the objective, subjective, and normative validity claims. Validity claims are "portions of the possible meaning one could read from a social act" (p. 113).

Carspecken asserts five categories of reference and claim within the horizon of meaningful acts: intelligible, legitimate/appropriate, subjective state, identity, or objective state (1996, p. 104). Pragmatic horizon analysis allows for understanding, both tacit/remote (backgrounded) and meaning referenced more centrally in the act (foregrounded). This analysis provides for both "horizontal" (objective, subjective, and normative validity claims) and "vertical" analysis (foregrounded, i.e., explicit, and backgrounded, i.e., implicit, claims) (p. 110). Understanding meaning, "includes understanding the reasons an actor could provide to explain expressions" (p. 111).

Race, gender, and ethnicity are "primarily cultural as experienced by individuals and will take on very specific cultural articulations within particular sites" (Carspecken, 1996, p. 197). Pragmatic horizon analysis could be very useful with tacit themes such as race, ethnicity, and gender. Some themes regarding race, ethnicity, or gender could be remote (backgrounded) or immediate (foregrounded) within the objective, subjective, or normative validity claims. For example, using horizon analysis, a researcher would analyze a speech act, examining vertical meaning related to validity claims and horizontal meaning related to how outwardly a claim is referenced (foregrounded and backgrounded).

As the participant and researcher build trust and understanding, the tacit claims related to race and gender can become more foregrounded, or more explicit. In Carspecken's (1996) example of racial nuances, what were at first backgrounded possibilities move toward the foreground as the researcher and participant become clearer about what the other intends. Here, I was interested in claims made regarding racial and gender identity and ideologies related to race, oppression, and social justice. In the example of horizon analysis below, these claims became more explicit through analysis of possible validity claims.

The following is an example of a horizon analysis from a discussion I had with a woman about her experiences in college:

A: *Well, there isn't anyone in the class who really looks like me.* [Said with head down.]

Possible Objective Claim

> *Quite foregrounded, quite immediate*
>
> "Everyone in the class looks different than me." OR
>
> "I am Black and most of my peers are White."
>
> *Less foregrounded, less immediate*
>
> "I am noticeably different from my peers."
>
> *Backgrounded, Remote*
>
> "Others might notice that I do not look the same."
>
> *Highly backgrounded, Remote*
>
> "I am not accepted as one of the group in the classroom."

Possible Subjective Claim

> *Quite foregrounded, quite immediate*
>
> "I feel different from my peers."
>
> *Less foregrounded, less immediate*
>
> "I wish that there were others who looked like me."
>
> *Backgrounded, Remote*
>
> "The fact that no one looks like me makes me uncomfortable."
>
> *Highly backgrounded, Remote*
>
> "I do not feel like I belong."

Possible Normative-Evaluative Claims

> *Quite foregrounded, quite immediate*
>
> "Looking different is a negative thing." OR
>
> "I should have peers who looked like me."

Less foregrounded, less immediate

"People should not have to feel the way that I feel." OR

"Diversity in the classroom would be beneficial."

Backgrounded, Remote

"People should feel accepted in the classroom." OR

"It is wrong that I feel this way."

Highly backgrounded, Remote

"White people should work harder to accept me." OR

"There is a particular way that people should look."

Possible Identity Claim

Quite foregrounded, quite immediate

"I am unique and different."

Less foregrounded, less immediate

"I am odd or strange."

Backgrounded, Remote

"Maybe something is wrong with me."

Highly backgrounded, Remote

"I am not valuable in the classroom."

Both the meaning field analysis and the reconstructive horizon analysis lay the groundwork for coding. These two preliminary forms of analysis provide a way to delve deeper into the data before coding so that the codes can be more representative of the intended meanings of the participants.

Coding

Using the concepts and depth obtained from the meaning fields and reconstructive horizon analysis, I coded the data, using both low-level and high-level codes. Low-level codes are those that "require little abstraction," primarily objective codes (Carspecken, 1996, p. 147). As I began low-level coding, I coded the statements, putting them into categories such as "access to college," "racial issue," "gender issue," or "college experience." High-level codes require "greater amounts of abstraction" and should be used with caution and backed up with horizon analysis (p. 148). For example, as I moved into high-level coding, I used codes such as "too White or too ghetto?" "the spotlight and invisibility of being Black on campus," etc.

Duality of Identity: Imposed Identity

Using the identity claims from the reconstructive horizon analysis, I developed another layer of analysis. I allowed clusters of identity or groups of identity claims to emerge from the data (e.g., I am strong, I am a survivor, I am a hard worker). These identity clusters were often not explicitly stated in the discussion but were implicit in the way the women self-identified and talked about themselves and their experiences. For instance, as a woman discussed her experiences, if she talked in terms of "surviving," the identity would be "I am a survivor."

To further understand identity inherent in the ways women talked about themselves, I analyzed the data temporally, identifying each statement as being the past, present, or future and in first, second, or third person. Additionally, I identified the type of statement that was made (e.g., autobiographical, questioning, informing, demanding). This allowed me to understand how the women saw themselves as the same or changing through time—the past, present, and future. If the women switched from first person to second or third person when talking about an emotionally difficult issue such as racist experiences, this could indicate that they were trying to detach themselves from the issue at hand (shifting from a personal explanation to a more generalizable explanation).

I also identified whether the women were talking in a monological (e.g., giving a monologue or speech) or dialogical manner (e.g., conversing with oneself during an explanation, such as "I said . . ."). For example, sometimes the women would switch from giving a monologue of their experiences to actually having a dialogue with themselves (e.g., "And then I was like, 'You should work harder.'"). This self-dialogue allowed me to understand the ways in which the women made sense of their experiences within themselves, thus, allowing me to better understand their identity.

Finally, I coupled the above-mentioned normative and identity statements to create imposed identity codes: codes that coupled the normative-societal, self-imposed or other-imposed messages with the person's identity claims (e.g., you should work harder if you want to make it here). Then I coded each entire document for more general codes, using all of the meaning-making tools described above (Carspecken, 1996). After identifying many individual codes, I grouped the codes into categories representing imposed identity themes. To view an example of the full data analysis, see Appendix C.

Relating Analysis to the Unchosen Me

In examining the imposed identity codes and relating them to the general codes, a series of dual structures emerged. The African American, Biracial, and Black Latina women in this study categorized their college experiences and the construction of identity within their experiences in a series of dualities. In other words, the women discussed issues of identity and self-identification in a series of polarities or dichotomous categories. For instance, among African American women in the study, the concept of being "too White" or "not Black enough" was often contrasted with being "too Black" or "too ghetto." While these concepts certainly do lie on a continuum, the women described themselves and their experiences as if there were only two dichotomous choices, meaning that it would be inappropriate to place themselves somewhere in the middle of the continuum.

The dualities were experienced as forced choices to the women. As they forced to decide among polarized choices, often ones that did not fit, this facilitated the acceptance of Unchosen Me aspects of identity. Thus, they would seemingly *choose* among the dualities, although the choice itself was imposed on them, and they were often afforded no other viable (i.e., socially recognizable) alternative. The lack of options or viable alternatives is an indication that the women felt pressured to accept unchosen characteristics: they chose among available options, even though the options were often uncomfortable, if not painful. Thus, the themes and sub-themes that emerged from the data were often dualistic, representing the forced choices in the women's lives.

Because I felt that it was important to connect this micro-level understanding with system or macro-level concepts, I began to conduct systems analysis in order to clarify the way in which the women's experiences were influenced by the larger social structure. In addition, the women's experiences reflected, and at times reinforced or recreated, macro-level inequalities.

Systems Analysis

After conducting the aforementioned lifeworld-level analysis, concerned with culture, norms, beliefs, and values, I conducted systems analysis. This form of analysis is concerned with the aggregate action consequences. This allows the researcher to look at "findings in light of existing macro-level social theories" by comparing data to cultural routines found in earlier forms of analysis (Carspecken, 1996, p. 202). Systems analysis allowed me to consider my participants' access to "economic, political, and cultural resources" (p. 204). This form of analysis, "penetrate[s] social sites and group cultures" (p. 206). The systems-level analysis technique differs from hermeneutic-reconstructive analysis in that it can move outside the bounds of the discursive research to study issues that influence participants (i.e., music, movies, and media). It should only be conducted after reconstructive analysis because reconstructive analysis should be used to ensure the validity of systems analysis (Carspecken, 1996). While the general assumption about qualitative research is that it is micro-level research, Carspecken argues that "analysis of systems relations is both epistemologically possible and absolutely crucial to gain a full understanding of qualitative research findings" (1987, p. 194).

To consider systems-level issues, I kept a log of the types of music, movies, and television programs that the students mentioned. I then listened to and/or watched the programs to better understand the macro-level issues that the participants referenced. In addition, I considered the interaction between the individual participants and the larger society. I examined the way in which one's race or gender is both individual and internalized, and socially constructed in the media, family, and larger society.

RELATIONSHIPS BETWEEN THEORY AND DATA

In social science research, there are typically three ways in which theory is used in empirical research (Denzin & Lincoln 2003; Crotty, 1998): (1) as a methodological meta-theory, (2) as substantive meta-theory, and (3) as the findings themselves. I used theory in all three of these ways. Figure B.1 provides a visual representation of the use of theory in research, and the way in which theory is used in this study.

Methodological meta-theory provides the epistemological framework, or "theory of knowledge embedded in the theoretical perspective and thereby in the method" (e.g., feminist epistemology, critical epistemology,[1] etc.) (Crotty, 1998, p. 3). The foundation of this critical ethnographic study is critical epistemology. Critical inquiry is rooted in critical theory; thus, the methodological meta-theory in this project is critical inquiry as it is informed by critical theory. I chose critical inquiry because the epistemology or the

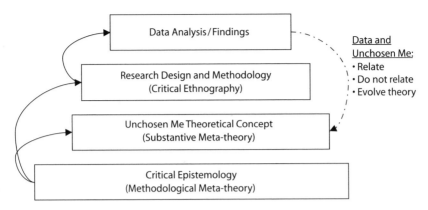

Figure B.1 The interaction between theory and findings

theory of knowledge that is embedded within it was strongly convincing to my commit-ment to social justice and to my understanding of research. My use of methodological meta-theory, critical epistemology in this case, guided the construction of my research questions, my methodological choices (e.g., the way I organized and structured the sister circles), and my data analysis.

This epistemology does not rule out other epistemological theories (e.g., feminist epistemology) because the idea that they can be incorporated within each other is consis-tent with a critical perspective. Most importantly, critical inquiry that is rooted in critical theory, as my methodological meta-theory was, affects the subsequent use of theory in relation to data. In critical inquiry, there is a constant dialogue between the theory and the data—as if the theory and the data are in conversation with one another through the research process (Kincheloe & McLaren, 2003; Carspecken, 1996). This dialogue allows the researcher to delve deeper into the meaning within the data and simultaneously evolves the theory.

Substantive meta-theory, or social theory, is a theory that is developed before, during, and after the research process. It is a "philosophical stance informing the methodology and thus providing a context for the process and grounding of its logic and criteria" (Crotty, 1998, p. 3). In this project, my development of the Unchosen Me theoretical con-cept, which was rooted in critical theory (Habermas, 1984, 1987) and Mead's (1934/1967) pragmatist philosophy, is substantive theory. Because this is a critical research project, my substantive theory (the Unchosen Me) should be in constant dialogue with the find-ings. Thus, I provided a dialogue at the end of each theme that discusses the interaction between the Unchosen Me and the data.

Finally, the third use of theory in social science research, particularly in qualitative research, is the creation of theory from the findings themselves. This is the process high-lighted by grounded theory (Creswell, 1998), whereby a researcher develops a theory from the findings. However, this is not the way I used theory in this particular project. In my project, there was an inter-play or dialogue between theory emerging from my findings and the Unchosen Me theoretical concept. This process *could have* resulted in a rejection of my theoretical concept. However, in this study, the dialogue between the data and the Unchosen Me resulted in an evolution and refining of the initial Unchosen Me theoretical concept.

Figure B.1 provides an illustration of the above discussion, describing the way that theory interacts with the data. The methodological meta-theory, critical epistemology in this study, provided the foundation for the study, influencing the research design and methodology as well as the development of the Unchosen Me theoretical concept. In this study, critical epistemology guided my decision to use critical ethnographic methods that comprise the research design. The critical ethnographic methods then influenced the nature of the data that emerged from the study. Notice that the Unchosen Me concept does not influence the data analysis or the findings that emerged from the study. Finally, the findings are in constant dialogue with the Unchosen Me concept, as denoted by the dotted line in figure B.1, to determine if the findings relate or do not relate to it and/or the way in which the data changes and evolves the Unchosen Me.

LIMITATIONS

The limitations of the methodology used in this study were: (1) the lack of generalizability; (2) the potential for extreme responses due to the bonding in the sister circles; and (3) the potential for researcher bias. Here, I address each limitation and briefly discuss the techniques that I employed to address these limitations.

One of the primary critiques of qualitative research is that it is not generalizable to larger populations because of limited sample sizes (Denzin & Lincoln, 2003; Creswell, 1998). For example, this study, at one predominantly White institution (PWI), could not be generalized to *all* institutions of higher education. However, there is some transferability in the findings, meaning that aspects of the findings may be similar to findings at other PWIs. To address the issue of generalizability, I took caution in the way that I interpreted the data. For example, I did not claim that the women's experiences were necessarily representative of the experiences of *all* women of color. Rather, I discussed the women's experiences in terms of the importance of the uniqueness of their experiences. Additionally, I included multiple sister circle groups (9 total) in order to compare the data across the sister circles. This allowed me to begin to consider ways that the findings may or may not be transferable other women on campus.

Secondly, because the women in the sister circles met for a long period of time (9 months), many of the groups became very bonded. While this had a positive influence on the women's experience with the study itself (i.e., they claimed that the study was empowering to them and that they enjoyed the sister circles as a support network), this could have influenced the type of data that emerged. It is possible that as the women bonded and talked with one another that their experiences emerged as *more* extreme due to the rapport-building within the groups. In the social psychology literature, there is evidence that at times a sense of "group think" can emerge whereby group members begin to think as a group rather than as individuals (Janis, 1972; Park, 2000). In this study, I attempted to mediate this limitation through the triangulation of data collection. I conducted individual interviews with many of the women in order to compare the data to the focus group data. The same themes emerged in the interviews as in the sister circles. In addition, I conducted observations (i.e., social settings, lunches, classes, conferences) to corroborate the sister circle data. Again, the same themes emerged from the observations.

The third potential limitation of this methodology was researcher bias. Because I used critical inquiry and the advocacy approach consistent with this form of inquiry, I became very attached to my participants. Below, I provide a detailed description of the ways that I attempted to address my own bias as a researcher (i.e., member checks, peer debriefing, checking personal biases).

VALIDATION METHODS

Validity in qualitative research is a unique challenge because there is more than one way to validate the research, and some scholars argue whether or not the word "validity" is in fact relevant to qualitative inquiry. Many words are used to identify validation techniques in qualitative research: "trustworthiness," "credibility," "transferability," "dependability," "confirmability," "verification" (Creswell, 1998, p. 197). Constructivist researchers often search for "authenticity" (Lincoln & Guba, 2003, p. 278); and some poststructuralist scholars call validation "transgressive" (Lincoln & Guba, 2003, p. 281). Regardless of the terms, the trustworthiness/validity/verification of research design, analysis, and implications needs to be addressed. Adapting from the critical ethnographic methods of Carspecken (1996), I employed the following validation methods: (1) an examination of own biases and value orientations; (2) an exploration of my theoretical background; (3) a consideration of the data in a way that moved beyond the multiple realities approach; (4) member checks; (5) peer debriefing; (6) strip analysis; (7) negative case analysis; and (8) prolonged engagement in the field.

Examination of Biases and Value Orientations

Before beginning research, I examined my own research biases and considered my research value orientations. This validation method, called "reflexivity" by some scholars (Gergen & Gergen, 2003, p. 579), aided in my construction of a "socially critical epistemology" (Kincheloe & McLaren, 2003, p. 467). This "self-conscious" validation method is a process whereby I became aware of my own ideological positions and my own subjective, intersubjective, and normative reference claims with regards to the research (p. 453). I needed to consider my own investment in the research, my biases, and my expected findings. Throughout the research process, I reflected on my biases and value orientations through my field notes and journal. If and when findings differed from my expected findings, I examined these surprises and considered my potential biases for or against them.

Examination of Theoretical Background

Alongside or possibly informing my value orientations was my theoretical foundation. While I do not wholly accept the base-superstructure model presented by Marxist philosophy, this structuralist conception of oppression, maintaining that the social structure imposes and determines oppressive forces, does guide some of my thinking about equality.

I root my thinking in a Habermasian (1984, 1987) approach to oppression and equality. While the "totalizing critique of modern society" is the root of Habermas's work because of his affinity for critical theory, he posits a "reconstructive" critical approach rooted in critical hermeneutics (Delanty, 1997, p. 83). Habermas's aim is to "reconstruct the emancipatory potentials in modern society." Therefore he, "rejects the idea of a 'negative dialectic' in favor of a 'critical hermeneutical' [approach]" (p. 83). That is, Habermas takes communication as the starting point of his critique, and not instrumental domination (Delanty, 1997). Emancipation, or liberation, finds its way into his thinking in a real way. I used Habermas's (1984, 1987) conception of emancipation through communicative rationality to consider emancipation in my work.

Beyond a "Multiple Realities" Approach

Related to the issue of validation, I moved beyond the constructivist "multiple realities" approach (Kincheloe & McLaren, 2003, p. 467) in my research. As Carspecken (1996) suggests, I differed between the ontological categories (subjective, objective, and normative-evaluative) rather than "realities" in my analysis of the data in this project.

Member Checks

Another validation method that I used was conducting member checks throughout the data collection and analysis process. I sent the transcripts to the participants to ensure that their voices were represented appropriately. If the participants asked me to change the grammar or wording that they used in their explanations, I followed their requests. If the participants did not request a change in wording, even if their grammar was informal, I did not change the transcripts. In addition, once the data was analyzed, I discussed my interpretations with participants. Again, if my interpretation was questioned by the participants, I used discussions with them and my colleagues to resolve the discrepancy. This was particularly necessary in my analysis of meaning fields, reconstructive analysis, coding, and systems analysis. In my desire to include the participants in the design and analysis of research as much as possible, I was ethically inclined to record the participant's feedback, especially if it differed from my own interpretation. What is represented in this book is the culmination of this interactive process between the participants and me.

Peer Debriefing

To check my interpretation of the research findings, I used peer debriefers to check my biases or absences in my meaning field analysis, reconstructive analysis, coding, and systems analysis. I asked peer debriefers to review my data and analyze the data, using the techniques that I employed to test whether they would come up with similar results. I also had the peer debriefers read reports of the data, looking for potential biases in my reporting. As a White researcher working with participants from a variety of ethnic backgrounds, it was important to find peer debriefers from these backgrounds to capture the nuances, depth, and potential misunderstandings of the cultural concepts and racialized experiences. Since my participants were African American women, I worked with two African American female colleagues who helped me peer debrief my analysis and the reporting of the data. The insights of these two colleagues were invaluable to help me check my own biases and to the deeper interpretation of this data.

Strip Analysis and Negative Case Analysis

One particularly important aspect of the research findings is what some refer to as the "outliers" in quantitative work. What I mean by this is that it is important to understand findings that vary from the primary themes or norms of the analysis. Carspecken (1996) recommends what he calls "strip analysis," or the analysis of small chunks of the primary record to examine if they fit the constructed themes, codes, or systems (p. 141). If these small chunks do not fit the larger general findings, I analyzed these pieces further and worked with participants and my peer debriefers to understand why these pieces do not fit the larger puzzle of analysis. Carspecken (1996) calls this method whereby I found incidents that did not seem consistent with the larger analysis and considered an explanation for the lack of fit "negative case analysis" (p. 141). For example, at times, these pieces led to different themes or to deeper analysis of the existing themes.

Prolonged Engagement in the Field

Another validation method that I employed was prolonged engagement in the field. I was in the field for a period of nine months. In the early stages of research, I worked to gain trust with participants through informal social meetings and discussions unrelated to the research (chapter 3). Then, I conducted interviews and/or sister circles and observations with participants multiple times to meet this requirement for validation.

CONCLUSION

The use of critical inquiry was important for substantive reasons as well as for the rigor and validation of this study. Critical inquiry, and the theoretical tradition on which it is based, allowed for an advocacy approach in this research, encouraging me as the researcher to attempt to equalize power within the research process. I found this particularly important, given that I was conducting research across color lines. Additionally, I would not have ethically been able to simply watch as the women struggled if I knew that I had the information or resources to attempt to help them in their college experiences. Critical research fosters a researcher role that allows the researcher to advocate, help, or become involved in the lives of participants in meaningful ways. Yet the five forms of data analysis that I used in this research fostered rigor in the interpretation of the data that helped to alleviate potential biases of my role in the researcher process. That is, by using such extended methods of data analysis, the findings become clearer and one is able to better illuminate the meaning behind participants' statements. All statements are bounded, and the role of data analysis within critical inquiry, in this case, is to uncover these boundaries in order to rigorously interpret the data. Additionally, the multiple methods of data analysis become validation techniques whereby one form of analysis either does or does not validate the findings from another form of analysis; thus, the analysis becomes an iterative, interactive process. If there are discrepancies, this encourages the researcher to go back and re-analyze the data in a more thorough and systematic manner. Finally, I used the data analysis techniques in my creation of and evolution of theory. While I developed the Unchosen Me as a philosophical concept, based on previous work in social psychology, higher education, sociology, and psychology, through the data analysis, I was able to revise and evolve this concept so that it is now grounded in empirical findings.

Examples of Data Analysis

The examples below are excerpts from a focus group discussing the women's transition into the campus environment.

MICHELLE: *I think that a lot of people have this picture of how it will be, that it will be all of us together and we will be hanging out with everybody. You know, it was just all White people, you know . . . it wasn't really a lot of you know. I think that my freshman year I would say I'm acting for a degree.*

→ Identity: I am an actor
→ Identity: I am Black
▶ Autobiographical/reflecting statement—1st person—monological

Codes: Campus Culture—All White people, acting for a degree

Imposed identity code: I have to act for degree / I can't be myself on campus even though White people can

> Meaning Field: I have to act differently to get the degree AND I am not being myself while getting this degree AND/OR I am acting like White people to get this degree AND There are more White people here than Black people AND I feel like a minority here
> Reconstructive Horizon:
> *Highly Foregrounded*
>> Objective: There are a lot of White people here.
>> Subjective: I feel like I am different than the White people here.
>> Normative: People should act a certain way here.
>> Identity: I am different than White people.
> *Foregrounded*
>> Objective: Black people are in the minority.
>> Subjective: I feel alone.
>> Normative: White people are the normal people here.
>> Identity: I act the same as those around me.
> *Backgrounded*
>> Objective: Black people act different than White people.
>> Subjective: I feel like an outsider.

Normative: It is not okay to act different than the majority of the people.
Identity: I have to act a certain way here.
Highly Backgrounded
    Objective: White people are the norm here.
    Subjective: I am a different person than who they think I am.
    Normative: People should act like White people here.
    Identity: I have to act White to get my degree.

MICHELLE: *But, other than that, we do assimilate. You know what I'm saying? I guess, it's different faces. You know? Like, with me at home it's kind of like me at home. You know? But, like here you have to conduct yourself in a professional manner. Here, at MU you have to be professional. It depends on who you are talking to and stuff.*
→ Identity: I am a person with different faces
→ Identity: I am successful because I assimilate
▶ Autobiographical/describing statement—1st/2nd person—dialogical

Codes: Imposed/Assimilation—professional, different faces, success means acting different

Imposed identity code—I should assimilate and have different faces

<u>Meaning Field:</u> Sometimes I feel like I have to assimilate AND I have different faces in different contexts AND/OR Being professional is assimilating AND/OR At MU I have to assimilate
<u>Reconstructive Horizon:</u>
Highly Foregrounded
    Objective: She acts different in different contexts
    Subjective: Sometimes I do have different faces.
    Normative: People should act different in different contexts
    Identity: I am different in different contexts
Foregrounded
    Objective: She fits into the context
    Subjective: I do assimilate
    Normative: People should fit in.
    Identity: I assimilate.
Backgrounded
    Objective: She acts professional
    Subjective: Being professional is assimilation and at MU I have to act professional
    Normative: People should be professional.
    Identity: I am professional.
Highly Backgrounded
    Objective: She assimilates to the context around her.
    Subjective: At MU I have to assimilate
    Normative: People should assimilate.
    Identity: I am not the same person here.

TINA: *I think that is just a part of life. Um, when you around different people there are certain ways that you act, like if you are in the Business world. Or, like if you are with your friends. There are just different roles you have to play. And I just think that if you are at home, you know you can let your hair down and do your thing. And when someone comes to your house they have to accept your as whatever you are. But, if you are out in public, you have to there's just some things . . . like you don't know who's watching you. So, you have to just play that role like somebody's watching me so I have to be a little more cautious about what I say or how I act. I think that's just how it is in our society.*

→   Identity: I am different in different contexts

▶   Reflecting/describing statement-2nd person-dialogical

Codes: Identity-roles, different ways of acting, Be cautious of what you say and do

Imposed identity code: I must be cautious and play different roles

Meaning Field: I act differently here and at home AND I am being watched AND There are certain ways that I am supposed to behave AND I play different roles in different contexts.

Reconstructive Horizon:

Highly Foregrounded
   Objective: She acts differently at different times.
   Subjective: I act different in different contexts.
   Normative: People should act a certain way.
   Identity: I am complex.

Foregrounded
   Objective: Some environments require particular ways of acting.
   Subjective: I play different roles at different times
   Normative: One should be cautious about how they act.
   Identity: I play multiple roles.

Backgrounded
   Objective: There is a particular way to act.
   Subjective: I feel like I am being watched.
   Normative: People should try to fit in.
   Identity: I am a different person in different contexts

Highly Backgrounded
   Objective: Not all people can act the right way.
   Subjective: I feel more comfortable at home than here.
   Normative: One should adapt themselves to their situation.
   Identity: I have multiple selves.

RENEE: *I remember my mom tried to get me to have a Black friend when I was in like third grade. She invited me over one time. She like made people be friends with her. Like [my boss] said when I came in she said that I was a White girl and that I was her project to make me Black. I think that is not a good attitude to have.*

→   Identity: I am too White

▶   Autobiographical—1st—monological

Codes: "Too White" / "not Black enough," background experiences

Imposed identity code: I change myself to be Black

<u>Meaning Field:</u> I was not Black enough AND I was too White AND It made me uncomfortable to have her boss try to change me AND/OR I struggle with my racial identity AND/OR I did not have many Black friends growing up AND/OR I have not been around Black people much

<u>Reconstructive Horizon:</u>

Highly Foregrounded

   Objective: I am her project.

   Subjective: I am culturally White.

   Normative: People should be changed.

   Identity: I am Multiracial.

Foregrounded

   Objective: She wants to change me.

   Subjective: I don't feel comfortable

   Normative: People should be Black.

   Identity: I am both Black and White.

Backgrounded

   Objective: She doesn't accept me.

   Subjective: I don't want to be told who I should be.

   Normative: People should fit into their group.

   Identity: I am culturally White.

Highly Backgrounded

   Objective: She doesn't see me as Black.

   Subjective: I am not Black enough.

   Normative: Only certain people can be Black.

   Identity: I don't want to be Black.

Sister Circle Protocols

Topic Domain: Transition into Midwest University

Covert Categories of Interest: college choice decision-making, identity changes, identity dissonance, support networks, racial climate, gender climate, general campus environment, belongingness, friendship decisions

Guiding Questions:

1. Tell me about the process that you underwent in your decision to attend Midwest University.
   a. What did you expect MU to be like?
   b. Describe the top three factors in your decision-making process.
   c. What role did you family play in your decision-making process?
   d. What role did your friends play in your decision-making process?
   e. How did finances play a role in your decision-making process?
   f. Did you have a mentor or someone who influenced you greatly in your decision? If so, describe that person's role and they way that he/she influenced you.

2. Describe to me your first day in classes at Midwest University.
   a. Describe your very first class. How did you feel? What were you thinking about?
   b. What feelings did you experience?
   c. In what ways was the campus the same as what you had expected?
   d. In what ways was the experience different than you had anticipated?
   e. Did you feel like the campus fit you?
   f. In what ways did you act differently than you would act with your family/friends?
   g. In what ways did you act the same?
   h. In what ways did you feel different than you did before coming to MU?
   i. In what ways did you feel the same?
   j. Talk about the initial friendships that you made.
   k. What type of support system did you come from?
   l. How did you get through that first day of class?

INTERVIEW AND SISTER CIRCLE PROTOCOL 2

Topic Domain: Campus Culture

Covert Categories of Interest: institutional racism, imposed identity, institutional sexism, belonging on campus, institutional fit, campus culture, campus climate/environment

Guiding Questions:

1. If I were new to Midwest University and you were helping me to fit in here, what types of things would I need to know or do to belong?
   a. How should I act to fit in here?
   b. Would I be surprised by the way that others act sometimes?
   c. What happens if a person does not act this way?
   d. Which of these norms do not fit well for you? Why?
   e. How do these norms differ from ways that you would act with friends or family off campus?

2. Describe to me a typical class experience at MU.
   a. How big is the class?
   b. How do you feel walking into the class?
   c. Who do you sit next to in the class?
   d. Do you talk during the class? Why / why not?
   e. What types of things would make the class experience better?

3. Describe to me your favorite extracurricular activities on campus.
   a. Why did you choose these activities?
   b. In what ways do these activities help you to belong on campus?
   c. Discuss the types of friendships you have made in these activities.
   d. Are these activities the types of things that most students on campus would be involved with?
   e. In what ways are these activities unique from the types of things that most students do?

4. Describe to me your closest friendship.
   a. Is this person at MU?
   b. How does this friendship differ from other types of friendships/acquaintances that you have?
   c. In what ways do you act differently with this friend? Why do you not act this way with others?
   d. What role does race or gender play in your friendship?
   e. Are there particular groups of people with whom you feel most comfortable?
   f. Describe a typical Friday night with this friend. What types of things will you do together?

Topic Domain: Who Am I?

Covert Categories of Interest: definitions of self, role choices, identity dissonance, identity salience, support networks, racial climate, gender climate, general campus environment, belongingness, friendship decisions, self conceptions

Guiding Questions (AFTER completing the "Who am I?" worksheet):

1. Discuss the top three characteristics you listed.
    a. How do you feel about these characteristics?
    b. Were the characteristics positive or negative?
        a. Are there times when these descriptions do not fit you?
        b. Are there times when these are good descriptions for you?
        c. Did you choose these characteristics?
        d. Are there others on campus who would also describe themselves this way?
        e. Are there people on campus who would NOT describe themselves this way?

Activity Example: Who am I?

1. _____
2. _____
3. _____
4. _____
5. _____
6. _____
7. _____
8. _____
9. _____
10. _____
11. _____
12. _____
13. _____
14. _____
15. _____
16. _____
17. _____

18. _____

19. _____

20. _____

INTERVIEW AND SISTER CIRCLE PROTOCOL 4

Topic Domain: Who Am I NOT?

Covert Categories of Interest: definitions of self, role choices, identity dissonance, identity salience, support networks, racial climate, gender climate, general campus environment, belongingness, friendship decisions, self conceptions

1. *Guiding Questions (AFTER completing the "Who am I NOT?" worksheet): Describe to me the three characteristics that you really dislike.*
   a. How do these characteristics make you feel?
   b. Were the characteristics positive or negative?
   c. How do these characteristics relate to the characteristics you listed on the "Who am I?" worksheet?
   d. Are there times when you feel like you have to take on some of these characteristics? If so, when? Why do you think that you have to take on these characteristics?
   e. Which characteristics most accurately describe you when you are on campus?
   f. Which characteristics most accurately describe you when you are with your family / in your hometown?
   g. Which characteristics most accurately describe you when you are with friends?

Activity Example: Who am I NOT?

1. _____

2. _____

3. _____

4. _____

5. _____

6. _____

7. _____

8. _____

9. _____

10. _____

11. _____

12. _____

13. _____

14. _____

15. _____

INTERVIEW AND SISTER CIRCLE PROTOCOL 5

Topic Domain: Who Do I Want to Be in the Future?

Covert Categories of Interest: definitions of self, role choices, identity dissonance, identity salience, support networks, racial climate, gender climate, general campus environment, belongingness, friendship decisions, self conceptions

Guiding Questions (AFTER completing the "Who do I want to be in the future?" worksheet):

1. Describe the one or two things that you are most excited about.
   a. How do these characteristics make you feel?
   b. Were the characteristics positive or negative?
   c. How do these characteristics relate to the characteristics you listed on the "Who am I?" and the "Who am I NOT" worksheet?
   d. Are there times when you feel like you have to take on some of these characteristics? If so, when? Why do you think that you have to take on these characteristics?
   e. Which characteristics most accurately describe you when you are on campus?
   f. Which characteristics most accurately describe you when you are with your family / in your hometown?
   g. Which characteristics most accurately describe you when you are with friends?
   h. In what ways does your experience here at MU relate to what you wrote in this activity?

Activity Example: Who do I want to be in the future?

1. _____   _____

2. _____

3. _____

4. _____

5. _____

6. _____

7. _____

8. _____

9. _____

10. _____

11. _____

12. _____

13. _____

14. _____

15. _____

INTERVIEW AND SISTER CIRCLE PROTOCOL 6

Topic Domain: Meaning of a College Degree / Future

Covert Categories of Interest: identity associated with having a college degree, future aspirations, constraints on aspirations, institutional discrimination, societal discrimination, gender roles, racial/ethnic roles, meaning of a college degree, uplift / giving back to community, motivation for getting a degree, degree choice decision-making process

Guiding Questions:

1. Why is it important to you that you get a college degree?
   a. How does your family feel about you getting your degree?
   b. What do your friends from high school think about you getting a college degree? Are they also going to college at this time?
   c. What does this degree mean to you?
   d. What will you do with this degree?

2. Have you chosen a major? If so, why did you choose that major?
   a. What types of jobs are available with this major?
   b. Was money a factor in your decision?
   c. In what ways did your family influence your choice of major?
   d. In what ways did your friends influence your choice of major?
   e. Do you like your classes?
   f. When did you first hear about this major?
   g. Do you know others who have this major?
   h. What will you do with this degree?

3. What are your plans after graduating from college?
   a. What is your dream job? What are your aspirations?
   b. What do you expect to be doing?
   c. Will you work near your family?
   d. How important is it to you that you stay near your friends?
   e. Will you have many loans to pay off after graduating?
   f. How important is it that you make money after graduating?
   g. What will change after you get this degree?
   h. How important is it that you give back to the community that you came from?

INTERVIEW AND SISTER CIRCLE PROTOCOL 7

Topic Domain: Roles

Covert Categories of Interest: role differences on and off campus, roles and identity, self conceptions, self discrepancy, identity salience, belonging on campus, institutional fit, campus climate, imposed roles/identity

Guiding Questions:

1. Take a few minutes and list the various roles that you play both on campus and off campus. You can write, draw, list them, write a poem, or whatever feels comfortable to you.
   a. In what ways do the roles fit together?
   b. In what ways to the different roles conflict with one another?
   c. Are there ways that you act differently on campus versus off campus?
   d. How are the roles that you play with your family different from the roles that you play with your friends?
   e. Do you feel like some roles are more difficult to play while you are at MU?
   f. Do you think that others have similar roles to yours?

2. Describe a situation since you have been at MU when you felt like you didn't know what role to play. Or, describe a time when you didn't quite know how to act.
   a. How did you feel at that time?
   b. Were you surprised to see others acting this way? What was surprising about it?
   c. Who was there with you?
   d. Why do you think it was difficult to know what role was appropriate?
   e. Was it easy for some people to play that role?
   f. How did you learn about this particular role?
   g. Are there times when you would like to play this role?
   h. How should I act to fit in here?

3. Discuss a time since you have been at MU when you knew exactly how to act.
   a. Were there others there who did not know how to act?
   b. Who was there with you?
   c. How did it feel to know exactly how to act in this situation?

INTERVIEW AND SISTER CIRCLE PROTOCOL 8

Topic Domain: Implicit Aspects of Self

Chameleon Activity:

1. Talk about a time/situation when you adapted yourself to a particular situation or group of people.

2. Describe some parts of yourself that you often hide from those around you.

3. What parts of yourself do you have to adapt like a chameleon when you are on campus?

Notes

CHAPTER 1. THE "PROBLEM" OF RACE AND GENDER

1. Throughout this book, I refer to those Americans who self-identify with European, Anglo, or Caucasian heritage as "White." I also use White and White privilege to refer to a system of norms that privilege those with White pigmentation, or with ways of behaving that are associated with being White. Whiteness refers to a system of advantage that holds up a particular White-centric way of being or knowing as the norm or as the ideal (Delgado & Stefanic, 1997).

2. Throughout this text, I use the words "Black" or "African American" to refer to the women in the study who self-identified within these groups who were of African, Caribbean, Multiracial (claiming Black / African American as one identity), or Black Latina / Black Hispanic (claiming Black / African American as part of their identity) heritage. There was some debate among the women in the study regarding these terms, and, ultimately, consensus was not reached. Some women felt that all women with a particular experience or pigmentation should be referred to as Black in order to include Multiracial women and those from Caribbean or Hispanic descent. However, some women clearly identified with African traditions or heritage and felt strongly that they should be called "African American." Thus, I refer to the women as they referred to themselves, using both "Black" and "African American" to describe the women in these pages. This is to give merit to the debate that occurred among the women, to foster the self-claiming of racial categories among the women, and to underscore the sometimes transitory nature of racial categories.

3. For a historical view of the biological perspective on racial difference, see Graves, 2002.

4. Among African American high school graduates, only 41.9% were enrolled in college in 2006 (Census Bureau, 2008b).

5. Among the larger population, only 13% of African Americans had obtained a bachelor's degree in 2007 as compared to 20.7% of their White counterparts (Census Bureau, 2008a).

6. Tinto initially adapted his work from Spady (1971).

7. Assimilation theories about the larger U.S. population were initiated as immigrant populations made their way to the United States and the country was faced with the tensions that arose as different cultures came into contact. For more information on assimilation theories, see Alba & Nee, 1997; Lieberson, 1980; and Ripley, 1909. The paradox of

assimilation is that while assimilation was (and debatably still is) the American way of life, some people, namely, those of African descent, were historically disallowed from full assimilation because of physical appearance (Lieberson, 1980). A similar concept, acculturation, refers to the process whereby one culture comes into contact with another, changing the cultural patterns of *both* groups; often resulting in the gradual loss of identity of one group—usually a marginalized group (e.g., see Cardona, Busby, & Wampler, 2004).

8. For more work that looks at the influence of student financial aid trends on student success in college, see Baum, 2003; Ficklen & Stone, 2002; Hearn & Holdsworth, 2004; Heller, 2003, 2004; Longanecker & Blanco, 2003; St. John, 2002; St. John, Chung, Musoba, & Simmons, 2004.

9. For examples of work that does consider African American students' experiences at predominantly White institutions, see Benson, 2000; Branch Douglas, 1998; Cureton, 2003; Cuyjet, 1997; Davis et al., 2004; Winkle-Wagner, 2009a. For further research with African American students, particularly around the issue of their choice to attend college or of a particular college, see Freeman, 1997, 1999a, 1999b, 1999c; Freeman & Cohen, 2001; Freeman & Thomas, 2002; Perna, 2000.

10. For work on the journeys of Black female scholars in academia, see the work of Theodorea Regina Berry and Nathalie Mizelle (2006). See Winkle-Wagner, 2009a, for a discussion of the navigation of family relationships among African American college women.

11. Fordham and Ogbu (1986) first identified the "acting White" concept among adolescent African American males as an oppositional culture where peer groups fostered anti-intellectualism.

12. The foundational theories related to identity in the field of higher education, called college student development theories, are rooted in a psychological tradition, particularly the scholarship of Erickson, Piaget, Rodgers, and Jung (Evans, Forney, & Guido-DiBrito, 1998).

13. There are four primary types of foundational student development theories that often take a phase or stage-based approach: (1) Psychosocial theories rooted in the work of Erickson (1968, 1980), examining individuals' personal and interpersonal lives as primarily a sequential, stage-based, age-related process that is influenced by crises (see Chickering, 1969; Chickering & Reiser, 1993; Marcia, 1966); (2) Cognitive-structural theories based in the psychology of Piaget (1952), addressing the way that people think, principally in a series of linear sequential stages (see Baxter Magolda, 1992; Gilligan, 1993; Kohlberg & Hersh, 1977; Perry, 1981); (3) Typological theories stemming from Jungian psychology examining differences in the way people view and relate to the world, identifying traits or mainly inborn characteristics (see Holland, 1992; Kolb, 1984; Myers, 1980); and (4) Person-environment interaction theories rooted in the scholarship of Rodgers (1990), exploring the interaction of a student with the environment (see Astin, 1985; Sanford, 1966; Schlossberg, 1989).

14. For example, Cross's (1991, 1995) theory of Nigrescence (the process of becoming Black) describes a stage-based, linear process of becoming Black to explain the racial identity development of African Americans. Race is most closely aligned with an input

perspective in this theory because "Blackness" or being African American leads one to develop a particular identity associated with being Black.

15. Many of the foundational studies were conducted with only White men.

16. For further examples of such advances, refer to: Atkinson, Morten & Sue's (1979, 1989) minority identity development model; the refinement of this model by Sue and Sue (1990); Cross's (1991, 1995) psychological theory of Nigrescence; Helms's (1995) adaptation of Cross's model to other minority groups; or Cass's (1979, 1984) development of a model for gay/lesbian identity development.

17. For example, Renn (2000) considered a situational identity where students exhibited different identity characteristics in various settings. Reynolds and Pope (1991) explored the influence of oppression on one's identity, finding that many people experience a sense of multiple identities rather than a singular identity. Jones's (1997) work with college women identified multiple *categories* of identity, all related to a core category. In a grounded theory study of college women, Jones and McEwen (2000), and later, Abes, Jones, and McEwen (2007), offered that there are multiple *dimensions* of identity, creating intersecting circles around a "core identity."

18. Some of the more recent theories, at times spinning out of critiques to foundational theories and their lack of applicability to non-mainstream groups, are less stage-oriented, moving the field in a new direction. For examples, see Robinson & Howard-Hamilton (1994) or Renn (2000).

19. For example, Henri Tajfel (1982) focused on individuals' membership in groups and the way the group to which one belongs (i.e., political group, race, nationality, etc.) provides a definition of who one is based on the defining characteristics of that the group. The group characteristics influence one's self-concept within one's mental processes/ cognitions and also affect behavior (Hogg, Terry, & White, 1995). Tajfel's (1982) work on membership in groups considered the way "in-groups" (i.e., inclusion within a particular group) and "out-groups" (i.e., exclusion within a particular group) were fostered. The study of "in-group" and "out-group" behavior led Tajfel (1982) to theoretically consider the way that both individuals and groups may be stereotyped, leading to ethnocentrism, dehumanization, discrimination, and even individual internalization of negative impressions of one's group. Tajfel's work can be best classified as taking a psychological perspective because this line of thinking begins with the individual and then shifts toward considerations of ways that individuals are grouped, come into contact with groups, and behave in relation to groups. Additionally, he assumes a singular notion of identity.

20. This could be one reason why many grounded theory studies, allowing the data to emerge into theory, assert different types of identity development that are not necessarily stage-based (e.g., Renn, 2000).

21. Sociological identity work indicates that students from racially underrepresented groups often report a sense *multiple identities* whereby they act one way with their ethnic group and another way when they are the minority (Arroyo & Zigler, 1995; Linville, 1987; Oyserman et al., 2003; Spears & Manstead, 1988; Thoits, 2003).

22. For further examples of work using the sociological perspective in the study of college students' experiences, see Ethier & Deaux, 1994; Higgins, Klein, & Strauman, 1985; McCall, 2003; Serpe and Stryker, 1993; Swann and Pelham, 2002.

23. Rather than referencing multiple "categories" of identity associated with a "core identity," as the work of Jones (1997) and her colleagues suggests (Jones & McEwen, 2000; Abes, Jones, & McEwen, 2007), in the sociological perspective, a student could simply have multiple identities that are dynamic and fluid.

24. For examples of scholarship that uses a multiple-identities sociological perspective, see Oyserman et al., 2003; Arroyo & Zigler, 1995; Linville, 1987; Thoits, 2003.

25. Stryker (1980, 2000) developed a way to empirically test identity through the study of one's roles in society, the commitment that one feels to those roles, and the resulting salience of particular identities due to those social commitments (i.e., identities are more salient if one is particularly committed to a role).

26. Perhaps there is a common ground between the two perspectives. The psychological perspective emphasizes cognitions or mental processes, while the sociological perspective assumes a direct link (through identity) between self and society. In this spirit, Hogg, Terry, and White (1995) conclude that perhaps the psychological perspective can provide the missing cognitive/mental process dimension, and the sociological perspective can keep identity work away from psychological reductionism.

27. In particular, I use George Herbert Mead's identity work (1934/1967) to guide the development of the Unchosen Me.

28. To protect the participants, I chose not to cite the institution name. I use pseudonyms for all institutions, places, and people in this project.

CHAPTER 2. THE UNCHOSEN ME

1. Scholarship in the field of higher education primarily uses a psychological perspective rooted in the work of psychologists such as Erickson (1959/1980), Piaget (1952), or Rodgers (1990).

2. On the contrary, with Cross's (1995) psychologically based theory of Nigrescence (the process of becoming Black), for example, a student would move through stages in an attempt to learn how to navigate the social structure *within her/his own cognitions*. The social structure or environment would either facilitate or impede a students' ability to move through the stages with a potential implicit assumption, perhaps even a misinterpretation of Cross's intent, that a student who is unable to progress through these stages is deficient.

3. I first became acquainted with Mead through my reading of Habermas's *Theory of Communicative Action* (1984, 1987). Following this, I became more centrally concerned with Mead's writing. In Mead's (1934/1967) theory of society, he links action to understanding, meaning that most action is geared toward fostering an understanding with others. Habermas (1987) critiques the primacy of action oriented toward understanding in Mead's theory of society, arguing that some action is goal oriented. He identifies *both* goal oriented action (e.g. instrumental action or strategic action) and action geared toward understanding in society. I use Mead's (1934/1967) theory of the self and then examine it in contexts of inequality that are better captured in Habermas's theory of communicative action. For example, in his critique of Mead's notion of society, Habermas (1987) maintains that society is not just a large communicative group; it is a cultural construct that is also linked to communicative action. Here, I focus on Mead's theory of

the *self,* not on his theory of society where the distinction between action orientations becomes more relevant.

4. James (1890/1968) was the first to consider the possibility of multiple aspects of self and multiple selves. One's sense of self is in part linked to one's interaction with others and sense of feeling recognized by others. However, James did not adequately conceptualize the relationship between self and society, leaving room for the work of Cooley and Mead.

5. By dialectical, I mean that tradition rooted in Hegel (1977/1952), where an argument is provided with a counter-argument or a series of contradictions and tensions. As one considers a dialectical process, one begins by defining a concept as "not this," "not that"; and this begins to create or define what a concept *is.*

6. The sense of vanishing that I allude to here is adapted from Derrida's (1973) notion of "trace."

7. For an elaboration on infinite recognition and for another explanation of the I and Me relative to spirituality and the creation of knowledge, see Carspecken, 2009.

8. The concept of recognition desires that I describe here is adapted from Hegel (1977/1952) and applied to Mead's work. Mead may or may not have applied recognition desires to his concepts of self.

9. For example, Mead (1934/1967) uses the idea of a baseball game, where a player would need to understand the other players' roles and attitudes in order to know what do next in the game. The player would, for example, know that the pitcher needs to throw the ball and that the pitcher would expect someone to attempt to hit that ball.

10. Mead does not explicitly mention expectations, but in the Unchosen Me, one may accept aspects of self that are not chosen because one perceives the expectations of others.

11. There is generally thought to be one I and multiple Me's in one's self in this perspective.

12. Recognition desires were not explicated in Mead's initial depiction of the I/Me parts of self. As I link Mead's I/Me parts of self to a Hegelian dialectic, this discussion becomes post-Meadian, meaning that it is an expansion or development of Mead's original conception.

13. Brewer (1991) discussed these contrasting tendencies in her theory of optimal distinctiveness whereby groups determine the rules of in-group and out-group membership. See also Brewer & Silver, 2002.

14. Many scholars in sociology use Stryker's (2000) elaboration of Mead's identity theory to examine the way college experiences influence identity for students. For examples, see the research of Burke & Reitzes, 1991; Owens & Serpe, 2003; Serpe & Stryker, 1987; Stryker & Serpe, 1994; Thoits, 2003.

15. Goffman (1959) previously alluded to these social roles and the ways that one's identities or roles may change in different contexts with his/her situational identity.

16. For example, in Serpe and Stryker's (1987) questionnaire regarding the college transitions related to identity salience, the findings from a study of college freshmen indicated that students exhibited more identity stability if they were successful in establishing social relationships consistent with their salient identities. This finding has implications for diversity on college campuses. For example, an African American student attending a predominantly White postsecondary institution may find it more difficult to establish

social relationships that are consistent with previous salient identities. If this is the case, the findings of Serpe and Stryker (1987) indicate that the student would have a less-stable sense of identity and potentially be less successful in college.

17. Ethier and Deaux (1994) studied identity salience among Latino college students, finding that the students' commitment to their ethnic identity before entering college was central to their identity salience. Students with a salient ethnic identity had a greater likelihood of reinforcing that identity (through extracurricular involvement / peer groups) once they entered college.

18. For another example of work that considers the intergenerational transmission of norms and values of upper-class status, see Lamont's (1992) comparison of upper-class males in the French and American contexts.

19. Jasper (1997) considered notions of ascribed identity in his work on social movements and protests. This linked to the study of collective identity, which primarily focused on group mobilization, protest, and social movements. By "ascribed identity," Jasper was referring both to the identity that came from belonging to a social movement and to the identity-related ascriptions related to categories such as race. In this case, ascribed identity is used as a tool to describe the outcomes of social grouping and social movement. Ascribed identity is largely a descriptive tool, differentiating it from the Unchosen Me, which refers to the *process* or one's experience of managing aspects of identities that feel as if they are not chosen.

20. Goffman (1959) also examined social roles and the ways that one presents oneself in various social settings, the notion that one's identities may change in different contexts, calling this idea situational identity, or the "art of impression management" (Goffman, 2004). Subsequent research expanded this notion to consider such topics as: the way one manages impressions that others have of one's identity (Goffman, 2004); the experiences of multiracial students in college regarding situational identity (Renn, 2000); the ethnic identities of college students in predominantly White settings or the notion of identity stability in changing contexts (Ethier & Deaux, 1994); the identity-related expression of emotions in particular settings (Felson, 1978); and identities within organizations (Ashforth & Mael, 2004; Ginzel, Kramer, & Sutton, 2004).

The Unchosen Me is distinguished from this line of work because of the emphasis on roles and impression management within this scholarship. While roles are one aspect of the Unchosen Me, and one's roles would in fact change in various contexts, the Unchosen Me is not only about the roles one feels compelled to play. It is also not only about managing the impressions that others have of the self. Rather, with this concept I am arguing that there is a process through which people experience impositions or pressures on their identity. While contexts or situations may make this pressure more or less salient, the process may occur at any time—it is not necessarily context dependent. At times, this occurs *before* one commits to play a role in a social group: one experiences identity pressures or a sense that aspects of one's identities are not chosen. For example, prior to playing the role of a student, one already is experiencing the impositions of race, class, or gender that may influence the way one enacts this role. Additionally, situational identity does not necessarily allow for a consideration of the *process* and way in which one's identities develop in a dynamic, fluid manner in relation to one's interactions with others and society. So *The Unchosen Me* attempts to uncover the sometimes unforeseen pressures that exist in social settings that impose particular notions of identity on one's sense of self. This could in many ways influence the "situational identity" that one is able to enact.

21. Arroyo and Zigler (1995) examined African Americans' integration into higher education, finding that many African Americans achieve success academically by adopting behaviors and attitudes that are distant from their culture of origin.

22. Helms's (1995) model maintains a psychological perspective in its stage-based notion of racial identity development. This model examines the process that one undergoes in identifying or choosing one's racial category. I argue with the Unchosen Me that this process itself may not be chosen, resulting in unchosen aspects of identities.

23. As an example of the way this memory of former Me's might work, in Swann and Pelham's (2002) use of a Self-Attributes Questionnaire (SAQ-S) to study female college students' self-verification among college roommates, they found that students who were certain of their self-views desired roommates who validated their preexisting view of self. This self-reflection led to a self-awareness that influenced students' social relationships.

CHAPTER 3. RESEARCH ACROSS THE COLOR LINE

1. Advocacy in critical methodology can take multiple forms. In this case, I attempted to provide support and resources for the women throughout the research process. Additionally, I advocated for this group of women on the campus where the research was conducted, meeting with top administrators and faculty to attempt to create a better environment for future groups of African American women.

2. Epistemology is a way of knowing, how one knows what one knows, or a view of the world.

3. For instance, I did not anticipate that the women would describe their identities in terms of dualities or polarities as they do in the chapters that follow. Nor did I think that I would find evidence for the concept of "acting White" (Fordham & Ogbu, 1986), described in chapter 6, because that concept initially emerged among adolescent African American males.

4. For example, in chapter 7, the women describe very traditional women's roles that actually made me uncomfortable, given my own feminist orientation. Yet I felt it was important to grapple with the way they experienced and described gender even though it was different from my own values about gender roles.

5. I chose to study women because the evidence of a "chilly" institutional climate for women provides a compelling case for further study of women's experiences (Whitt et al., 1999).

6. Objective claims refer to third-person claims to which all have access (i.e., that which can be seen, touched, tasted, smelled, or heard by others). Subjective claims are first-person claims, generally what one would say from her own perspective. Normative-evaluative claims refer to that which is considered to be moral or ethical. Identity claims are the overarching references that one makes to oneself or one's identity within a statement.

7. For a more detailed explanation of the validation of cross-racial research, see Winkle-Wagner, 2009b.

8. W.E.B. Du Bois first noted the problem of the color line in his *Souls of Black Folk* (1903/2003).

9. For example, see Denzin and Lincoln's (2003) volume on qualitative research.

CHAPTER 4. WALKING IN ENEMY TERRITORY

1. For more scholarship that identifies feelings of isolation and alienation within African American students, see Allen, 1992; Davis et al., 2004; Feagin et al., 1996; Loo & Rollison, 1986; Nilsson et al., 1999.

2. Psychologically based, psychosocial theories of college student development such as those of Marcia (1966, 1980, 2002) or Josselson (1973, 1987) are rooted in Erik Erikson's (1980) work. Erikson maintained that one progressed through a series of stages whereby progression was predicated on a psychosocial crisis. If one were to use these theories to interpret this data, for example, the "culture shock" would be a catalyst toward development. Yet this fails to recognize the way the women here described culture shock and isolation as a painful, unequal experience that was largely detrimental to the development of their identities and sense of self more generally.

3. For more information on hostile racial climates on campus, see Hurtado & Carter, 1997; Hurtado, Carter, & Kardia, 1998; Hurtado, Carter, & Spuler, 1996. For work that considers potential solutions to hostile climates, see Hurtado, Milem, Clayton-Pederson, & Allen, 1998.

4. For more information about students' experiences with racism in college, see Swim et. al, 2003.

5. These programs are called early intervention programs because they attempt to help disadvantaged students get to college. Typically, these programs begin early in a students' academic career, in junior high or high school.

6. The Trio Summer Program is a pseudonym for a federally based program the university had adopted to assist in providing access to higher education for underrepresented students.

7. For further information on federally funded TRIO programs, see Carey, Cahalan, Cunningham, & Agufa, 2004; Kuenzi, 2005.

8. This corroborates previous work regarding the importance of early intervention programs (St. John, Musoba, & Simmons, 2003; Musoba, 2004).

9. See Winkle-Wagner, 2009a, for more information on the sense of homelessness felt by African American women in college.

CHAPTER 5. ACADEMIC PERFORMANCES

1. If one were to use one of the psychologically based theories of college student development that particularly deal with women's development, for example, Josselson's (1987) psychosocial theory, Lisa might be considered to be in the "identity diffusions" status because she is withdrawing from this situation. Yet this would fail to

highlight the impositions of race that are placed on Lisa in this situation because of her minority status: she is made to feel simultaneously that she must speak on behalf of her race, and that if she doesn't choose to speak for her race, she should remain silent.

2. The pressure to represent one's racial group could manifest itself in a "stereotype threat" whereby students feel the need to dispel potential stereotypes through their behaviors (Steele, 1995, 1997). In Steele's experiments, the threat of stereotypes did have a deleterious impact on academic achievement. Many of the women's experiences in this chapter relate to the issue of either implicit or explicit stereotypes.

3. Claudia's angry response to her White peers here could put her in the "Immersion-Emersion" stage of development if one were to use Cross's (1995) theory of Nigrescence. In this stage, one feels anger toward White people and ways of being. But, this could potentially miss the way Claudia's experiences with her White peers influences the identities that she sees as available. Here, she is made to feel different because of her White peers' actions. Rather than placing the onus of this situation on Claudia, the sociological perspective emphasizes inequalities in the social structure that lead to "ignorance," as Claudia puts it, and to her own feelings of difference.

4. For further information on the aspirations of African American students generally, see D. F. Carter (2001).

5. Here Lisa implicitly places boundaries around what it means to belong within a group. The discrepancy between in-group and out-group membership (Brewer & Silver, 2000) has been useful in sociologically based identity perspectives in attempting to understand issues related to college student experiences and academic success, particularly for racially underrepresented students (Spears & Manstead, 1988).

CHAPTER 6. "TOO WHITE" OR "TOO GHETTO"?

1. Fordham & Ogbu (1986) and Ogbu (1987) first developed the concept of "acting White" in their study with African American adolescent boys, suggesting that "acting White" was linked to an oppositional anti-intellectual peer culture whereby the adolescent African American males associated "acting White" with doing well academically. Here the women used the words "too White" to refer to actions, thoughts, or speech patterns that were associated with being White. Perhaps because they were enrolled in college, these women have already resisted the anti-intellectualism that they may have experienced in their adolescence or earlier schooling.

2. For more recent revisions to the "acting White" concept and work that considers the concept relative to African American women, see Carter, 2006; Ogbu & Davis, 2003; Tyson, 2002; Tyson, Darity & Castellino, 2005.

3. Willie (2003) asserted an "acting Black" concept in her study of African American alumni's reflections of their college experiences. However, this concept was not compared to an "acting White" phenomenon as it is here.

4. Renee's statement also relates to Renn's (2000) notion of situational identity in Multiracial students where she associates with a different aspect of her identity in different situations.

5. Using the racial identity theories that are predominant in the higher education literature, Renee could be considered to be in a stage with a "high negative salience to being Black" (Torres et al., 2003, p. 42). Or, using a Multiracial identity model, since Renee is technically Multiracial (although she self-identifies as Black), this could be a situational identity whereby the salience of particular aspects of her identity changes in different contexts (Renn, 2000). However, this evidence indicated the pervasiveness of strong imposed messages that work to define *for* Renee and other women regarding what racial group they might belong to, which also reveals the creation of race and gender in the larger social structure.

6. This relates to the student engagement literature, maintaining that as students become integrated in social organizations outside of the classroom, they are more likely to persist and may have better college experiences (see Kuh, 1993, 2001; Kuh, Hu, & Vesper, 2000).

7. Krystal's desire to be disassociated from Blackness relates to earlier racial identity theories such as Cross's theory of Nigrescence (1991, 2001). In Cross's stage theory, he asserts that African American students undergo a series of stages whereby they interact with societal oppression and begin to understand their own racial identity (Torres et al., 2003). One familiar with Cross's theory may classify Mercedes or Krystal as being in a pre-encounter or encounter stage, a lower-level stage where they may carry a "high negative salience to being Black" (Torres et al., 2003, p. 42). Ultimately, this puts the onus on the individual students, as if they are not advanced enough in their identity, rather than placing the responsibility on the larger society. In large part, this would have missed the continual imposition of racial categories that worked to create racial stereotypes and racial inequalities. This would also largely ignore the influence of past experiences and associations of behavior with these experiences. Through a sociological perspective on identity, I focused on the impositions or pressures that Mercedes and Krystal experienced in which they felt that they needed to alter aspects of their identity to fit within the boundaries of either their African American peer group or the White mainstream on campus. Rather than highlighting the way they did or did not advance through stages, this allowed for a central consideration of the way that larger social inequalities are reenacted or created through interactions between one's self, others, and society.

8. This famous quote was part of Justice Potter Stewart's dissenting opinion for *Jacobellis v. Ohio*, citing the First and Fourteenth Amendments regarding the government's role in censoring pornography, positing that the government was limited in claiming criminality only for "hard-core pornography."

9. For a longer discussion of the way this concept differs from the "acting White" concept developed by Fordham and Ogbu (1986), see chapter 8.

CHAPTER 7. LEARNING TO BE A "GOOD WOMAN"

1. In the main, gender identity is not addressed on its own within psychologically based college student development theories. Rather, gender is considered within existing notions of development, primarily considering women as a new or alternative participant/subject group on which to study other theories. For example, Josselson (1973, 1987)

built on Erikson's (1959/1980) stage-based, psychosocial identity development (the examination of personal and interpersonal lives). Or, as another example, theorists built on Perry's (1981) cognitive-structural theory that considered the way people think to include women's perspectives (see Baxter Magolda, 1992; Belenky, Clinchy, Goldberger, & Tarule, 1986; Gilligan, 1993).

2. The link between gender and behavior or the exhibition of particular traits relates to West & Zimmerman's (1987) article, "Doing Gender," and West & Fernstermaker's (1995) article, "Doing Difference."

3. The negative gendered experiences on campus corroborate previous research on a "chilly" climate for women on campus (Jacobs, 1996; Whitt et al., 2001).

4. For more research that considers students' academic self-concept related to their achievement, see Cokley & Chapman, 2008; Awad, 2007.

5. This is one of the few instances where the women's peer groups identified being smart in negative ways similar to those described by Fordham and Ogbu's (1986) "acting White" concept.

CHAPTER 8. THE UNCHOSEN ME AND THE INTERACTIONS
THAT CREATE RACE AND GENDER

1. For another example of this perceived pressure for Black people to act differently among White than among African American people, see the work of Charisse Jones and Kumea Shorter-Gooden (2003).

2. The women's stories concur with evidence that many students of color experience a sense of "double consciousness" or multiple pressures on their identities on predominantly White campuses, feeling that they have to act differently in different contexts in ways that majority students do not (Arroyo & Zigler, 1995; Oyserman et al., 2003).

3. Since the women were enrolled in college, they may have already identified strategies for negotiating the "acting White" issue in ways that adolescents would not have had the opportunity to do.

4. On the contrary, when the spotlight notion, for example, was enforced by professors, that was largely experienced in negative terms by the women in this study.

5. The concept of "acting Black" has been offered by Willie's (2003) study of African American alumni from a predominantly White institution. She asserted that students created norms for "acting Black," the name of her book, but it was not connected with acting "too White" as it was in this study.

6. For other work that builds on the "acting White" concept among various populations or age groups, see Carter, 2006; Fordham, 2008; Ogbu & Davis, 2003; Tyson, 2002; Tyson, Darity, & Castellino, 2005.

7. In the Color of Privilege, Aida Hurtado (1996) argues against this normative model based on only White women's experiences. Maxine Baca Zinn and Bonnie Thornton Dill (1999) submit a "multiracial feminism" that takes into account that structures of domination in society, in particular, the importance of race in understanding the social construction of gender. In Black Feminist Thought, Patricia Hill Collins (2000) examines the importance of self-defined knowledge as one road to group empowerment.

8. For another example of work that examine the not-Me aspect of identities, see Mc-Call (2003).

9. Recall that the psychological perspective maintains the theoretical priority of the individual and not society, emphasizes cognitions, roots the self in these cognitions, assumes a single self/identity, and discusses concepts such as traits, characteristics, personality, and individuals' perceptions of membership within groups (Styker, 1997). In contrast, the sociological perspective argues that the self develops out of interaction, roots the self in society (society develops first and identity stems from socialized roles), locates the self in social structures, maintains that the self works to organize social life, assumes a multiple selves/identities perspective, places reflexivity or reflection as a central aspect of the self, and emphasizes roles, commitment to roles, and identity salience (Stryker, 1997).

10. For more work that compares the sociological and psychological perspective, see Hogg, Terry, & White, 1995; Stryker, 1997.

11. For example, psychologically based racial identity theories from the higher education literature primarily do emphasize stages (e.g., Cross's theory of Nigrescence, 1995; Helms, 1995). While not all college student development theories are stage-based, the foundational theories do generally assert a series of developmental stages or phrases (Evans, Forney, & Guido-DiBrito, 1998; Torres, Howard-Hamilton, & Cooper, 2003).

12. For examples of theories that describe these early stages in primarily negative or less-advanced terms, see Cross, 1991, 1995; Helms, 1995.

13. For more information about putting money in the right places, see Winkle-Wagner, 2008.

14. For a cautionary tale that considers the potential detriments of such contact, especially as it relates to White people having paternalistic attitudes toward people of color, see Jackman, 1994.

15. I have chosen a pseudonym for the program so as not to identify the research site.

16. For information on the success rates and recent funding issues associated with TRIO programs, see Carey, Cahalan, Cunningham, & Agufa, 2004; Kuenzi, 2005.

APPENDIX B. DATA ANALYSIS AND VALIDATION

1. Epistemology is most simply stated as the way one knows what one knows. It can also be referred to as a worldview or a way of knowing. Critical epistemology links with critical theory and is associated with a way of knowing that links to considerations of power, oppression, and the uncovering of inequalities.

References

Abes, E. S., Jones, S. R., & McEwen, M. K. (2007). Reconceptualizing the model of multiple dimensions of identity: The role of meaning-making capacity in the construction of multiple identities. *Journal of College Student Development, 48*(1), 1–22.

Alba, R., & Nee, V. (1997). Rethinking assimilation theory for a new era of immigration. *International Migration Review 31*(4), 826–874.

Allen, W. (1992). The color of success: African-American college student outcomes at predominantly white and historically black colleges and universities. *Harvard Educational Review, 62*(1), 26–44.

Allen, W., Epps, E. G., & Haniff, N. Z., (Eds.). (1991). *College in black and white: African American students in predominantly white and in historically black universities*. Albany: SUNY Press.

Allen, W., & Jewell, J. O. (1996). The miseducation of Black America: Black education since 'An American Dilemma.' In O. Clayton Jr., ed., *An American Dilemma revisited: Race relations in a changing world* (pp. 169–90). New York: Russell Sage Foundation.

Arroyo, C. G., & Zigler, E. (1995). Racial identity, academic achievement, and the psychological well-being of economically disadvantaged adolescents. *Journal of Personality and Social Psychology, 69*(5), 903–914.

Ashforth, B. E., & Mael, F. (2004). Social identity theory and the organization. In M. J. Hatch & M. Schultz, *Organizational identity: A reader* (pp. 134–160). Oxford: Oxford University Press.

Astin, A. W. (1985). *Achieving educational excellence: A critical assessment of priorities and practices in higher education*. San Francisco: Jossey-Bass.

Astin, A. W. (1993). *What matters in college: Four critical years revisited*. San Francisco: Jossey-Bass.

Astin, A. W. (1996). Involvement in learning revisited: Lessons we have learned. *Journal of College Student Development, 37*, 123–134.

Atkinson, D. R., Morten, G., & Sue, D. W. (1989). *Counseling American minorities: A cross-cultural perspective* (3rd ed.). Dubuque, IA: William C. Brown.

Awad, G. H. (2007). The role of racial identity, academic self-concept, and self-esteem in the predication of academic outcomes for African American students. *Journal of Black Psychology, 33*(2), 188–207.

Banton, M. (1998). *Racial theories* (2nd ed.). Cambridge: Cambridge University Press.

Baum, S. (2003). The role of student loans in college access: Research report. *Report from the National Dialogue on Student Financial Aid and the Pathways to College Network, RR-5*. New York: College Entrance Examination Board.

Baxter Magolda, M. B. (1992). *Knowing and reasoning in college: Gender-related patterns in students' intellectual development*. San Francisco: Jossey-Bass.

Bean, J. P., & Eaton, S. B. (2001). The psychology underlying successful retention practices. *Journal of College Student Retention, 3*, 73–89.

Beil, C., Reisen, C. A., Zea, M. C., & Caplan, R. C. (1999). A longitudinal study of the effects of academic and social integration and commitment on retention. *NASPA Journal, 37*, 376–385.

Belenky, M. F., Clinchy, B. M., Goldberger, N. R., & Tarule, J. M. (1986). *Women's ways of knowing: The development of self, voice, and mind*. New York: Basic Books.

Benson, K. F. (2000). Constructing academic inadequacy: African American athletes' stories of schooling. *Journal of Higher Education, 71*(2), 223–246.

Berry, T. R., & Mizelle, N. (2006). *From oppression to grace: Women of color and their dilemmas within the academy*. Sterling, VA: Stylus Publishing.

Blau, J. (2004). *Race in the School: Perpetuating white dominance?* Boulder, CO: Lynne Rienner Publishers.

Blum, L. (2008). White privilege: A mild critique. *Theory and Research in Education, 6*(3), 309–321.

Bonilla-Silva, E. (2003). *Racism without racists: Color-blind racism and the persistence of racial inequality in the United States*. Lanham, MD: Rowman & Littlefield Publishers.

Bourdieu, P. (1984). *Distinction: A social critique of the judgment of taste*. (R. Nice, Trans.). Cambridge, MA: Harvard University Press.

Branch Douglas, K. (1998). Impressions: African American first-year students' perceptions of a predominantly white university. *Journal of Negro Education, 67*(4), 416–431.

Braxton, J. M. (2000). Reinvigorating theory and research on the departure puzzle. In J. M. Braxton (Ed.), *Reworking the student departure puzzle*, 257–274. Nashville, TN: Vanderbilt University Press.

Braxton, J. M., & McClendon, S.A. (2001). The fostering of social integration and retention through institutional practice. *Journal of College Student Retention, 3*, 57–71.

Braxton, J. M., & Mundy, M. E. (2001). Powerful institutional levers to reduce college student departure. *Journal of College Student Retention, 3*, 91–1118.

Brewer, M. B. (1991). The social self: On being the same and different at the same time. *Personality and Social Psychology Bulletin, 17*, 475–482.

Brewer, M. B., & Silver, M. D. (2000). Group distinctiveness, social identification, and collective mobilization. In S. Stryker, T. Owens, & R. White (Eds.). *Self, identity and social movements*. Minneapolis: University of Minnesota Press.

Burke, P. J., & Reitzes, D. (1991). An identity theory approach to commitment. *Social Psychology Quarterly, 54*, 239–251.

Cardona, J. R. P., Busby, D. M., & Wampler, R. S. (2004). No soy de aqui ni soy de alla: Transgenerational cultural identity formation. *Journal of Hispanic Education, 3*(4), 322–337.

Carey, K. (2004, May). *A matter of degrees: Improving graduation rates in four-year colleges and universities—Report by the Education Trust*. Retrieved on August 19, 2004 from www2 .edtrust.org/NR/rdonlyres/11B4283F-104E-4511-B0CA-1D3023231157/0/highered.pdf.

Carey, N., Cahalan, M. W., Cunningham, K., & Agufa, J. (2004). *A profile of the Student Support Services Program: 1997–98 and 1998–99 with select data from 1999–2000*. Washington, D.C.: Mathematica Policy Research, Inc. prepared for U.S. Department of Education.

Carnoy, M. (1995). *Faded dreams: The politics and economics of race in America*. New York: Cambridge University Press.

Carspecken, P. F. (1996). *Critical ethnography in educational research: A theoretical and practical guide*. New York: Routledge.

Carspecken, P. F. (1999). *Four scenes for posing the question of meaning: And other essays in critical philosophy and critical methodology*. New York: Peter Lang.

Carspecken, P. F. (2009). Limits to knowledge with existential significance: An outline for the exploration of post-secular spirituality of relevance to qualitative research. In R. Winkle-Wagner, C. A. Hunter, & J. H. Ortloff, *Bridging the gap between theory and practice in educational research: Methods at the margins* (pp. 47–62). New York: Palgrave, Macmillan.

Carter, D. F. (2001). A dream deferred? Examining the degree aspirations of African American and White college students. In P. G. Altbach (Ed.), Studies in Higher Education, Dissertation Series. New York: Routledge Falmer.

Carter, P. (2005). *Keepin' it real: School success beyond Black and White*. Oxford: Oxford University Press.

Carter, P. (2006). Straddling boundaries: Identity, culture, and school. *Sociology of Education, 79*, 304–328.

Case, K. A. (2007). Raising male privilege awareness and reducing sexism: An evaluation of diversity courses. *Psychology of Women Quarterly, 31*(4), 426–435.

Cass, V. (1979). Homosexual identity formation: A theoretical model. *Journal of Homosexuality, 4*, 219–235.

Cass, V. (1984). Homosexual identity formation: Testing a theoretical model. *Journal of Sex Research, 20*, 143–167.

Census Bureau. (2008a). Proportion of 18- to 24-year-olds enrolled in college. In *The Chronicle of Higher Education, Almanac Issue 2008–2009, LV(1)*, A13.

Census Bureau. (2008b). Trends in the proportion of high-school graduates enrolling in college in the fall following graduation. In *The Chronicle of Higher Education, Almanac Issue 2008–2009, LV(1)*, A13.

Chickering, A. W. (1969). *Education and Identity*. San Francisco: Jossey-Bass.

Chickering, A. W., & Reiser, L. (1993). *Education and identity* (2nd ed.). San Francisco: Jossey-Bass.

Christie, N. G., & Dinham, S. M. (1991). Institutional and external influences on social integration in the freshman year. *Journal of Higher Education, 62*, 412–436.

Clark, K. B., & Clark, M. K. (1939). The development of consciousness of self and the emergence of racial identification in Negro preschool children. *Journal of Social Psychology, 10*, 590–599.

Cokley, K. O., & Chapman, C. (2008). The roles of ethnic identity, anti-White attitudes, and academic self-concept in African American student achievement. *Social Psychology of Education: An International Journal, 11*(4), 349–365.

Cooley, C. H. (1902). *Human nature and the social order.* New York: Scribner's Press.

Cosby, W. H., & Poussaint, A. F. (2007). *Come on people: On the path from victims to victors.* Nashville, TN: Thomas Nelson, Inc.

Creswell, J. W. (1998). *Qualitative inquiry and research design: Choosing among the five traditions.* Thousand Oaks, CA: Sage Publications.

Cross, W. E. Jr. (1995). The psychology of Nigrescence: Revising the Cross model. In J. G. Ponterotto, J. M. Casas, L. A. Suzukli, & C. M. Alexander (Eds.), *Handbook of multicultural counseling* (pp. 93–122). Thousand Oaks, CA: Sage Publications.

Crotty, M. (1998). Introduction: The research process. In M. Crotty, *The foundations of social research: Meaning and perspectives in the research process* (pp. 3–17). Thousand Oaks, CA: Sage Publications.

Cureton, S. R. (2003). Race-specific college student experiences on a predominantly white campus. *Journal of Black Studies, 33*(3), 295–311.

Cuyjet, M. J. (1997). African American men on college campuses: Their needs and their perceptions. In *New Directions for Student Services, 80* (pp. 5–16). San Francisco: Jossey-Bass Publishers.

Davis, M., Dias-Bowie, Y., Greenberg, K., Klukken, G., Pollio, H. R., Thomas, S. P., & Thompson, C. L. (2004). "A fly in the buttermilk": Descriptions of university life by successful black undergraduate students at a predominantly white southeastern university. *Journal of Higher Education, 75*(4), 420–445.

Denzin, N. K., & Lincoln, Y. S. (Eds.). (2003). *The landscape of qualitative research: Theories and issues* (2nd ed.). Thousand Oaks, CA: Sage.

Delanty, G. (1997). *Social science: Beyond constructivism and realism.* Minneapolis: University of Minnesota Press.

Delgado, R., & Stefanic, J. (Eds). (1997). *Critical White studies: Looking behind the mirror.* Philadelphia, PA: Temple University Press.

Derrida, J. (1973). *Speech and phenomena and other essays on Husserl's theory of signs.* Evanston, IL: Northwestern University Press.

DeSousa, J. (2001). Reexamining the educational pipeline for African-American students. In L. Jones, *Rethinking African Americans in higher education: Challenging paradigms for retaining students, faculty and administrators.* Sterling, VA: Stylus Press.

DesJardins, S., Ahlberg, D., & McCall, B. (2002). A temporal investigation of factors related to timely degree completion. *Journal of Higher Education, 73*(5), 555–581.

Du Bois, W.E.B. (1903/2003). *The souls of Black folk.* New York: Barnes and Noble Classics.

Durkheim, E. (1897/2006). *On suicide.* London: Penguin Books.

Erikson, E. (1959/1980). *Identity and the life cycle.* New York: Norton.

Ethier, K. A., & Deaux, K. (1994). Negotiating social identity when contexts change: Maintaining identification and responding to threat. *Journal of Personality and Social Psychology, 67*(2), 243–251.

Evans, N. J., Forney, D. S., & Guido-DiBrito, F. (1998). *Student development in college: Theory, research, and practice.* San Francisco: Jossey-Bass Publishers.

Feagin, J. R. (1991). The continuing significance of race: Antiblack discrimination in public places. *American Sociological Review, 56*(1), 101–116.

Feagin, J. R., & McKinney, K. D. (2002). *The many costs of racism.* Lanham, MD: Rowman and Littlefield Publishers.

Feagin, J. R., Vera, H., & Imani, N. (1996). *The agony of education: Black students at White college and universities.* New York: Routledge.

Felson, R. B. (1978). Aggression as impression management. *Social Psychology, 41*(3), 205–213.

Ficklen, E., & Stone, J. E. (Eds.). (2002). *Empty promises: The myth of college access in America. A report of the Advisory Committee on Student Financial Assistance.* Washington, D.C.: Advisory Committee on Student Financial Assistance.

Fleming, J. (1984). *Blacks in college: A comparative study of students' success in Black and in White institutions.* San Francisco: Jossey-Bass.

Fordham, S. (1995). *Blacked out: Dilemmas of race, identity and success at Capital High.* Chicago: University of Chicago Press.

Fordham, S. (2008). Beyond Capital High: On dual citizenship and the strange career of acting white. *Anthropology & Education Quarterly, 39*(3), 227–246.

Fordham, S., & Ogbu, J. U. (1986). Black students' school success: Coping with the "burden of 'acting white.'" *The Urban Review, 18*(3), 176–206.

Freeman, K. (1997). Increasing African Americans' participation in higher education: African American high-school students' perspectives. *Journal of Higher Education, 68*(5), 523–551.

Freeman, K. (1999a). The race factor in African Americans' college choice. *Urban Education, 34*(1), 4–25.

Freeman, K. (1999b). Will higher education make a difference? African Americans' economic expectations and college choice. *College and University Journal, 75*(2), 7–12.

Freeman, K. (1999c). No services needed? The case for mentoring high-achieving African American students. *Peabody Journal of Education, 74*(2), 15–27.

Freeman, K., & Cohen, R. T. (2001). Bridging the gap between economic development and cultural empowerment: HBCUs challenges for the future. *Urban Education, 36*(5), 585–506.

Freeman, K., & Thomas, G. E. (2002). Black college and college choice: Characteristics of students who choose HBCUs. *Review of Higher Education, 25*(3), 349–358.

Fries-Britt, S. (1998). Moving beyond Black achiever isolation: Experiences of gifted Black collegians. *Journal of Higher Education, 69*(5), 665–576.

Fries-Britt, S., & Griffin, K. A. (2007). The Black box: How high-achieving Blacks resist stereotypes about Black Americans. *Journal of College Student Development, 48*(5), 509–524.

Fries-Britt, S. L., & Turner, B. (2002). Uneven stories: Successful black collegians at a black and a white campus. *Review of Higher Education, 25*(3), 315–330.

Garvey, J., & Ignatiev, N. (1997). Toward a new abolitionism: A race traitor manifesto. In M. Hill (Ed.). *Whiteness: A critical reader.* New York: New York University Press.

Gergen, M. M., & Gergen, K. J. (2003). Qualitative inquiry: Tensions and transformations. In N. K. Denzin & Y. S. Lincoln (Eds.). *The landscape of qualitative research* (2nd ed.) (pp. 575–610). London: Sage Publications.

Gilligan, C. (1982/1993). *In a different voice: Psychological theory and women's development.* Cambridge, MA: Harvard University Press.

Ginzel, L. E., Kramer, R. M., & Sutton, R. I. (2004). Organizational impression management as a reciprocal influence process: The neglected role of the organizational audience. In M. J. Hatch & M. Schultz, *Organizational identity: A reader* (pp. 223–274). Oxford: Oxford University Press.

Giroux, H. (1997). Rewriting the discourse of racial identity: Toward a pedagogy and politics of Whiteness. *Harvard Educational Review, 67*(2), 285–320.

Glazer-Raymo, J. (1999). *Shattering the myths: Women in academe.* Baltimore: Johns Hopkins University Press.

Goffman, E. (1959). *The presentation of self in everyday life.* Garden City, NY: Doubleday.

Goffman, E. (2004). The art of impression management. In M. J. Hatch & M. Schultz, *Organizational identity: A reader* (pp. 35–55). Oxford: Oxford University Press.

Graves, J. L. (2002). *The emperor's new clothes: Biological theories of race at the millennium.* New Brunswick, NJ: Rutgers University Press.

Guifridda, D. A. (2003). African American student organizations as agents of social integration. *Journal of College Student Development, 44,* 304–317.

Guinier, L. (2000). Confirmative action. *Law and Social Inquiry, 25*(2), 565–584.

Habermas, J. (1984). *The theory of communicative action: Reason and the rationalization of society* (T. McCarthy, Trans.). Boston: Beacon Press.

Habermas, J. (1987). *The theory of communicative action: Lifeworld and system: A critique of functional reason* (T. McCarthy, Trans.). Boston: Beacon Press.

Hale, J. (2001). *Learning While Black: Creating educational excellence for African American children.* Baltimore: Johns Hopkins University Press.

Hammersley, M. (2005). A response to Barbara Korth on feminist ethnography. *Methodological Issues and Practices in Ethnography, 11,* 169–74.

Harper, S. R. (2006). Peer support for African American male college achievement: Beyond internalized racism and the burden of 'acting White.' *Journal of Men's Studies, 14*(3).

Harper, S. R. (2008). Realizing the intended outcomes of Brown. *American Behavioral Scientist 51*(7), 1030–1053.

Harper, S. R., & Quaye, S. J. (2007). Student organizations as venues for Black identity expression and development among African American male student leaders. *Journal of College Student Development, 48*(2).

Hatch, L. R., & Mommsen, K. (1984 June). The widening gap in American higher education. *Journal of Black Studies, 14*(4), 457–476.

Hearn, J. C., & Holdsworth, J. M. (2004). Federal student aid: The shift from grants to loans. In E. P. St. John, *Readings on Equal Education, 19, Public policy and college access: investigating the federal and state roles in equalizing postsecondary opportunity.* New York: AMS Press, Inc.

Hegel, G. W. F. (1952/1977). *Phenomenology of spirit*. (A.V. Miller, Trans.). New York: Oxford University Press.

Heller, D. E. (2003). State financial aid and college access: Research report. *Report from the National Dialogue on Student Financial Aid and the Pathways to College Network, RR-4*. New York: College Entrance Examination Board.

Heller, D. E. (2004). State merit scholarship programs. In E. P. St. John, *Readings on Equal Education, 19, Public policy and college access: Investigating the federal and state roles in equalizing postsecondary opportunity* (pp. 99–108). New York: AMS Press, Inc.

Helms, J. E. (1994). Racial identity and career assessment. *Journal of Career Assessment, 2(1)*, 99–209.

Helms, J. (1995). An update of Helms's White and people of color racial identity models. In J. Ponterotto, J. Casas, L. Suzuki, & C. Alexander (Eds.), *Handbook of multicultural counseling* (pp. 181–198). Thousand Oaks, CA: Sage.

Helms, J. (2000). *A race is a nice thing to have: A guide to being a white person or understanding the white persons in your life*. Topeka, KA: Content Communications.

Hernstein, R. J., & Murray, C. (1994). *The bell curve: Intelligence and class structure in American life*. New York: Simon and Schuster.

Higgins, E., Klein Tory, R., & Strauman, T. (1985). Self-concept discrepancy theory. *Social Cognition, 3*, 51–76.

Hill Collins, P. (2000). *Black feminist thought: Knowledge, consciousness, and the politics of empowerment*. New York: Routledge.

Hogg, M. A., Terry, D. J., & White, K. M. (1995). A tale of two theories: A critical comparison of identity theory with social identity theory. *Social Psychology Quarterly, 58(4)*, 225–269.

Holland, D. C., & Eisenhart, M. A. (1990). *Educated in romance: Women, achievement, and college culture*. Chicago: University of Chicago Press.

hooks, b. (2000). *Feminist theory: From margin to center* (2nd ed.). Cambridge, MA: South End Press.

Horvat, E. M., & Lewis, K.S. (2003). Reassessing the "burden of 'acting white'": The importance of peer groups in managing academic success. *Sociology of Education, 76(4)*, 265–281.

Howard-Hamilton, M. F. (1997). Theory to practice: Applying development theories relevant to African American men. *New Directions for Student Services, 80*, 17–30.

Howard-Hamilton, M. F. (Ed.) (2004). *Meeting the needs of African American women: New directions for student services, 104*. San Francisco: Jossey-Bass.

Hu, S., & St. John, E. P. (2001). Student persistence in a public higher education system: Understanding racial and ethnic differences. *Journal of Higher Education, 72(3)*, 265–286.

Hurtado, A. (1996). *The color of privilege: Three blasphemies on race and feminism*. Ann Arbor: University of Michigan Press.

Hurtado, S., & Carter, D. F. (1997). Effects of college transition and perceptions of the campus racial climate on Latino college students' sense of belonging. *Sociology of Education, 70*, 324–345.

Hurtado, S., Carter, D. F., & Kardia, D. (1998). The climate for diversity: Key issues for institutional self-study. *New Directions for Institutional Research, 25*(2), 53–63.

Hurtado, S., Carter, D. F., & Spuler, A. (1996). Latino student transition to college: Assessing difficulties and factors in successful college adjustment. *Research in Higher Education, 37,* 135–157.

Hurtado, S., Milem, J. F., Clayton-Pederson, A. R., & Allen, W. R. (1998). Enhancing campus climates for racial/ethnic diversity: Educational policy and practice. *Review of Higher Education, 21*(3), 279–302.

Jackman, M. R. (1994). *The velvet glove: Paternalism and conflict in gender, class, and race relations.* Berkeley: University of California Press.

Jacobs, J. A. (1996). Gender inequality and higher education. *Annual Review of Sociology, 22,* 153–185.

James, W. (1890/1968). The self. In C. Gordon & K. J. Gergen (Eds.), *The self in social interaction,* vol.1. New York: Wiley Press.

Janis, I. L. (1972). *Victims of groupthink.* Boston: Haughton Mifflin.

Jasper, J. M. (1997). *The art of moral protest.* Chicago: University of Chicago Press.

Jencks, C., & Phillips, M. (Eds.). (1998). *The Black-White test score gap.* Washington, D.C.: Brookings Institution Press.

Jones, C., & Shorter-Gooden (2003). *Shifting: The double lives of black women in America.* New York: HarperCollins Publishers.

Jones, S. R. (1997). Voice of identity and difference: A qualitative exploration of the multiple dimensions of identity development in women college students. *Journal of College Student Development, 38*(4), 376–386.

Jones, S. R., & McEwen, M. K. (2000). Conceptual model of multiple dimensions of identity. *Journal of College Student Development, 41*(4), 405–414.

Josselson, R. (1973). Psychodynamic aspects of identity formation in college women. *Journal of Youth and Adolescence, 2,* 3–52.

Josselson, R. (1987). *Finding herself: Pathways to identity development in women.* San Francisco: Jossey-Bass.

Keating, A. (1995, December). Interrogating "Whiteness," deconstructing "race." *College English, 57,* 901–918.

Keister, L. A., & Moller, S. (2000). Wealth inequality in the United States. *Annual Review of Sociology, 26,* 63–81.

Kerckoff, A. C. (1995). Institutional arrangement and stratification processes in industrial societies. *Annual Review of Sociology, 21,* 323–347.

Kincheloe, J. L., & McLaren, P. (2003). Rethinking critical theory and qualitative research. In N. K. Denzin & Y. S. Lincoln (Eds.). *The landscape of qualitative research,* (2nd ed.). London: Sage Publications, 433–488.

King, M. L. Jr. (1968, March 31). Remaining awake through a great revolution. Speech at National Cathedral, Washington, D.C.

Kohlberg, L., & Hersh, R. H. (1977). Moral development: A review of the theory. *Theory into Practice, 16,* 53–59.

Kolb, D. A. (1984). *Experiential learning: Experience as the source of learning and development.* Englewood Cliffs, NJ: Prentice Hall.

Korth, B. (2005). Choice, necessity, or narcissism? A feminist does feminist ethnography. *Methodological Issues and Practices in Ethnography, 11,* 131–68.

Knottnerus, J. D. (1987). Status attainment research and its image of society. *American Sociological Review, 52,* 113–121.

Kuenzi, J. J. (2005). *Trio and GEAR UP Programs: Status and issues. CRS Report for Congress.* Washington, D.C.: Congressional Research Service, Library of Congress.

Kuh, G. D. (1993). In their own words: What students learn outside the classroom. *American Educational Research Journal, 30*(2), 277–304.

Kuh, G. D. (2001). Organizational culture and student persistence: Prospects and puzzles. *Journal of College Student Retention, 3,* 23–39.

Kuh, G. D., Hu, S., & Vesper, N. (2000). They shall be known by what they do: An activities-based typology of college students. *Journal of College Student Development, 41,* 228–244.

Lamont, M. (1992). *Money, morals, and manners: The culture of the French and American upper-middle class.* Chicago: University of Chicago Press.

Lareau, A. (1987). Social class difference in family-school relationships: The importance of cultural capital. *Sociology of Education, 60,* 73–85.

Lareau, A. (1993). *Home advantage: Social class and parental intervention in elementary education.* Philadelphia: Palmer Press.

Lareau, A. (2003). *Unequal childhoods: Class, race, and family life.* Los Angeles: University of California Press.

Lee, V. E., & Burkam, D. T. (2002). *Inequality at the starting gate: Social background differences in achievement as children begin school.* Washington, D.C.: Economic Policy Institute.

Lemann, N. (1999). *The big test: The secret history of the American meritocracy.* New York: Farrar, Strauss and Giroux (ED434949).

Lieberson, S. (1980). *A piece of the pie: Blacks and White immigrants, 1880–1930.* Berkeley: University of California Press.

Lincoln, Y. S., & Guba, E. S. (2003). Paradigmatic controversies, contradictions, and emerging influences. In N. K. Denzin & Y. S. Lincoln (Eds.). *The landscape of qualitative research* (2nd ed.). London: Sage Publications, 253–291.

Linville, P. (1987). Self-complexity as a cognitive barrier against stress-related illness and depression. *Journal of Personality and Social Psychology, 5,* 797–811.

Locks, A. M., Hurtado, S. Bowman, N. A., Oseguera, L. (2008). Extending notions of campus climate and diversity to students' transition to college. *Review of Higher Education, 79*(2), 183–207.

Longanecker, D. A., & Blanco, C. D. (2003). Student financial assistance. In *Student success: Statewide P-16 systems.* Denver, CO: SHEEO.

Loo, C. M., & Rollison, G. (1986). Alienation of ethnic minority students at a predominantly white university. *Journal of Higher Education, 57*(1), 58–77.

MacLeod, J. (1987). *Ain't no makin' it: Leveled aspirations in a low-income neighborhood.* Boulder, CO: Westview Press.

Mahoney, M. R. (1997). In R. Delgado & J. Stefanic (Eds.), *Critical white studies: Looking behind the mirror.* Philadelphia: Temple University Press.

Marcia, J. (1966). Development and validation of ego-identity status. *Journal of Personality and Social Psychology, 3*, 551–588.

Marcia, J. (1980). Identity in adolescence. In J. Adelson (Ed.), *Handbook of adolescent psychology* (pp. 159–187). New York: Wiley.

Marcia, J. E. (2002). Identity and psychosocial development in adulthood. *Identity: An International Journal of Theory and Research, 2*(1), 7–28.

Massey, D. S., Charles, C. Z., Lundy, G. F., & Fischer, M. J. (2003). *The source of the river: The social origins of freshmen at America's selective colleges and universities.* Princeton, NJ: Princeton University Press.

McCall, G. J. (2003). The Me and the Not-me: Positive and negative poles of identity. In P. J. Burke, T. J. Owens, R. T. Serpe, & P. Thoits, *Advances in identity theory and research* (pp. 11–26). New York: Kluwer Academic/Plenum Publishers.

McDonough, P. M. (1997). *Choosing colleges: How social class and schools structure opportunity.* Albany: State University of New York Press.

McEwen, M. K., Roper, L. D., Bryant, D. R., & Langa, M. J. (1990). Incorporating the development of African American students into psychosocial theories of student development. *Journal of College Student Development, 31*(5), 429–436.

McIntosh, P. (1992). White privilege and male privilege: A personal account of coming to see correspondence through work in Women's Studies. In M. Anderson & P. H. Collins (Eds.), *Race, class, gender.* Belmont, CA: Wadsworth Publishers.

McWhorter, J. (2001). *Losing the race: Self-sabotage in Black America.* New York: Free Press.

Mead, G. H. (1934/1967). *Mind, self, and society: From the standpoint of a social behaviorist,* (C. W. Morris, Ed.). Chicago: University of Chicago Press.

Mehan, H., Hubbard, L., and Villanueva, I. (1994). Forming academic identities: Accommodation without assimilation among involuntary minorities. *Anthropology of Education Quarterly, 25*, 91–117.

Morgan, D. L. 1997. *Focus Groups as Qualitative Research.* Thousand Oaks, CA: Sage.

Museus, S. D., Nichols, A. H., & Lambert, A. D. (2008). Racial difference in the effects of campus racial climate on degree completion: A structural equation model. *Review of Higher Education, 32*(1), 107–134.

Musoba, G. D. (2004). Postsecondary encouragement for diverse students: A reexamination of the Twenty-first Century Scholars Program. In E. P. St. John, *Readings on Equal Education, 19, Public policy and college access: Investigating the federal and state roles in equalizing postsecondary opportunity* (pp. 153–177). New York: AMS Press.

Myers, I. B. (1980). *Gifts differing.* Palo Alto, CA: Counseling Psychologists Press.

Myers, R. D. (2003). *College success programs: Executive summary.* Washington, D.C.: Pathways to College Network Clearinghouse.

NECS (U.S. Department of Education, National Center for Education Statistics). (2005). Postsecondary institutions in the United States: Fall 2000 and degrees and other awards conferred: 2002–03. In *A shared agenda: A leadership challenge to improve college access and success.* Washington, DC: Pathways to College Network.

Ness, E. C., & Tucker, R. (2008). Eligibility effects on college access: Under-represented student perceptions of Tennessee's merit aid program. *Research in Higher Education, 32*(1), 107–134.

Nilsson, J. E., Paul, B. D., Lupini, L. N., & Tatem, B. (1999). Cultural differences in perfectionism: A comparison of African American and White college students. *Journal of College Student Development, 40*(2), 140–150.

Nora, A. (2004). The role of habitus and cultural capital in choosing a college, transitioning from high school to higher education, and persisting in college among minority and nonminority students. *Journal of Hispanic Higher Education, 3*(2), 180–208.

Norvilitis, J. M., Szablicki, P. B., & Wilson, S. D. (2003). Factors influencing levels of credit-card debt in college students. *Journal of Applied Social Psychology, 33*(5), 935–947.

Ogbu, J. (1987). Variability in minority school performance: A problem in search of an explanation. *Anthropology of Education Quarterly, 18*(4), 312–344.

Ogbu, J. U., & Davis, A. 2003. *Black American students in an affluent suburb: A study of academic disengagement.* Mahwah, NJ: Lawrence Erlbaum Associates, Publishers.

Oliver, M. L., & Shapiro, T. M. (1997). *Black wealth/White wealth: A new perspective on racial inequality.* New York: Routledge.

Omi, M., & Winant, H. (1994). *Racial formation in the United States: From the 1960s to the 1990s* (2nd ed.). New York: Routledge.

Owens, T. J., & Serpe, R. T. (2003). The role of self-evaluation in identity salience and commitment. In P. J. Burke, T. J. Owens, R. T. Serpe, & P. Thoits, *Advances in identity theory and research* (pp. 85–104). New York: Kluwer Academic/Plenum Publishers.

Oyserman, D., Kemmelmeier, M., Fryberg, S., Brosh, H., & Hart-Johnson, T. (2003). Racial-ethnic self schemas. *Social Psychology Quarterly, 66*(4), 333–347.

Padilla, R. V., Trevino, J., Gonzalez, K., & Trevino, J. (1997). Developing local models of minority students success in college. *Journal of College Student Development, 38,* 125–135.

Park, W. (2000). A comprehensive empirical investigation of the relationship among variables in the groupthink model. *Journal of Organizational Behavior, 21,* 873–887.

Pascarella, E. T., & Terenzini, P. T. (2005). *How college affects students: A third decade of research,* Vol. 2. San Francisco, CA: Jossey-Bass.

Pathways to College Network. (2003, August). *A shared agenda: A leadership challenge to improve college access and success.* Washington, D.C.: Pathways to College Network.

Perna, L. W. (2000). Differences in the decision to attend college among African Americans, Hispanics, and Whites. *Journal of Higher Education, 71*(2), 117–141.

Perry, W. G. Jr. (1981). Cognitive and ethical growth: The making of meaning. In A. W. Chickering and Associates, *The modern American college: Responding to the new realities of diverse students and a changing society* (pp. 76–116). San Francisco: Jossey-Bass.

Piaget, J. (1952). *The origins of intelligence in children.* New York: Norton.

Rendòn, L. I. (1994). Validating culturally diverse students: Toward a new model of learning and student development. *Innovative Higher Education, 19,* 35–51.

Rendòn, L. I., Jalomo, R. E., & Nora, A. (2000). Theoretical considerations in the study of minority student retention in higher education. In J. M. Braxton (Ed.), *Reworking the student departure puzzle* (pp. 127–156). Nashville, TN: Vanderbilt University Press.

Renn, K. A. (2000). Patterns of situational identity among biracial and multiracial college students. *Review of Higher Education, 23*(4), 399–420.

Reskin, B., & Padavic, I. (1994). *Women and men at work.* Thousand Oaks, CA: Pine Forge Press.

Reynolds, A. L., & Pope, R. L. (1991). The complexities of diversity: Exploring multiple oppressions. *Journal of Counseling & Development, 70*, 174–180.

Ripley, W. Z. (1909). Three Black histories. In T. Sowell (Ed.), *Essays and data on American ethnic groups* (pp. 7–64). Washington: The Urban Institute.

Robinson, T. L., & Howard-Hamilton, M. F. (1994). An Afrocentric paradigm: Foundation for a healthy self-image and healthy interpersonal relationships. *Journal of Mental Health Counseling, 16*(3), 327–340.

Rodgers, R. F. (1990). An integration of campus ecology and student development: The Olentangy project. In D. G. Creamer & Associates, *Colleges student development: Theory and practice for the 1990s* (pp. 27–70). Alexandria, VA: American College Personnel Association.

Roscigno, V. J., & Ainsworth-Darnell, J. W. (1999). Race cultural capital, and educational resources: Persistent inequalities and achievement returns. *Sociology of Education, 72*, 158–178.

Sanford, N. (1966). *The American college.* New York: Wiley.

Schlossberg, N. K. (1989). Marginality and mattering: Key issues in building community. In D C. Roberts (Eds.), *Designing campus activities to foster a sense of community. New Directions for Student Services, 48.* San Francisco: Jossey-Bass.

Schwartz, R. A., & Washington, C. M. (2002). Predicting academic performance and retention among African American freshmen men. *NASPA Journal, 39,* 355–370.

Serpe, R., & Stryker, S. (1987). The construction of self and the reconstruction of social relationships. In E. J. Lawler & B. Markovsky (Eds.), *Advances in group process,* Vol. 4. Greenwich, CT: JAI Press.

Serpe, R., & Stryker, S. (1993). Prior social ties and movement into new social relationships. In E. J. Lawler & B. Markovsky (Eds.), *Advances in group process,* Vol. 10. Greenwich, CT: JAI Press.

Sewell, W. H., Haller, A. O., & Portes, A. (1969). The educational and early occupational attainment process. *American Sociological Review, 34,* 82–92.

Sewell, W. H., & Hauser, R. M. (1972). Causes and consequence of higher education models of the status attainment process. *American Journal of Agricultural Economics, 54,* 81–861.

Shapiro, T. M. (2004). *The hidden cost of being African American: How wealth perpetuates inequality.* Oxford University Press.

Spady, W. (1971). Dropouts from higher education: An interdisciplinary review and synthesis. *Interchange, 1,* 64–85.

Spears, R., & Manstead, A. S. R. (1988). The social context of stereotyping and differentiation. *European Journal of Social Psychology, 19,* 101–121.

Spencer, M. B., Noll, E., Stoltzfus, J., & Harpalani, V. (2001). Identity and school adjustment: Revisiting the 'acting white' assumption. *Educational Psychologist, 36*(1), 21–31.

St. John, E. P. (2002). The access challenge: Rethinking the causes of the new inequality. Policy issue report. *Indiana Education Policy Center: Policy Issue Report R-2002–01.* Bloomington, IN: Education Policy Center.

St. John, E. P., Cabrera, A. F., Nora, A., & Asker, E. H. (2000). Economic influences on persistence reconsidered: How can finance research inform the reconceptualization of persistence models? In J. M. Braxton (Ed.), *Reworking the student departure puzzle*, (pp. 29–47). Nashville, TN: Vanderbilt University Press.

St. John, E. P., Chung, C. G., Musoba, G. D., & Simmons, A. B. (2004). Financial access: The impact of state finance strategies. In E.P. St. John, *Readings on Equal Education, 19, Public policy and college access: Investigating the federal and state roles in equalizing postsecondary opportunity* (pp. 109–129). New York: AMS Press, Inc.

St. John, E. P., Musoba, G. D., & Simmons, A. B. (2003). Keeping the promise: The impact of Indiana's Twenty-first Century Scholars Program. *Review of Higher Education, 27*(1), 103–123.

St. John, E. P., & Noell, J. (1989). The effects of student financial aid on access to higher education: An analysis of progress with special consideration of minority enrollment. *Research in Higher Education, 30*(6), 563–581.

Steele, C. M. (1995). Stereotype threat and the intellectual test performance of African Americans. *Journal of Personality and Social Psychology, 69*(5), 797–811.

Steele, C. M. (1997). A threat in the air: How stereotypes shape intellectual identity and performance. *American Psychologist 52*(6), 613–629.

Stewart, D. L. (2008). Being all of me: Black students negotiating multiple identities. *Journal of Higher Education, 79*(2), 183–207.

Stryker, S. (1980). *Symbolic interactionism: A social structural version.* Menlo Park: Benjamin/ Cummings Publishing.

Stryker, S. (1989). Further developments in identity theory: Singularity versus multiplicity of self. In J. Berger, M. Zelditch Jr., & B. Anderson (Eds.), *Sociological theories in progress: New formulations.* Newbury Park, CA: Sage.

Stryker, S. (1994). Freedom and constraint in social and personal life: Toward resolving the paradox of self. In G. M. Platt & C. Gordon (Eds.), *Self, collective behavior and society: Essays honoring the contributions of Ralph H. Turner.* Greenwich, CT: JAI Press.

Stryker, S. (1997). In the beginning there is society: Lessons from a sociological social psychology. In C. McGarty & A. Haslam (Eds.), *Message from social psychology: Perspective on mind in society.* London: Blackwell.

Stryker, S. (2000). Identity theory. In E. F. Borgatta & R. J. V. Montgomery (Eds.), *Encyclopedia of Sociology.* New York: Macmillan.

Stryker, S., & Serpe, R. (1994). Identity salience and psychological centrality: Equivalent, overlapping, or complementary concepts? *Social Psychological Quarterly, 57,* 16–35.

Swann, W. B. Jr., & Pelham, B. (2002). Who wants out when the going gets good? Psychological investment and preference for self-verifying college roommates. *Self and Identity, 1,* 219–233.

Swim J. K., Hyers, L. L., Cohen, L. L., Fitzgerald, D. C., & Bylsma, W. H. (2003). African American students' experiences with everyday racism: Characteristics of and responses to these incidents. *Journal of Black Psychology, 29*(1), 38–67.

Tajfel, H. (1978). Social categorization, social identity and social comparison. In Tajfel, H. (Ed.), *Differentiation between social groups: Studies in social psychology of intergroup relations* (pp. 61–76). London: Academic Press.

Tajfel, H. (1982). Social psychology of intergroup relations. *Annual Review of Psychology, 33*, 1–39.

Tajfel, H., & Turner, J. C. (1985). The social identity theory of intergroup behavior. In S. Worchel & W. G. Austin (Eds.), *Psychology of intergroup relations* (2nd ed.), Chicago: Nelson-Hall, 7–24.

Tatum, B. D. (2000). The complexity of identity: "Who am I?" In M. Adams, W. J. Blumsfeld, R. Castañeda, H. W. Hackman, M. L. Peters, & X. Zúñiga (Eds.), *Readings for diversity and social justice: An anthology on racism, anti-Semitism, sexism, heterosexism, ableism, and classism* (pp. 9–14). New York: Routledge Publishers.

Taylor, J. D., & Miller, T. K. (2002). Necessary components for evaluating minority retention programs. *NASPA Journal, 39*, 266–282.

Taub, D. J., & McEwen, M. K. (1992). The relationship of racial identity attitudes to autonomy and mature interpersonal relationships in black and white undergraduate women. *Journal of College Student Development, 33*(5), 439–446.

Thoits, P. (2003). Personal agency in the accumulation of multiple role-identities. In P. J. Burke, T. J. Owens, R. T. Serpe, & P. Thoits, *Advances in identity theory and research* (pp. 179–194). New York: Kluwer Academic/Plenum Publishers.

Tierney, W. G. (1992). An anthropological analysis of student participation in college. *Journal of Higher Education, 63*(6), 603–618.

Tierney, W. G. (1999). Models of minority college-going and retention: Cultural integrity versus cultural suicide. *Journal of Negro Education, 68*, 80–91.

Tierney, W. G. (2000). Power, identity, and the dilemma of college student departure. In J. M. Braxton (Ed.), *Reworking the student departure puzzle* (pp. 213–134). Nashville, TN: Vanderbilt University Press.

Tierney, W. G., & Jun, A. (2001). A university helps prepare low income youths for college: Tracking school success. *Journal of Higher Education, 72*(2), 205–225.

Tilghman, S. M. (2007). Expanding equal opportunity: The Princeton experience with financial aid. *Harvard Educational Review, 77*(4), 435–441.

Tinto, V. (1975). Dropouts from higher education: A theoretical synthesis of recent research. *Review of Higher Educational Research, 45*, 89–125.

Tinto, V. (1993). *Leaving college: Rethinking the causes and cures of students' attrition.* Chicago: University of Chicago Press.

Tinto, V. (1997). Classrooms as communities: Exploring the educational character of student persistence. *Journal of Higher Education, 68*(6), 599–623.

Tinto, V. (2000). Linking learning and leaving: Exploring the role of the college classroom in student departure. In J. M. Braxton (Ed.), *Reworking the student departure puzzle* (pp. 213–134). Nashville, TN: Vanderbilt University Press, 81–94.

Torres, V. (1999). Validation of bicultural orientation model for Hispanic college students. *Journal of College Student Development, 40*(3), 285–299.

Torres, V. (2003). Mi casa is not exactly like your house: A window into the experience of Latino students. *About Campus*, May-June.

Torres, V., Howard-Hamilton, M. F., Cooper, D. L. (Eds.). (2003). *Identity development of diverse populations: Implications for teaching and administration in higher education.* In A. Kezar (Series Ed.), *ASHE-ERIC Higher Education Report, 29*(6).

Turner, R. H. (1960). Sponsored and contest mobility and the school system. *American Sociological Review, 25*(6), 855–867.

Tyson, K. (2002). Weighing in: Elementary-age students and the debate on attitudes toward school among Black students. *Social Forces, 80*(4), 1157–1189.

Tyson, K., Darity, W. D., & Castellino, D. R. (2005). "It's not a "black thing": Understanding the burden of acting white and other dilemmas of high achievement. *American Sociological Review 70*(4), 582–605.

U.S. Department of Education. (2008). 6-year graduation rates of 2000–1 freshmen at 4-year institutions. In *Chronicle of Higher Education, Almanac Issue 2008–2009, LV(1)*, A13.

West, C., & Fenstermaker, S. (1995). Doing difference. *Gender and Society, 9*(1), 8–37.

West, C., & Zimmerman, D. H. (1987). Doing gender. *Gender and Society, 1*(2), 125–151.

Whitt, E. J., Edison, E. T., Pascarella, E. T., Nora, A., Terenzini, P. T. (1999). Women's perceptions of a "chilly climate" and cognitive outcomes in college: Additional evidence. *Journal of College Student Development, 40*(2), 163–177.

Whitt, E. J., Edison, E. T., Pascarella, E. T., Terenzini, P. T., & Nora, A. (2001). Influences on students' openness to diversity and challenge in the second and third years of college. *Journal of Higher Education, 72*(2), 172–204.

Wilds, D. J. (2000). *Minorities in higher education, 1999–2000: Seventeenth annual status report.* Washington, DC: American Council on Education.

Willie, S. S. (2003). *Acting Black: College, identity and the performance of race.* New York: Routledge.

Willis, P. (1977). *Learning to labor: How the working class kids get working class jobs.* New York: Columbia University Press.

Williams, J. (2006). *Enough: The phony leaders, dead-end movements, and culture of failure that are undermining Black America—and what we can do about it.* New York: Random House.

Winkle-Wagner, R. (2008). Putting money in the right places: Policy suggestions for supporting first-generation African American women in College. *ASHE-Lumina Policy Brief Series, 6,* 1–8.

Winkle-Wagner, R. (2009a). The perpetual homelessness of college experiences: The tensions between home and campus for African American Women. *Review of Higher Education.*

Winkle-Wagner, R. (2009b). Get real: The process of validating research across racial lines. In R. Winkle-Wagner, C. A. Hunter, & J. H. Ortloff, *Bridging the gap between theory and practice in educational research: Methods at the margins* (pp. 127–146). New York: Palgrave, Macmillan.

Zarembo, A. (2002, September 16). Death of the male. *Newsweek.*

Zhang, L. (2008). Gender and racial gaps in earnings among recent college graduates. *Review of Higher Education, 31*(3), 257–285.

Zinn, M. B., & Dill, B. T. (1999). Theorizing difference from multiracial feminism. In R. D. Torres, L. F. Miron, & J. Xavier, *Race, identity, and citizenship: A reader.* Blackwell Publishing.

Index

Page numbers in *italics* indicate figures and tables.